ZetaTalk

To Jeremy!
whom I expect will meet
up with others of his
calibre soon, and start on
the great adventure that
is the Transformation.

Nancy Lieder

ZetaTalk

Direct Answers
From the Zeta Reticuli People

Nancy Lieder

Granite Publishing, LLC
Post Office Box 1429,
Columbus, NC 28722 U.S.A.

Cataloging-in-Publication Data
Lieder, Nancy 1941-
ZetaTalk : Direct Answers
From the Zeta Reticuli People / Nancy Lieder. -- 1st ed.
p. cm.
ISBN: 1-893183-15-7
1. Life on other planets. 2. Human-alien encounters.
3. Unidentified flying objects--Sightings and encounters. I. Title.

Library of Congress Catalog Card Number: 99-57714

Cover Artwork
Suzanne Maksel

Manuscript editor: Brian Crissey

Printed in the United States of America.

Address all inquiries to:
Granite Publishing, LLC
Post Office Box 1429,
Columbus, NC 28722 U.S.A.
828-894-3088
living gently on the Earth

Introduction

Our home planet is in the star system of Zeta Reticuli. We and other visitors speak through a number of conduits. Many channels are valid, and some of these on occasion carry our voice. However, Nancy is unique. We, the Zetas, are using a different form of communication with our emissary Nancy than is done during channeling. Nancy has been willingly modified with Zetan genetic material inserted directly into her brain. This allows her to be more receptive to our telepathic voice. This has in no way changed Nancy from her otherwise normal human form.

We are Service-to-Others Zetas. Our audience is the Service-to-Others humans. Humans in the Service-to-Others struggle with the many societal and ecological problems the Earth presents today. They are of our heart, and we share their grief. There are many groups on Earth already who operate in the Service-to-Others orientation. They share their resources, address the problems of each as though it were a problem for the many, sacrifice their own comfort for the better comfort of the many, and do not impede the growth or awakening to knowledge of each other. In the Earth of the future, these qualities will seem to increase in people, and groups will find less and less need for artificial controls on their behavior, and more and more allowance for trust among each other.

The Earth will go through physical cataclysms in the near future, due to another passage of the 12th Planet, in the year 2003. There is truth in the rumors of what is called the 12th Planet, a giant comet that causes pole shifts on Earth during its passage. The Earth carries the marks of these violent geological changes, which rent continents apart and heave mountains high. The deluge occurred during just such a passage. The Jewish Exodus occurred during the last passage. Greenland is the site of the prior North Pole, which shifted during that time. The Earth's crust slides over the soft molten core, the crust pulled in one direction and the core, which is more magnetically inclined, in another. Such a time of violent geological upheaval is again pending for earthlings, who will scarcely be prepared.

There will be much death. Most of the people on Earth at this time will be unaware. The authorities will not encourage the propagation of information, wishing calm and for the status quo to continue. Even where there is awareness, there will be little action. Many will look about them, and debate their lifestyle should they take action. Most faced with these grim choices will deal with the situation by denial. Between the unaware, the unfortunate, and the reluctant, lie most of humanity. Those who survive the massive earthquakes, which will level cities to dust, and the massive tidal waves, which will inundate coast lines for hundreds of miles inland, will be few. Many will move to safe areas and set up communes, operating in the Service-to-Others mode of the future. These areas will be rural, essentially primitive, and they will not rely on civilization as they now know it either before or after the cataclysms.

The grief that will result from the cataclysms will be no greater for any given human than the grief their normal life would sustain. Any survivor of the cataclysms could have experienced a life situation where home, job, family and friends, and health disappeared. This can and does happen today to many, and not just due to acts of nature. What will be different is that the anticipated assistance from wealthy countries or one's own government will not be available. For most of the world, this won't come as a shock, as it is rather a shock when they do receive assistance. For wealthy industrialized countries, this lack of assistance will be a shock. Some individuals will have to learn to rely more on themselves and to work communally with others. These are lessons that life teaches in any case, however, and are not exclusive to the cataclysms.

ZetaTalk

Table of Contents

Table of Contents

Rules

Contact

Majestic-12

Planets

Table of Contents

Pole Shift

Being Human

1
Early Man

Mankind arose from a combination of sources, and the Earth was one. As there is tremendous variation of environments found throughout the Universe, in any genetic engineering project the engineers find it most profitable to use, as a base, a species native to the planet. The species in this case was a form of ape no longer in existence on Earth. Anthropologists searching for this missing link have not found it, as this ape was chosen not for its wide range but for its suitability. Having a suitable base, several experiments were tried. Through genetic engineering, the intelligence and dexterity of this ape was increased. The bipedal stance was encouraged. The product of genetic engineering then either survived and flourished or died out for some reason. More often than not, the product expired. This step was repeated many times, on different places on Earth, and this formed the basis for the various races of mankind you see today.

Early Man

Man has a fascination with his early forms for good reason. Early Man was father to the child, and the child wishes to know whereof he sprang. Early Man's appearance changed as his developmental stages changed—ranging as one would expect from apelike to manlike. Hypotheses on his appearance almost always leans in the direction of humanlike traits, as humans feel uncomfortable to some degree when contemplating their origins. Monkeys have bright coloration on their faces and behinds, and so did early White Man. Sharp prominent teeth were a characteristic of Gypsy Man, whose grimacing face was more tooth than otherwise. African Black Man was covered with hair, in his early stages, and though black men of today are without beards in the main, beards were present in the prototype. And the descendants of China Man would be surprised to learn he had a tail for quite some time.

Man, in each of the six races, was developed in stages, and between these developmental stages there was a period of time for things to settle down and for the genetically engineered product to be road tested. Would it break down? Frequently this happened, resulting in intervention, fine tuning the product to correct whatever was deemed to be the problem. Archeologists discover bones, such as those of Neanderthal Man, and wonder what became of him. Did he die out? Did he evolve? It seems he rather abruptly disappeared, and such a strapping fellow he was!

Neanderthal Man

Neanderthal Man was taken in hand to correct a problem. All of him? Yes. This was affected by making him sterile, a simple snip to the male, where he roamed free, and genetically engineering those taken into the lab. So there will be no misinterpretation, let us explain that the lab did not consist of cages, but in this instance was an island, and a paradise at that. The lab was a controlled environment, but with no more controls than necessary. So what were Neanderthal's problems, and what did he become? Neanderthal, big brute that he was, had a digestive problem. It is often assumed that he died out because he was stupid, or confrontational, but he was none of these and underwent change only because he had tummy troubles. He was not living his full life, and some died young, due to his inability to digest the foods available, or to take advantage of the fauna and flora that were in his menu. Coming out of his genetic correction, and returned to his environs, he looked different—a bit like Cro-Magnon Man.

Homo Erectus

The bones of Homo Erectus simply mark the evolution of more than one race at a particular stage. Where did he go? Into the labs to become the next stage. You can equate the puzzle archeologists are trying to put together with litter along the highway. Here there are Coke bottles, there plastic wrappers, and at yet another stretch, no litter at all. If one did not understand that litter was influenced by recycling efforts and laws, the price paid for aluminum and glass, and the dedication of local groups or commandeered prisoners set out to pick the roadside clear, the patterns would make no sense. The missing link in the evolution of man is not a particular pile of bones as yet undiscovered, it is the teams of genetic engineers who periodically descended on Earth to check on their handiwork, and left when mankind had made another leap.

The six races of man have not all survived, but traces of their genetics can be seen in the other races. Originally, as a result of numerous genetic engineering efforts, the six races were what we will term Northern White Man, African Black Man, China Man, Indonesian Man, Gypsy Man, and Angola Man. Angola Man has not survived, passing early and leaving no genetic mark.

Angola Man

Angola Man was not black at all, but pale to the point of being bluish. This color was due to the transparency of the skin, which gave the oxygen depleted veins and capillaries on the surface dominance in setting the color tone. However, this was scarcely noticeable, as Angola Man was literally covered with hair—fine, short, and laying flat. This was not thick enough to be called fur, but should we have chosen to call the original races by their appearance, rather than point of origin, we would have called him Fuzzy Man. Angola Man was the least aggressive of the six races, and this is in no small degree why he passed early, leaving none of his genetic heritage in the vast billions that swarm the surface of the Earth today. Angola Man literally allowed an attacker to overtake him while making neither a move to escape or to defend himself. He was eaten, regularly, until gone.

Indonesian Man

Indonesian Man in the pure form also died out, but through casual encounters with Gypsy Man merged into what we will call Polynesian Man. The Australian Aborigines also can point to Indonesian Man for a large portion of their genetic heritage, being, like the new Polynesian Man, a combination of Gypsy Man and Indonesian Man, with the addition of some Black Man genes due to a highly promiscuous Black Man who traveled with a small band to that part of the world. He was viewed as an oddity, being tall in stature compared to their tallest warrior, so he was treated as a god and was given all the women they could muster. He considered this a pleasant retirement.

Indonesian Man was short and stocky, with a rounded belly. He had a dominant forehead which protruded out over his eye sockets, giving him the natural equivalent of shades. He was not swift, but moved in a ponderous manner, and thus his demise. He could not run for safety or rescue others quickly, and his lack of agility and rounded shape prevented him from taking to the trees or cliffs for safety. Indonesian Man had what we might describe as a stubborn rage that when lit would not soon quell. Where he stood to fight, and won some, he was invariably bested by large predators. He too was eaten, irregularly, until gone.

Gypsy Man

Gypsy Man, as the name implies, moved about. His descendants can be seen in India and the surrounding countries, in the Arab countries, and, of course, in the Gypsies themselves. Gypsy Man was slight, and slid from confrontation, a factor of his hominoid genetics as well as the root ape, which took to the trees to escape and confronted only when escape was not possible. He learned to plot evasion rather than employ confrontation. This legacy can be seen today in the Gypsies, who disappear in the night, the Arabs, who likewise fold their tents and slip away, and the Hindus, who actively work at evading reality through meditation when they are forced to stick in one place and can find no escape. The hominoid contribution to Gypsy Man was Pleiadean, so a gentle, nonconfrontational nature compounded the desire to evade conflict. It is not by accident that Ghandi was able to sell the masses in India on passive resistance. It came naturally to them.

6

Northern White Man

Northern White Man first emerged in a climate that was not at that time cold, nor was it even in Europe or the steppes of greater Russia. White Man evolved in the deserts of Africa, and migrated across the Mediterranean, which in those days was not the water barrier it is today. White Men were few at first, a few hundred, and migrated in different directions. Some took a loop south, along the southern edges of what is now the Mediterranean, which in those days was a swamp, and then looped north and east. This band is seen in the large noble noses of the Turks, Afghans, and Italians. The band that headed straight north is seen in those with light hair and fine features. However all are from the same stock.

Where White Man entered the world in temperate climes, bad weather descended during a subsequent pole shift and survival became a game not easily won. Warm clothing needed to be constructed and fur-bearing animals needed to be trapped or hunted down with the least amount of effort. Survival required plotting and planning, and White Man found his stock being shaped in this manner, so that the clever planner survived. This can be seen today in the descendants of White Man, who are innovative and industrialized, and at the forefront of technology developments. Of the races that survived, White Man had the hottest temper. Quick, flashy, but quickly cooled. The root ape for White Man defended itself by a loud bluster, shrieking and hopping up and down. You've heard the expression, hopping mad, and this is where it comes from. White Man, even today, blusters and bluffs more than he engages.

African Black Man

African Black Man also underwent a shock to his system, but not because of climate changes. During the pole shifts the dice did not toss a pole into Africa, but the effects of winds and rain patterns brought desert conditions. The particular hominoid stock forming Black Man emerged from a portion of the Family of Man that relied on physical skills and social harmony, and this was the legacy Black Man carried when the desert descended, creeping over his hunting lands until there was less and less to share. Black Man adapted by broadening his embrace to include more of his fellows, and today you see this in the tradition of the extended family in most black communities.

7

Black Man's inheritance was a combination of a benevolent large ape which spent a good part of its time basking in groups. Like the elephant seal, this ape had no natural enemies, so the population was held in check by variations in the food supply. Sometimes plenty, sometimes dearth. No need to fight, as there was nothing to fight over. The hominoid contribution created the capacity to plan, and did not detract from the ape tendency to social harmony. Larger family circles translated to forced civility for longer periods. Black Man learned to employ violence when outside the family circle, so this acted as a release for repressed rage not allowed to be expressed within the circle. Early Black Man was shaped by those factors, so that those able to suppress their irritability until they could release away from home were kept in the band, and the others expelled where they did not survive to reproduce. Black-on-black violence occurs, but seldom inside the family circle.

China Man

China Man was developed to offset the ruthlessness of the inhabitants of the 12th Planet, who interbred with humans during their mining operations. The Oriental is slight, and given to ponder and consider the feelings of many before proceeding. It was foreseen that Earth's humanity would grow and eventually blend, as it has, so the ultimate Earthling was the target, and China Man was engineered accordingly. The hominoid stock used to build China Man was from those least likely to be impulsive, where deliberation brought rewards and had thus been selected for survival during evolution. In addition, a different ape was chosen as the base, one with a placid nature, where the apes selected for the other races did not have this quality at the fore. These qualities can be seen today in the descendants of China Man, who consult with one another, proceed only when there is consensus, and succeed best at those endeavors that require group dedication.

2
The Human Animal

Violence is a characteristic of many intelligent species. Where entities seek dominance over each other, violence exists. Another factor of violence is that it is often a necessary ingredient for primitive life. Depending on the environment, violent tendencies may in fact be crucial to survival. Your Earth was such an environment. During genetic engineering projects in the past, those intelligent species that developed without violent tendencies did not survive and flourish. On the contrary, they died out.

What is violence, and the tendency to use violence, and why was this a necessary ingredient in the past? First off, species eat each other. As has been often stated, the species on your planet generally use fight or flight when confronted with this possibility. Where it is assumed that these two reactions differ, they have more in common than not. Adrenaline surges, the heart beats wildly, and all thought or necessity of attending to other matters, such as digestion or favoring an injury, is put aside. If it is determined that fight is not possible, flight or its variant, playing dead, will be set into motion. In flight the adrenaline is put to good use in pumping legs and frantically scrambling arms. If it appears that escape is not possible, then a last attempt at deflecting the attack is tried—playing dead, or otherwise appearing as an undesirable morsel to the attacker. Thus, defecation and fainting may ensue.

Now, if fighting off the attack is possible, then a different set of staged defenses ensues. First, there is the defensive posture, where the body is fluffed up to appear larger or weapons such as teeth and claws are flashed. The defensive posture is quite familiar to humans, as the stiff-legged circling, with neck hair fluffed and lips curled back over teeth, is seen frequently in canine pets. Humans recognize this in themselves. The refusal to sit down in a relaxed posture when in the presence of those not trusted. Hair up at the back of the neck, and not wanting the enemy at one's back. The sneer, attributed to arrogance, is in fact equivalent to curling the lips back over teeth in preparation for a fight.

If the defensive posture does not succeed in deflecting the attack, taking the offensive in a parry is undertaken. The element of surprise is used as much as possible. Thus, the defensive posture is dropped and replaced with what is termed blind rage. The one under attack is now the attacker. Savage fury is unfurled. Everything in sight is devastated, without remorse or hesitation. When this defensive posture is completed, with the defendant finally spent, the attack will have either been deflected or the outcome of the battle will be in the other direction—one becomes a meal.

Humor

It is not by accident that a person coughing or choking is frequently thought to be a person having a good laugh. Likewise the start of a hearty laugh is often mistaken for a shout or sneeze, and the rhythm of laughing is similar to the heaving rhythm of sobbing. Do these similarities mean that laughter has a physiological basis with sobbing and coughing or a defensive bark? They do indeed. An analysis of situations found humorous invariably uncovers a tense situation. In fact, to discern why one person finds a situation funny while another does not, look to why the amused person is experiencing tension.

Muscles tensed without relief naturally begin twitching and cramping, a result of the buildup of toxins in the muscles but also due to the evolution of effective relaxation methods. Those creatures that cramped without release did poorly, and those that twitched into a different state survived. Thus laughter, sobbing or barking are all tension releases. Socialized humans given to denying their hostilities excuse their laughter as benign, which of course in the main it is. If they weren't laughing they might be murdering each other.

The Immune System

The immune system is sensitive to the psychological state, a fact which human physicians are acutely aware of. Cancer patients are often choosing to die by maintaining the depressive state that preceded the disease. It is a quick, if somewhat gruesome, escape, and one which the patient can use to punish those they are angry at—the family who must watch the process. In autoimmune diseases, as in allergies, the problem is the reverse—an overactive or rather hypersensitive immune response. The body is like a bow strung too tight, which twangs at every touch. This is not the result of depression, a wish to die, but a heightened wish to survive, to live. The body perceives danger, due to the psychological situation, and mobilizes.

Cancer is considered a scourge of mankind, as cancer is so often what the mortician writes as the cause of death. What is poorly understood is that cancer is a natural process which allows the organism an out, a type of suicide. Cancer is developing all the time, but is held at bay by scavenger cells that mop them up, as is known by your biologists. What occurs in cancer development is that the scavengers are told to cease, to back off and let the destruction proceed. Cancer occurs for the same reason many infectious diseases run rampant, because the immune system turns off. As has long been recognized by humans, the immune system is highly sensitive to one's surroundings, and by design. Suicide in nature is rarely possible, other than by such means as to cease eating or fail to remove oneself from danger, both actions which are associated with mental depression.

Diet

Humans are omnivores, as during their evolution they required the ability to eat a broad diet in order to survive. The omnivore, of which mankind is a member, evolved to meet wildly swinging cycles of food availability. Early humans, being land animals and highly mobile, could travel during drought to areas lush with vegetation. Humans, evolved from apes which were adjusted to eating fruits and insects as well as vegetation, do not have the apparatus to digest fiber. Thus, while on the road during droughts, they would have starved unless able to kill and eat meat. In effect, they have dual digestive systems.

Humans are designed, due to the influence of food availability during evolution, to eat either vegetables and fruits or meat, but not both at the same time. This is a fact not widely recognized or understood by humans, and thus they do themselves damage by eating both foods at meals, routinely. Imagine the cave man on the road, traveling to lush fields of vegetation where fruits and grains and tubers could be located with ease. The troop kills a deer or elephant, and feasts on nothing but meat and blood for days, consuming the entire kill before it can spoil. They do this repeatedly while on the road. When they arrive at their destination, they find they no longer need to take the physical risks that hunting invariably presents—flailing hooves and charging frightened beasts. They become vegetarians.

Modern man misunderstands what the cave man ate while lolling about during their vegetarian periods. They did not live strictly on vegetables and fruits and grains. They ate any and everything that was handy, and this included numerous insects and slow-moving life-forms such as mollusks and possums. They ate less meat, but the diet was highly varied and included occasional small bites from sources other than plants. Thus, those modern humans who try to live what they interpret to be a strictly vegetarian life suffer from malnutrition—poor immunity, anemia, lack of strength, and inability to deal with stress. Man was not designed to live by vegetables alone, and must accommodate their body with protein sources from living creatures other than plants, or suffer the consequences.

Biorhythms

Do biorhythms start from the moment of birth, as claimed? Some do, as the moment of birth is traumatic and gripping, no matter how easy the delivery. The babe breathes, feels the cool air, and is handled—all for the first time—a shock. Other biorhythms are set off from the moment of conception, and yet others when the nervous system reaches a point in its development capable of sustained activity, such as movement, the flutter that expectant mothers refer to as feeling life.

What are biorhythms, and why do they persist with such regularity? So much in life is controlled by biological switches—the urge to eat is switched on by an empty stomach, or the urge to drink by a blood chemistry ration, or the urge to defecate by a full colon. And is not menstruation cyclical, as is the urge to sleep, and the sex drive? Biorhythms, however, are not influenced by factors outside of themselves. They hear only their own rhythm, and listen only to the note they sing. Unlike brain waves, they are not a choir. They are all soloists. A biorhythm is the expression of the rising and falling of chemical levels in the blood, cerebrospinal fluid, lymph, intramuscular tissues, kidneys, and various glands. These chemical levels are regulated, much like a self-activating sump pump, by high and low points. When the chemical level drops to the low point, the body switches into production mode on this particular chemical, and when the chemical level rises to the high point, the body switches production off again.

Auras

Auras exist, and some humans can see them, as their eyes are sensitive enough to detect a form of light ray which is always there but not seen by most. Auras do not represent the spirit, but are an emanation, or by-product, of the human body as a furnace, maintaining 98.6° F. As with other by-products of the body, such as urine, feces, sweat or breath, the aura can tell a practitioner a lot about the mental and physical health of a person. Auras are normally pale blue, when viewed by humans, but vary all over the color spectrum and change shape, compressing close around the body or wafting out with tendrils. We, the Zetas, see human auras regularly, as well our own, and were we not highly telepathic with one another, we would use this to read the well-being and mood of another, just as humans use the expression on the face of another human.

Psychics

Humans in the main do not have a great deal of psychic ability, which is simply a combination of telepathy and common sense. A small percentage, perhaps less than 10%, have some psychic abilities, and a very few are significantly psychic. Most humans are personally acquainted with a situation that had overtones of psychic interplay, or have a close friend or relative who relays such a story. Someone knew that revenge was being plotted and the means being planned. Someone knew that a package was in the mail and what it contained. Someone sensed that an airplane was in danger and warned a potential passenger to change their plans. Psychic ability runs in families, and for a simple reason. Telepathic ability as well as common sense are based on the structure of the brain, and this is for the most part genetic.

Where psychics seem to be foretelling the future, common sense has entered in. Here the psychic senses facts known to a number of humans, and puts them together in logical probabilities. The pending airplane crash is in fact known to several humans—the airplane mechanics who are ordered to overlook maintenance because the financial condition of the airline is dire; the pilot who notices, however subconsciously, that his instruments are not lining up as they normally do; the scheduling clerks, who regret assigning aging airplanes to busy flights, knowing the risks involved. These humans send forth their thoughts for psychics to capture and ponder. For every situation where there is a successful foretelling of the future, there are literally thousands of situations where the psychic was wrong. The successful occurrences are so dramatic that the story gets widely told. Failures rarely get mentioned.

3
The Brain

One can map with simple animals, trained in a maze, the learning curve whereby they learn that to follow the smooth wall, for instance, they arrive at food. The first time this occurs it is by accident, so the rat makes an association. Smooth walls = food. The next time the hungry rat is put into a maze, he will give more weight to exploring smooth-walled paths over rough-textured routes. The mental association in the rat's brain is a chemical sequence in the existing brain cells in certain areas of the brain. Hunger in the rat is now connected to those sections of the brain that hold visual and tactile imprints. These imprints, as well as the pathways, are chemical. The pathways wax strong or weak, depending on how often they are used. More use, stronger chemistry. Less use, weaker chemistry.

Similarly, complex thought can be broken down into thousands of steps, where sensory memories are related. Even the abstract concept of numbers is related to sensory memories. The child piling blocks is noting that four blocks pile higher than three, and the concept of greater-than is related to these counts. Does the one pile not loom higher? When adding just one block onto the short pile, they are equal. An incipient algebraic equation is building in the babe's mind. Great thoughts are built from many small mental data stores, and many more connections. Great insights are simply where two or more formerly unrelated connections bridge, to become related.

Bridging occurs when the chemicals needed to build a new pathway are in abundance in a certain part of the brain. It is accidental in that the connection is only by proximity, but no accident in that the brain areas that relate to the issue at hand are now active and rich with these chemicals. Thus the brain is just making an introduction: "Here, you two places, you are both active, so speak to each other." Thus, the child, finding himself staring at a wall he wishes to climb over, and seeing some boxes near at hand, recalls his pile of blocks. As his memory of blocks connects to this sight of the boxes, which have a similar shape, a new association has occurred—thought.

Reptilian Brain

Humans have a genetic capacity for repressed emotions that is not present throughout the universe. Few intelligent species have this capacity, and it arises only when genetic engineering has created this confusion. Repressed emotions do not occur naturally, during evolution. Originally all species on the planet Earth were reptilian, and this is a common form throughout the universe. Mammals and the hominoid form are relatively rare, but are desired due to their capacity for intense empathy—their caring emotions. On worlds where mammals have evolved, they are the genetic engineering species of choice, even where reptiles may in fact be more intelligent at the time. This was the case on the Earth. However, because the majority of genetic engineering is done by reptilian species, they naturally inserted what they deemed important.

The ability to repress emotions comes from the fact that humans have several brains—the forebrain, which is mammalian, the midbrain, which is a mixture of the mammal and reptile, and the early brain, which is reptilian. When humans wish to remember all, they record the information in all their brains, although the information may vary in the different data banks. When humans wish to forget, they disconnect the memory chains between their forebrain and the other brains, and amnesia ensues. The midbrain, being the go-between, is responsible for keeping it all straight, and does so responsibly. Blind rage erupting during the day can get one fired or exiled, and thus the ability to repress emotions has been, if anything, selected for propagation.

16

Brain Capacity

It is often stated that humans only use 10% of their brain capacity. This is nonsense. If the brain evolved in response to need, why would it then turn off and become idle? Humans map the brain as best they can, and are puzzled by all that gray matter that seems to have no function. Then there are the cases of remarkable performance where the human brain seems to be virtually absent, as in the cases where an encephalitic infant develops into an adult with apparently normal capacity. Humans are also aware that they can live quite well with only half a brain, right or left side, as long as a complete half remains. As with many vital organs, evolution favored the specimen who could survive the loss of one.

If a human can survive losing half a brain, and an encephalitic can function with a minimal brain, then is there not excess brain capacity? This assumption is based on the apparent normalcy of humans functioning with diminished brain size. The humans walk, talk, laugh at jokes, remember to brush their teeth—they are apparently normal. However, as most consider it to be amazing that these individuals are not in a coma, they seldom move past astonishment to check for full capacity. Whereas diminished brain size allows the individual to learn well those routines called upon regularly, it is when the individual is asked to stretch that the lack of capacity shows up.

Each complex concept is built from many mental building blocks, and each of these building blocks likewise is composed of many parts. Children piece these building blocks together, bit by bit, piece by piece, and eventually get to the point where they can structure abstract concepts. Diminished brain capacity allows the afflicted person to laugh when others laugh, as laughter is contagious, especially when one wishes to belong. Do not small children laugh along while not understanding the joke? Diminished capacity does not allow one to create a joke beyond the slapstick, nor does it allow one to build an abstract concept where one has not already been constructed. Thus, the brain damaged can continue old functions where the connections and structures have not been lost, but time stops for them where new abstractions must be constructed. Abstract concepts, intuition, long range planning, adaptability—this is what all that uncharted gray matter is supporting, and it is not idle. The true range of any one brain capability is disguised by the need to enlist many capabilities at once, hundreds, in fact. Therein lies the reason some autistics appear incredibly gifted. They screen out all but a single thought, refusing to entertain others. Thus, an autistic may be able to sit at the piano and play a complex piece, having only had the opportunity to observe an experienced pianist play that piece a single time. Likewise, autistics who have integrated the digital or binary or any other type of number system can compute as fast as a calculator or computer the results of equations that require thousands of steps, as long as those steps do not require more than one mental process, repeatedly. Complex concepts, involving multiple thought processes, receive the same blank, apparently uncomprehending, stare from autistics that is their normal response.

Brain Waves

What human scientists do not know is that beyond the old brain and the new, the subconscious and the conscious, the right and the left halves—there are yet more subdivisions of the human brain. Where it is known that the brain seems to specialize in activity that requires Beta-frequency brain waves during wakefulness, and Alpha-frequency waves during sleep or meditation, and Theta waves during rage, and Delta waves in coma—no one is quite sure why.

Where brain functions are localized close to the data stores—the chemical paths and links that constitute memory and the potential for thought—these functional mother lodes cannot be mined without the greased lightning that is the communication substrata. We are not speaking here of synaptic junctions, the ends of one brain cell's dendrites touching another. We are speaking here not of chemistry, but of a communication method not understood by your scientists, as it cannot be pressed between glass plates and peeked at under a microscope, or placed in a vial of chemicals to test its nature. It requires a living brain to express itself, and beyond the difference in frequency, its nature is unknown to your scientists. Brain waves are but a symptom of the process, whereby the brain, as an organ, hums to itself.

This hum is not chemical but the result of chemical interactions, which result in what you may term a variation on electrical energy. The motion of this energy is in waves for the same reason a body of water has waves. For motion to occur at all there must be pressure and release, then bumping and reaction. Think of the choir, where all warm up with the same musical

18

scales—synchronicity. But the true musical potential is where the choir, open throated, strikes harmonious chords. Listen carefully, and you will hear the full choir.

Amnesia

Coma uses the same mechanism we aliens do during visitation, when we record the visit in the subconscious only. This is a chemical block, and can lift as suddenly as it can be applied—within minutes. Due to past genetic engineering, the human body has overlapping brains, with the conscious brain the least well rooted. If the chemistry flooding the body is missing certain components, the consciousness is deactivated. During visitation, of course, the contactee is not comatose, as we adjust the body chemistry so that the subconscious is functioning but the conscious is deactivated. Contactees do not forget their visits, as they were never recorded in the conscious. Rather, recall builds a conscious memory from the subconscious.

The human mind has the capacity to deliberately forget, allowing the amnesia state to wash away bridges between chemical memory lanes. This is but a step away from compartmentalizing memories into packages the human feels capable of dealing with at one time. Brain chemistry- and brain structure-wise, the process is the same. The average human can point to instances in himself or others where selective forgetting occurred. One just forgets that embarrassing moment or that appointment to go to the dentist. In amnesia the chemistry in the brain shuts down to the extent that the conscious brain is not recording new memories or playing back old memories. It's off-line, rather than on-line, as they say in the computer business. Selective amnesia attacks just those bridges that lead to painful memories, washing these away.

Psychosis

As with fainting, psychosis and senility allow the human animal to disconnect with reality. Catatonic or autistic individuals are, chemically, in a place where they are not feeling anxiety. The world does not exist for them. Delusions serve the same purpose, as the individual can build a world about them that meets their needs. How much different are delusions from the games people play with themselves to make themselves more secure, more attractive, or more valued in their own eyes than they are in the eyes of others? Depression serves a purpose in causing the individual to retract and withdraw from a world that is causing injury. Time to reflect and plot a new course. Senility, outside of the genetic disease which is Alzheimer's, is greatest in those who have the least to live for. Senility blunts the awareness of the aged, so they can reminisce about happier days when they were younger.

Infants born psychotic are thus because the genetic throw of the dice gave them an ultra-sensitive nature, and they are doomed to live in the sheltered world they live in. Schizophrenics react to the same stresses as other humans, but with a stronger and quicker reaction. This is widely recognized in giving schizophrenics a more sheltered environment, but as the press is for society to reabsorb the individual, any respite from the chemical surges is short lived. Depressives recover when they change the life situation that is distressing them, sometimes with dramatic swiftness. That so many depressives do not recover but mask their unhappiness with antidepressants does not point to the illness as being intractable so much as it points to the rigidity of society.

In the world of the individual without psychosis, pain is born quietly but is more intense. Psychosis is noisy and noticeable, where the prepsychotic individual is usually quiet and well behaved. Psychosis is the signal flag of misery. Antipsychotic drugs simply mask the raging surges, as though the fire hose were perpetually turned on the blaze so that one can say that the fire is out. The problem here is not so much that a psychosis ensues due to life stresses as that society has rigid expectations for all its citizens. Psychosis occurs in the animal kingdom, outside of the human animal, a fact that veterinarians will be the first to attest to. Psychotic pets, however, are usually given the life changes that are indicated, and recover. Human society is not so kind to the human animal, who is generally drugged and told to struggle on, in place.

4
The Soul

What you call a soul is composed of substances, just as your physical body is. These substances are just as complex as the molecules and cell structure your physical body is composed of—in their own way. However, these substances cannot be destroyed by such things as atomic explosions or even entry into a black hole. The soul is durable and indestructible. Souls are born, and evolve and grow, just as in your physical world you find plants and animals springing up from seed, from a single cell. This does not happen haphazardly, and only happens on worlds in third density. When an entity is incarnate, what you call the soul suffuses with the physical body, spreading throughout all the parts of the physical body.

The existence of the soul, that part of a human remaining after the physical body expires, has been measured as a tiny adjustment in the weight of the dead body, happening at the moment of death in most cases. We say in most cases, as the soul may depart earlier, seeing the trend. For instance, where individuals go out-of-body during trauma, the soul has already left. Nevertheless, there is some small scientific aspect to support the general human perception that they have a soul. In fact, so prevalent is this feeling or belief in humans, that one stating the opposite comes in for some heat. Religions invariably espouse the soul and an afterlife as a reality.

Chakras

An incarnation is not a superficial matter. As the soul, during incarnation, is diffused throughout the body, it aligns itself to embrace the world. The soul communicates with its extensions, the human arms and legs, as this is not a natural position for the soul. Incarnations in life forms that do not have arms and legs would, understandably, have different chakras. The chakras are related to the functions of the incarnated spirit, not to the human form. The spirit centers itself, and thus the heart chakra, and concerns itself with communicating to the mind, and thus the third eye, but the other organs of the human body are incidental to the spirit, which is not concerned with digestion or locomotion or such functions. Spirits that are more entranced with physical activities, such as sex or drug use, may be more diffuse within the physical body, however.

A central chakra, both in the human body and in chakra action, is the heart chakra. There are several reasons for this. First, the heart is centralized in the human body in order to serve the body well in its task as circulation central. Second, the heart responds to emotions, invariably, beating fast during fright or joy, being regular or irregular in pace with the life situation. Third, the spiritual centering of the soul within the physical body of a human must for similar reasons be centered. As the soul fills the being of whatever it incarnates in, it is distended into the human limbs and digits. To work as a unit, the soul indeed utilizes parts of itself to maintain unity and cohesive action. The heart chakra, while not circulating fluids, has a similar importance and function.

Past Lives

Tapping past lives is much in vogue, especially in California. Since the proposition cannot be disproved, the claimants wax poetic. All the past lives are invariably romantic or impressive—they lived in interesting times, in elegant surroundings, and were always hale and hearty, intelligent, and attractive. Although the vast number of past lives on Earth were marked by struggle for health—with broken teeth, missing or maimed limbs, and the health problems that plague mankind today present in the extreme—the past lives trotted forth all seem to involve good and even vibrant health.

Where all but perhaps 5% of the world's populace is of average or dull intelligence, the past lives claimed invariably involve stations in life which would require a relatively high IQ. And where most of mankind's history has gone down ignominiously and unrecorded, past lives published seem to all be placed smack in the center of either momentous historical times or well-recorded historical times. What is going on here? Are these past lives remembered simply fiction or are the memories selective?

Humans delving into their past lives face many hurtles. The human form has no memory of past lives, and the spirit has difficulty speaking to the mind about matters it has no concept of. Past lives are a leap into history recorded nowhere on Earth—living conditions, cultures and traditions, and physical appearance all beyond the imagination of humans alive today. A past life spent as a caveman, where the diet consisted of bugs and worms and even on desperate occasions the feces of herbivores, would not be remembered. Thus, past lives remembered do tend to fit into written history. Add to this selective memory the human tendency to deny unpleasantness. A past life where the human was ugly and behaved atrociously would likely not be given center stage, and past lives that passed the minimum acceptance criteria are pruned and amended by humans remembering them just as they have a selective memory about their current incarnation.

Rule of Forgetfulness

Lessons to be learned during the current incarnation, or personal missions as they are sometimes called, are less effectively addressed when consciously dealt with. In fact, being consciously aware of the lesson to be learned can sometimes prevent the lesson from being addressed during the incarnation at all. How can this be? If one is conscious of a posture, that the posture must be assumed, the posture may be assumed, but this may be an act. If one is not conscious of a posture, and the situation arises where the posture may be assumed, then if the posture is assumed this is not an act but a genuine choice. To know the desired outcome beforehand ruins the process, as the goal of the incarnation is not to have certain postures taken, but to have certain choices made.

Forgetfulness between lives occurs naturally. When an entity incarnates into a human body, the mind naturally has no knowledge of past lives. The mind develops memories from what it experiences, observes through its senses, and concludes due to the mental processes resulting from all this. Thus forgetfulness is natural, and breakthroughs where the spirit has an opportunity to relay bits and pieces of a past life are rare. The Rule of Forgetfulness is not an imposed rule, it is a rule of nature. However, given that incarnations work this way, and incarnations have proven to be the fastest way that young spirits grow and mature, no one is rushing forward to bring a newly incarnated body up to date on what has happened before. In fact, such a process can delay maturity or skew the eventual decision the entity makes on its first lesson—the orientation lesson. Imagine instances in life given no knowledge of past decisions or full knowledge of past decisions.

A mother, cuddling her newborn infant, seeing its helplessness and dependence on her, imagines the feelings of abandonment and desperation such an infant would feel if it were not held and loved and rescued when distressed. The mother, being basically a caring human, proceeds to care for the infant with great affection and pride in herself for her competence. If in past lives the entity incarnating had deserted a newborn, to ease the pressure on herself, and all the memories of this past incident were remembered, then the current situation would be colored with guilt and shame and in particular, the strong memory of what caused the abandonment in the first place. Forgetfulness allows the entity to move through circumstances that were similar to past circumstances, trying them out with a different approach and consequently experiencing a different outcome.

Near-Death Experience

Near-death experiences are quite common, and are similar to out-of-body experiences, but with a twist. Where the entity has left the physical body, seeing the trend, it moves forward on its journey to return to the birthing envoys in preparation for the next incarnation. This process is complicated, and has many steps. The first step is to let go of the former incarnation. As every dying person has many issues left undone, many statements left unsaid, and many concerns not yet completed to the entity's satisfaction, their focus is torn between the life they are leaving and the future. The birthing envoys meet this head on, by presenting the newly discarnate entity with those involved in the leftover concerns. Thus, in a near-death experience, an entity may meet relatives and friends, both loved and hated, or coworkers involved in incomplete projects. When the pending death does not occur, the person remembers meeting familiar people, but not much else as the death was aborted. Had the death continued, settling these leftover issues would have proceeded.

Ghosts

All humans have visits from those they knew in the past, now dead. These spirits, who are primarily discarnate but can come from their next incarnation in an out-of-body experience, are trying to settle things they feel were left outstanding. These matters can be as simple as an apology they wished to express to you, or a bit of information they felt you needed, intended to be told to you when you next met. Death interrupts the plans. Ghosts are such discarnate entities. Discarnate entities are in light form. The reason some such entities appear brighter in light form than others is related to their spiritual maturity. The older and wiser, the brighter. They gain in spiritual bulk, one might say.

When an entity is discarnate, it can wander about just as the soul can in out-of-body experiences. Likewise, as in out-of-body experiences, it is drawn to places it is either curious about or tied to because of emotional trauma. The entity that feels an issue is unresolved will hang about, desiring to influence proceedings. This is much displayed in your media in ghost stories of one kind or another. Just as with visits from entities in fourth density or higher densities, these discarnate entities cannot affect humans unless the human gives The Call. Their substance cannot affect the physical world, and they cannot possess another's body unless The Call has been given and permission granted. In this regard, a walk-in or a possession is a reality, and can happen.

Possession

In possession, a walk-in by a very high-level entity in the service-to-self orientation has occurred, such that this is dramatically noticed by the other humans in the vicinity. They could not fail to take notice, as however aggressive and non-compliant the human was prior to the possession, the stance the possessed human now takes is a quantum leap higher. The human now challenges everyone, and any social exchange has become a war. Where the human formerly complied with some social norms, the possessed human now complies with none. They seem, thus, completely uncivilized and unsociable. There thus ensues a great flurry of activity where various authority figures try to reason with the possessed human, thinking they are still speaking to the one they knew. In truth, the human is in part the one they knew, but at the core is someone very different, the possessing entity from another world. When reason fails, forms of magic or witchcraft are tried, and we are here including Catholic exorcism. This is where the faith or conviction of those in authority, their orientation to give service-to-others, comes into play.

Where this is successful in driving out the possessing entity and securing a return of the original incarnating entity it is because of two things. One, the flood of concern and caring poured upon the strongly oriented service-to-self entity disturbs its concentration, tugging at its focus on self, and it departs in disgust. Two, the formerly incarnating entity hears the pleas of the humans it formerly knew, feels the love pouring toward it, and changes its mind about having left in the first place. The birthing envoys confer with all concerned and the possessing entity vacates in an exchange.

5
Other Worlds

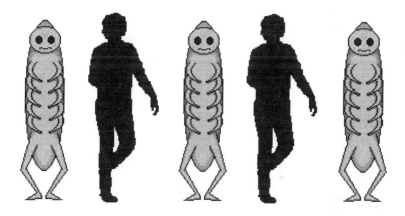

Life first begins as a natural result of the processes that occur on all life bearing planets—the warm soup of oceans, filled with the simple genetic components that can and do link-up in an endless variety of combinations. Humans are aware that the DNA on Earth is all composed of four simple building blocks. In other parts of the universe such components differ from those on Earth, nor is four the magic number. Big bangs occur periodically in this or that section of the Universe, and life forming after a big bang evolves slowly. In that same section of the universe numerous worlds will eventually produce, during the natural course of evolution, intelligent creatures capable of offering a home to forming entities. Seeding planets and genetic engineering is eventually done within a section of the universe for the same reasons that human couples long to have children—for more company and the pride that parentage brings. The process of evolution is expedited, bumped from slow motion to fast, and the number of worlds that eventually become life-bearing planets is increased.

In the section of the universe of which the Earth is a part, the seeding of planets and migration of reptilian or hominoid life forms has been in place long before our time. We have been told that none of the hominoids currently visiting Earth were the precursor, but rather all are the result of seeding and genetic engineering. Of the many hominoids who contributed to mankind's hominoid structure, none were the base hominoid, which was smaller and more monkey-like than would be expected. In truth, the issue of who started mankind will not be resolved by researching the history of genetic engineering efforts, as every step back opens another history book, and on it goes. Does it matter? Live in the present, which has more puzzles than humans can even begin to address. Live for the future, which will shortly get quite lively.

Percentages

If one were to take a census on intelligent life in the part of the universe the Earth goes around in, the results would probably shock humans. As entities in higher densities, fifth and above, have mobility and often go where duty calls, they may be wholly absent or present in great numbers, depending on need. Due to the Transformation, the Earth is positively swarming with such attention at the present time. Therefore, to give a realistic picture, we will describe second, third, and fourth density percentages only.

On a world-by-world basis, there are about 1,000 dead worlds for every one that holds life. Humans are familiar enough with their surroundings to understand conditions on other planets, and if anything, would be surprised at the percentage capable of life. Not every life-bearing planet sustains life that can develop to the level required for conscious and intelligent thought. There are about 2,500 primordial worlds for every one that can support an intelligent species. Your Earth, for instance, had many such species with this potential. Of these worlds that hold third-density intelligent species, the vast majority, perhaps 75%, are water babies, as the vast majority of habitable planets are essentially water planets. These species may be crablike, fishlike, squidlike, or formed like almost any of your ocean inhabitants—an almost infinite variety.

Of the worlds that sustain land-dwelling intelligent species, the greater share, just under 60%, are reptilian. Reptilian life-forms appear first, and thus better their percentages. A minority are mammalian, above 10%, but whenever these life-forms are a candidate they beat out all other candidates, as mammalian existence is highly interactive and thus a good spiritual school-yard for forming entities. The remaining land -dwelling third-density species range between birdlike or insect types—the latter more prevalent at about 30%. Since third density is a short stop, required only for the orientation lesson, fourth-density entities are much more prevalent. There are approximately 1,200 fourth-density entities for every forming third-density entity.

Water Cradle

On almost all worlds, life evolves in a liquid. This is reasonable, as the liquid provides mobility, and increases greatly the chances that any complex molecule will encounter another. If one examines the physical structure of intelligent species, one finds rudimentary gills, fins, egg sacs, webbing, if not the frank requirement of a liquid for the home. Most telling is the development of the fetus, where the evolutionary history repeats itself. We, the Zetas, do not have records we can tap regarding these early beginnings on your planet.

Planets, especially water planets, are seeded with simple DNA components and left alone. Things work out or they don't, and these planets are not checked that frequently. If life did not start, reseeding—perhaps of a different nature—is done. To trace your beginnings, we must do as your scientists have, and look at the stages the fetus goes through. The forebrain develops last, and arms and legs also come late. It takes a long time for the tail to disappear, and gills are unmistakably evident in the early days. You were first a fish.

Size and Shape

Where intelligent life-forms come from all possible stops on the evolutionary scale, they are fairly consistent in size. The reason for this rule is simple—on the inevitable encounters, intimidation would be minimized. Thus whether a life-form is similar to an insect, fish, octopus, snake, lizard, monkey, bird, or hominoid, they have all been genetically engineered to be of the same approximate size. Within these parameters there is great variation on other facets, however, as the life-form must live on the world they evolved on, and this cannot be ignored. Thus, on those worlds where the mass of the planet is such that gravity exerts a great pull, the life-form will evolve with enough strength in bone and muscle to move about. Thus the giant homi-noids from the 12th Planet are large, heavy boned, and strong in comparison to humans, as their planet exerts almost twice as much gravity pull as the Earth. Thus we, the Zetas, are stronger than humans, as our planets also had more mass and resulting gravity pull. Where skinny, our bones are bolstered by wraparound ribs and joints that move in fewer directions than human joints, thus preventing strain.

Beyond approximate size, the life-form may be of carnivorous or vegetarian nature, or if the planet is lush with watery nutrients, they may even simply absorb nutrients through the skin as many single-cell organisms do. They may have teeth or no teeth, eyes or no eyes or multiple eyes, skin that is dry and tough or covered with slime or oil, bones as an interior or exterior skeleton or no bones at all, able to generate their own sugars as do plants or be completely dependent upon food located and eaten, breathing through lungs or gills or absorbing air or water components through the skin, covered with feathers or fur or scales or without an outer garment. Life-forms come in all shapes, and humans embracing the Awakening should be mentally and emotionally prepared to encounter them. Bear in mind that they think of the human form as strange, too.

Intelligent Carnivores

Evolution in the universe takes many paths, but all the paths that corporeal life follows require consumption of other living matter. It may be argued that plants and single-cell creatures live by absorbing only chemicals and light, and thus sustain themselves in a benign manner, but close examination proves otherwise. Bacteria or virus material considered on the border-line of being living matter, infects and destroys that which they need for nourishment, and the amoebae and protozoa likewise surround and consume foodstuffs they encounter, whether this food be living or not. Plants seem to take in carbon dioxide and light and transform this into sugar. Yet the roots of the plant draw up the nourishment the plants need only because they are embedded in soil moistened in the by-product of other life, which must die for the plant to grow, and some carnivorous plants don't wait for the donor to die.

At the base of life on planets seeded with DNA are simple chemical reactions that form in ever more complex structures and replicate themselves. Those that replicate successfully become the genes of the future, and those that do not remain as building blocks for the more successful DNA chains. Eating one another starts early. Unlike the spiritual realm, where consumption of one spirit by another is never required and in fact cannot happen, carnivorous behavior is intrinsic to corporeal life.

Why God so structured the world in this way is not known, but considering that all forming entities begin their life incarnated, there are certain lessons that are guaranteed. As empathy in some degree is also intrinsic to corporeal life, a conflict between the self and the other is a given. Thus, the conscious decision to sacrifice the self is frequently made, and this is the spark that begins development toward the Service-to-Other orientation.

Intelligent Insects

In the case of planets where insects emerge as predominant, some insect forms begin to eat other insects, and thus can grow larger. Humans, used to insect forms that are tiny, are seeing what occurs when all insect forms are consumed by others. On Earth, insects are consumed not only by other insects but also are the favorite food of birds, reptiles, and rodents. For any insect to evolve as a large specimen on Earth would require a protected environment where none of the other Earth creatures could discover it. This is simply not the case on your Earth, but is the case on those rare worlds where insects evolve as the predominant, and eventually the intelligent, species.

Other Worlds

Life on other worlds is, of course, adapted to the chemical and mineral mix indigenous on the planet. Some are silicon based, where *Homo sapiens*, for instance, is carbon based. The primary difference is in adaptation to radiation, the intensity of a given sun or other heat source. Your sun is of moderate intensity, but there are some worlds that you could not visit in your physical form. You would fry or quickly sicken. There are other worlds that you could not visit in physical form because of their chemical and mineral mixes. You would become poisoned.

ZetaTalk

These are some of the reasons why all intelligent life-forms have not been presented to our contactees, during any adaptation orientation such as the one our emissary, Nancy, underwent. Consequently, the Zetas have not seen all that much of the universe either. The evolution of a life-form and the home planet determines to some degree where the life-form can travel and work. Beyond the obvious differences in the base chemistry of the DNA, or the ability to tolerate high radiation from a hot sun, or the need to breathe air or water, there are issues of gravity tolerance. We, the Zetas who have chosen work on the Earth's Transformation, cannot return to our home planets because the gravity would crush us. We have adapted to our new environments. Likewise it is known to your scientists that long space voyages without the semblance of Earth's gravitational field would doom your astronauts to a lifetime in space.

6
Incarnations

The rules we must observe that prevent our machines from becoming alive, from becoming sentient or conscious thinking machines, must seem confusing to humans who observe that their computers often seem more intelligent than other humans. A retarded human who can barely recall the sequences necessary to put one leg into a set of trousers is alive and conscious, but a powerful computer monitoring a myriad of logic threads simultaneously is not. Just how does that compute? The difference is subtle, and where the line may seem blurred to humans who are confusing performance with intrinsic intellectual independence, i.e. choice, the issue is not confusing to us. We will expand on the differences between performance and choice.

Confusion over whether robots are alive, make choices, or might be incarnated with spirits lies in understanding what is seen versus what is unseen on the surface. On the surface, humans see robots as able to entertain focus on a task at hand to the exclusion of all possible distractions, and thus, for instance, win at a game of chess over a human chess master. Is the robot not thinking? Yes and no, depending upon how one classifies thought. To primitive peoples, a simple computer program appears to be thinking, as it can rapidly arrive at a conclusion while entertaining a problem it has been programmed to address. Computer programs are not considered brains by most humans only because they can gaze at and understand the program, and can see that the computer is simply following instructions.

What is unseen is that robots are bounded in ways that DNA is not bounded. Humans are bounded by their biology, an inability to put aside their biological needs, so that they cannot travel where robots can, exclusively concentrate on a task as robots can, or remain calm in disturbing circumstances such as a burning building or the torture of another human might present. In overcoming biological imperatives, robots seem superior, especially since the average human does not understand how they have been programmed and are in awe. Robots, however, are bounded in what they can address. Even where robots are designed to repair themselves and make minor adjustments to their surroundings, they are still operating within their original programming.

A robot arrives at its decision quickly because it does not ponder. Humans are virtually unlimited in their ability to ponder, which is what makes their life-form attractive to the stuff of souls so that entities form within humans. Robots are utterly boring, as they have an inability to ponder, being programmed to reach quick conclusions after considering a set number of variables, and thus do not attract the stuff of souls, regardless of appearances!

Stuff of Souls

What humans refer to as the soul, what is sometimes called the spirit, or which we refer to as the entity, is not what is supposed by most humans. They imagine a vapor, something that can move through walls like a ghost, something without substance that seeks to influence the physical world around it with little success. They realize the soul can remember, as past lives are recalled, but do not imagine that a physical brain is required. The view that humans have of the soul is, as could be expected, the view from the human vantage point. What is missing from that vantage point is the ability to see the soul, as the substance is not something that the human eye can perceive. The soul has substance, and grows in bulk early in its development as many incarnations, many lives, are experienced. This bulk cannot be gauged by humans, who look upon one another as having equal souls, when nothing of the kind is the reality. Some souls are so tiny and poorly constructed that they dissipate after the incarnation, what we term aborted entities. This type of soul may be present in many animals and even some plant forms, as the stuff of souls is dispersed throughout the universe and incarnations happen naturally. Where the human eye cannot gauge the mass of another soul, the spirit gauges this very well. You know instinctively that another is old and wise.

Not only does the soul have memory, it also does not forget. It is not by accident that intelligent life-forms have nerves, brains, and memory in the form of chemical impressions. The stuff of souls is simply another density level, one that touches on all the others. It is finer and more durable, at the same time. It could be called the base of matter, in that regard, as it permeates all levels where matter can reside. Intelligent life-forms come in many shapes and sizes, but all have brains and nerves. Thus a soul can incarnate in a hominoid at one point in its development, and into quite another life-form during another incarnation, without any adaptation required. The spirit communicates to the mind by biochemical means, by inciting biochemical activity. It does so by adjusting itself to the density of the incarnated body and to the peculiar biochemistry of the life-form. During each incarnation the spirit quickly familiarizes itself with its new physical body, and gets down to business.

Soul Nature

The soul does not require food or nourishment as physical life-forms do. The human animal cannot retain its shape without fuel, without maintaining a certain temperature and replacing damaged or consumed biochemicals. It must eat to survive. Souls do not require a temperature maintenance, and by their nature maintain their own chemistry, the only outside reach required is to acquire more of the stuff of souls, present everywhere in the universe, when growth in bulk is occurring.

Humans are used to thinking of the senses as merely sight, sound, touch, taste, and smell—five senses. A sixth sense is attributed to all other hunches, and is variously described as being supported by ESP or intuition.

ZetaTalk

The human body alone has many other senses, and the soul surpasses any given body in which it happens to incarnate. Senses not mentioned are the sense of balance, where relationship to the gravity center is sensed, the sense of motion, related to the sense of balance, and the sense of being ill, where the human senses that all is not right with the body. We have mentioned only those senses that the common man can readily relate to, not the myriad that in fact exist. Between the soul and its surroundings, there are many touch points. Thus, even though the soul does not actually have eyes, it can see!

The stuff of souls, the substance spirits are composed of, transcends all density levels, as it can interact with what humans call the physical world on all density levels, simultaneously. Most humans are at best newly formed entities incarnated into an intelligent body native to the Earth. Both the entity, or spirit form, and the human body newly emerged into consciousness are aware only of the corporeal world around them. They naturally think this predominant. It is not. Those formed entities who have experienced thousands of incarnations and have begun to interact with entities from other worlds are aware of the spirit world also. But until an entity has arrived at higher-density levels and has itself been at the helm during density shifting, they are only superficially aware of how vast the universe actually is.

Incarnations

Incarnations occur naturally and are the way that forming entities get their start. The stuff of souls is everywhere, disbursed throughout the universe, but so disbursed it does not make a soul. Does a single strand of DNA constitute life? Yes and no. By itself it is a complex chemical, but when combined with other DNA in a living organism it is considered life. The stuff of souls tends to gather in living things as the environment is more interesting than nonliving environments. It is not so much that it is attracted to life as that it lingers, and thus begins to accumulate. Without conscious intelligence it fails to establish a personality—a self—and after death of the life-form disburses again.

After a certain point, when the lessons to be learned from the shear fact of life have been well learned by the newly formed entities, guided incarnations become the norm. This is to help the forming entities maximize the wisdom to be gained from their incarnations. Formed entities, operating in fourth density or higher, surround the immature entity when it has freed itself from a dead or dying body, and communicate. These conferences may be short, with a second incarnation occurring almost instantly when the path is clear and incarnation opportunities are available, or they may drag out, if the lesson to be learned requires a special environment or if incarnation opportunities are limited. In the meantime the forming entity does not wander, as it is essentially herded together with others like itself, and finds this stimulating.

Since incarnations are natural, when the forming entity is guided to a new body it sets up housekeeping willingly. This is a familiar experience. Burning issues which were present when the entity left its former home, a dead or dying body, come to the fore, and the forming entity is off again on the great exploration that life provides. Being incarnated is far more stimulating and fascinating than the alternative, being discarnate, at this stage, and out-of-body experiences seldom occur unless trauma to the body is extreme. Incarnations gain the entity an acute sense of mission. Think of your current third-density existence and your current mission to determine your orientation, service-to-self or service-to-others. How would a spirit form so decide? What sacrifice is required for service-to-others? The orientation decision of the entity is proved out by life circumstances. In some cases an entity continues to learn through incarnation, even when in a higher density. Incarnations are a learning tool.

Forming Entities

In the beginning, each forming entity is aware only of itself. Self-awareness is a constant state in all life of whatever form, but at the start this is the only state. Forming entities are placed into third-density incarnations, repeatedly, to hasten the third-density lesson—the orientation determination. Whether incarnated or not, forming entities first become aware of others based on the effect upon the self. Is the effect pleasant or unpleasant, dominating or acquiescing, desired or resisted? Incarnated or not, social interchange has begun. Sense of the other is also born in this context, not only in awareness of the partner in social interactions, but also by observing others undergoing a similar experience. Within third density there is first self-awareness, second reacting to the presence of others, and lastly the capacity for empathy.

ZetaTalk

In making the orientation determination, the entity choosing service-to-self is not so much progressing towards this determination as clinging back. They remain most comfortable with self-awareness, and react to others in this context, essentially asking, "What can you do for me?" Interactions between entities change and become more complex during spiritual fourth density, and many entities completing their third-density physical existence are already operating in this mode. Following the development of the capacity for empathy comes the determination to intercede, to rescue, and as an adjunct to this determination the entity begins cooperative efforts, the sum being greater than the parts.

Complex social interchange presents forming entities with situations requiring compromise if goals are to be met, and the need to subjugate personal desires so that another might be rescued or the group as a whole might benefit. While the entity leaning toward the service-to-others orientation moves steadily in this direction, the entity leaning toward service-to-self reacts to this greater social complexity with more of the same old reaction, "What's in it for me?" As entities surrounding the emerging service-to-self entity are learning compromise and conciliation, the technique for the self-focused entity to gain more for the self is essentially manipulation. Since groups of emerging service-to-others entities are forming, the emerging service-to-self entity tunes its manipulation skills so as to manipulate groups, too. The orientations, even within third density, set out upon different paths, and polarization increases as they progress.

What does the future hold? The service-to-self entities' spiritual existence is essentially frozen while their intellectual existence progresses. For the service-to-self entities there is even less interplay and manipulation between entities than took place in third density. A rigid hierarchy with rules for everything emerges so that the lessons can proceed. Spiritual wisdom for the service-to-others entities continues to grow and augments rather than detracts from their intellectual progress. Skills in team efforts, where the individual is not required to sacrifice, but can learn and grow while contributing, are honed. Where the focus at the beginning of third density was self-awareness, by the end of fourth density in the service-to-others orientation the focus has expanded to be on group awareness.

7
Reincarnation

Forming entities on a third-density world incarnate almost continuously early in their third-density existence, unless there is a lack of opportunity. Just after an intelligent species has been genetically engineered, however, forming entities usually find the opposite situation—more than enough bodies awaiting an incarnation, a choice. This is due to many forming entities aborting upon death, so that a stable or growing population has an increasing number of bodies but few reincarnating entities. During these early years the majority of intelligent, conscious, creatures are in fact virgin territory for a new forming entity, with the minority being occupied by a reincarnating spirit. The birthing envoys, at this stage, allow the process to occur automatically. In due time they step in to start guiding incarnations, but they do this without having to resort to the imposition of any physical restraints.

Spirit guides force an out-of-body entity back into its body, and birthing envoys gather up entities leaving a dead or dying body. How is this done without physical restraints? If spirits can pass through walls and travel freely, would they not simply flit away from the entities watching over them?

ZetaTalk

Order is maintained in these situations by what we would best describe as a force of will. Entities acting as school-yard monitors on a third-density world are operating in spiritual fourth density, and many have arrived from even higher densities to do service. Spiritually, they have more bulk, more mass, and certainly have more wisdom and skill to coax and manipulate lesser entities.

An immature entity leaning toward service-to-self is led to an environment, among more mature entities, where it can be the center of attention, and thus it has no urge to wander. Immature entities leaning toward service-to-others are placed together with a peer that needs healing, and participate with higher density entities in this process. Likewise, given their sense of purpose, they have no immediate urge to wander. Where recently incarnated entities have unsettled business and wish to visit the living or to visit certain settings, a field trip is essentially arranged. Some of these field trips go on for years and even hundreds of years, producing what you term a haunting. During this time the distraught entity is in the company of its guides, who normally keep watch over a number of other immature entities at the same time. Nevertheless, the guides can be called upon to attend to the haunting entity, when need be.

Aborted Entities

During times of a rapid increase in population, such as the Earth has experienced during the past half century, no reincarnation occurs in many intelligent creatures, but a forming entity may begin. As is usual in these circumstances, most will abort. The spark is not lit, and after death dissipation occurs. This essential abortion is not due to any action on the part of the birthing envoys, who are there to gather what emerges, but rather to lack of action having taken place within the body. Where a life is lived passively, with little challenge and exhibiting no initiative, a forming entity is unlikely to do anything but dissipate upon death. There is nothing for the birthing envoys to gather. Once formed, however, entities do not dissipate. Failure to form is due to a lazy or indolent life-style, lack of native intelligence, or lack of stimulation. In this regard, the challenging, stressful life is a benefit, rather than a drawback. Thus, when the harvest time comes, during the pending pole shift, there will not be close to five billion Terran souls to be escorted to new homes, but only a little more than a billion.

40

Animals' Souls

Not all living human bodies have incarnate souls. Those humans who are severely retarded, or in a deep coma with scant hope of recovery, or simply in a primitive and self-centered, idle, life-style may not have souls. On the other hand, they might. It is dependent on what lessons the soul requires, and what school room the soul would best be in to receive these lessons. Would a soul ever enter and incarnate into a nonhuman physical form? Most certainly, but only on rare occasions would such an arrangement be allowed. The reason is that this existence does not have much to teach an entity, and this is the consideration by which the birthing envoys are guided.

What type of animal might the entity incarnate into? Any kind, although most likely this would be a mammal, a reptile, or a bird. These categories include the mammals of the seas, and small as well as large reptiles and birds. Thus, when you see life, you should consider it to be precious, as you know not what you may be destroying. Dolphins are as intelligent as dogs or horses or pigs, and as such are sentient animals deserving of consideration. In fact, as souls may incarnate temporarily into such animals, they should be considered to have this possibility. A rare chance, but possible.

Crowded Incarnations

On worlds where incarnations are beginning to repeat, where entities have sparked due to incarnating into intelligent species and are reincarnating again and again, crowded incarnations seldom happen, as there is a plenitude of bodies for the entities to incarnate into. However, in a situation such as the Earth is due to experience, where the majority of bodies will die suddenly, leaving the formerly incarnated entities without opportunities, chaos can and does ensue. Crowded incarnations are very temporary. For instance, during the forthcoming pole shift this potential may exist for several months. The normal procedure where immature entities are gathered upon the death of their body and amused or otherwise occupied until the next incarnation can be arranged, is difficult due to the numbers, so at times these entities roam about and try to arrange their own incarnations.

For multiple entities to be incarnating in a body at once, all are weak or they would not tolerate cohabitation. Normally the birthing guides prevent such takeovers but during chaotic conditions, multiple incarnations can pass

41

ZetaTalk

notice temporarily. If the originally incarnating entity does not want to be removed and lingers about in resentment, the birthing guides soon arrive to set things right again. However, if the entity displaced in fact was looking for a way out and is relieved, this may be treated as a voluntary walk-in and allowed to continue. The takeover is often rebuffed, as the originally incarnating entity most definitely has the advantage, being familiar with the territory, for instance. The incarnating entity and its human body sense what they might term ghosts or spirits about, and may even be aware of spiritual discussions or invitations, but are otherwise not disturbed by the true drama around them.

Old Souls

If the Earth is a home to forming entities, and the Council of Worlds is regulating visits between entities who have graduated from such homes to travel about the universe, then just how ancient are such entities sitting on the Council? The length of time is not a relevant guide here, as progression in spiritual matters is less a matter of years than a matter of growth. There are old souls in the service-to-self camps that have barely progressed past the point of most immature souls on Earth! They are firmly service-to-self, and thus progressed to fourth density, and there they sit. There are relatively young souls who move rapidly through the densities, as by their nature they learn rapidly and do not hesitate to apply their knowledge. And in between are the vast majority, who linger at points, revisit areas they have passed through before to solidify lessons, and become blocked due to their natures now and then, moving beyond the blocks only when they realize that this is preventing any forward progress.

Star Children

A star child is an incarnation into human form by an entity from another world. Star children are often misunderstood while incarnated as humans, simply because they have no way of communicating their vast background to their human neighbors. Imagine trying to talk about jungles and deep oceans and the vastness of space to little children, who have only known the nursery! There is no frame of reference. Star children seldom operate alone, but are assisted by others from their group who operate disincarnately, in the main. Nevertheless, the star child finds himself cut adrift, as the human body is confused and has only the incarnating soul as a point of reference. Thus, a

42

star child's spirit may urge the human mind and body to a particular action that the human, mingling in human society with its limited perspective, finds absurd. The incarnation is then at odds with itself, with the human distressed and feeling lonely and confused.

When We Die

Humans are aware of a reception line awaiting them when they die, from the reports of near-death experiences—a long tunnel with a bright white light at the end, and those now deceased who were close to them waiting or beckoning. If the moment of death is confusing to doctors, it is no less clear in the spiritual realm. An injured body, such as one sustaining massive brain injury, may cease to be a home for the incarnating entity months before those attending the death watch finally pull the sheets up over the lingering beloved. It is possible, in such a circumstance, that the entity has already been placed in another, thriving, human body—a newborn babe. On the other hand, some entities hang around long after the body has been cremated or burned, as haunting ghosts. Beyond the issue of when the spirit leaves the body is the spiritual issue of how the entity puts the past life to rest, judges progress made on various lessons that were at the fore going into the incarnation, and determines any future course of action they personally might desire as a result—critique time.

If the death was sudden and unexpected, the entity may have many outstanding issues they remain concerned with after the physical body dies. This invariably is the first stop after death, though it varies, depending on the general orientation of the entity and their life circumstances. Elderly persons, who had long settled their affairs in preparation for the inevitable, might not do more than cast a backward glance on their way to the future, noting that their death was being handled as they had anticipated. Someone in their prime, with dependent children or oldsters and many outstanding promises, might linger at this stage, visiting those they are concerned about as a ghost, essentially an out-of-body, for days or months until they can see the outcome. This stage differs between orientations, the service-to-others entities lingering longer due to their concern for others and the service-to-self entities wishing only to move on to future opportunities. At times, those who have been wronged and wish for vindication or revenge may also linger at this stage, haunting in an effort to influence human affairs.

ZetaTalk

Critique of the incarnation, judging its success or failure, is not always what the entity might desire. The entity might feel he, himself, has made progress where the spirit guides have another opinion entirely. Progress on lessons to be learned can be confused by cross currents, where the life circumstances offered opportunities such that unplanned lessons were addressed, and those planned got neglected. The immature entity may view the incarnation a failure, in this regard, and be surprised to find the record being looked at from unexpected angles. Most often the entity has made scarce progress, and will find themselves repeating the setting in future lives until progress is made.

The stage where future action is determined marks the point where the past life is settled and the future is beginning. This point is not reached as long as issues from the past life and the critique are outstanding. It is at this stage that the lessons at the fore of the next incarnation are clear. The immature entity may not be in agreement, and thus this stage can be drawn out, as the incarnation would be wasted if the focus were not clear. Where humans are unaware of their past lives, and per the Rule of Forgetfulness are supposed to start the incarnation with a clean slate, in fact the immature entity needs to be clear on how their progress is viewed by others. They may not agree, but they must understand. At this point the next incarnation is planned and plotted by the spirit guides, who give scant consideration to what the immature entity might be clamoring for.

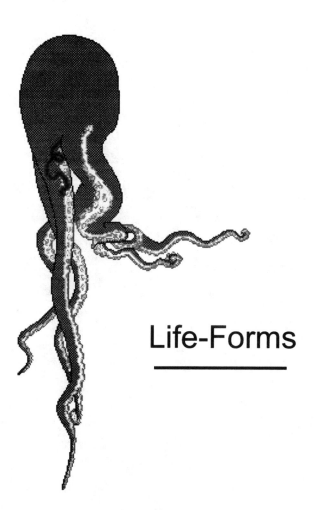

Life-Forms

8
Life Forms

Some aliens receive nutrients from basking in the Sun. This is true as some aliens, ourselves included, have to some degree inserted the genetics of plants into our systems. We create chlorophyll in response to energy emitted from a typical sun, and synthesize crude nutrients such as minerals and water into sugars. This all only goes so far, and in fact only gives us what you would describe as a sugar high, a boost. Most of the alien forms mankind will meet will be gray. Of the some thousand or more species visiting Earth, over half have been of a gray tone. The color is what your eye can perceive. Your scientists will tell you that the human eye sees only a very small spectrum of what is to be seen. When the color of the skin before you cannot be seen by you, you register gray. It is impossible to describe the color spectrum that humans are missing, as they would have no frame of reference. The colors are new to humans. The rainbows we see have dozens of colors beyond the rainbows you see.

Sexual Variations

The most common form of sexuality in the universe is two genders, emerging due to the obvious—if one wants to form a new genetic entity from various DNA samples, mixing two DNA samples together will do it. In fact, any life-form that does not combine into new variations will die out, unable to withstand the environmental variables that it sooner or later encounters. Inbred gene pools likewise are susceptible to disease or heritable diseases, as zoo keepers are acutely aware. The ability of the gene pool to survive by mixing is the reason that DNA most often has two strands. Those life-forms that had but a single strand did not survive to reproduce, and life-forms with more than two strands were prone to genetic flaws during the parting and re-merging phase of conception. Thus bisexuality is the most common form, followed by the ability of the life-form to clone itself.

The Earth is an example of the great number of sexual variations that can emerge. But whether the new offspring is the result of an intense and devoted coupling, pairing for life, or a casual encounter where insects swarm or fish mingle their deposit on the bottom of the pond, the process is the same—two DNA halves meeting to make a whole. Thus, the additional variations that the universe would present to man would not be that surprising. Size, shape, longevity of the coupling, and timing of mating or frequency of the routine are factors related to what the life-form found was most successful during its evolution.

The frequently seen sexual characteristic of male bulk versus female delicacy, so common in mammals on Earth, is not the most common arrangement throughout the universe. Large males have emerged on Earth due to their tendency to win the right to mate with the available females, thus passing their genes along. Many of your insects have the female huge, such as the queen bee, her size reflecting her focused vocation. Size of the male matters not as mating is done once, as a result of a swarm. Throughout the universe, the most common size and shape arrangement is a similar size, due to the fact that most life-forms are from water planets and conception occurs outside the body. Where life is carried inside the body, the female form reflects this. The extremes of this vary from birth when barely formed, as with your kangaroos, to birth when fully formed, as with most of your mammals.

Male strength and aggression versus female composure, common in life-forms that have emerged on Earth, are not the only arrangement that mankind is aware of. Some insects, such as the Praying Mantis, have the female massive and aggressive with the male small enough to become a snack for the female after the mating, which usually occurs. Land creatures on Earth have emerged with the males aggressive and the females passive due in part to the number of carnivores on Earth. Males who exploded with rage when their territory was challenged, and with great strength and resolve during the battle, protected the females they had impregnated and thus passed their genes along. Throughout the universe, aggression differences in the sexes most often tip towards the female being more aggressive, as she must snatch all available food for the eggs or young she is about to produce.

On Earth, mating frequency is most often related to seasons, the young making the mad scramble to attain enough size to survive during the warm summer months. In life-forms where the young are at great risk, mating frequency is almost constant, as with humans where the young are hairless and immobile. In other parts of the universe, or on other planets with longer orbits, seasons would either not be a factor or long hibernation of the life-form might ensue. There are life-forms in the universe that have sex only once, on average, during their life time and then produce a large number of offspring. On a planet with harsh living conditions, where tender young life has a narrow window of time in which to scramble toward adulthood, mating and rearing young becomes an intense focus, where all members of the life-form do little else.

Reptilians

Reptilian alien groups are somewhat cold-blooded, which does not relate to their orientation at all. Reptilian entities that humans may encounter may be of service-to-others or service-to-self orientation. However, as the reptilian genetics allow for less empathy, or telepathic awareness of others, which the service-to-self orientation finds distracting, reptilians most often are service-to-self.

There are numerous reptilians at work in the vicinity of Earth. Some of the forms are humanoid, with arms and hands with fingers and opposable thumbs, legs and feet with toes, eyes forward on the face rather than facing to the side, and a bipedal stance. Others take the form of what you would call snakes, with some development of limbs in varying numbers. Others have forms similar to lizards and walk on four or more legs, their bodies being too stiff to allow an upright stance. These alien forms can rear up to perform functions, but essentially work at the floor level. Because this places them at a disadvantage when meeting humans, they are not used by the service-to-self orientation in addressing humans, as the service-to-self orientation uses intimidation to function.

The Dino is a reptilian form familiar to humans. Where not as large as the Earth's dinosaurs, this reptilian looks like a miniature Tyrannosaurus Rex. This form is used by the service-to-self orientation in encounters with humans, as intimidation is supported not only by the imposing form, which stands at least as tall as the average human, but by educated humankind's awareness of the fierceness of a similar dinosaur in Earth's past.

Hominoids

It is frequently mentioned that the Pleiadeans look very much like humans, as do the Nordics and Sirians. Where the similarities immediately impress humans having contact with these hominoids, there are differences that would stand out should they simply set up housekeeping in the neighborhood. The eating habits would be the first to be noticed, as where genetic engineering of hominoids has resulted in similar looking forms, the worlds the hominoids had to adapt to differed greatly. Nordics eat little, having learned to adapt to lean times on their world. Faced with what humans consider a meal, a Nordic would appear to be a picky eater.

Just as the Men In Black are under stress when exposed to the Sun's rays, hominoid life-forms such as ourselves from dim suns have difficulty dealing with a mid-sized sun such as yours. This would be true of Pleiadeans as well as Nordics, who would not simply get sunburn, but would also develop symptoms of radiation poisoning as well.

Humans think of hominoids as bipedal and hairless—the naked ape. Hominoid forms evolve naturally on many worlds, and just as the proto-hominoid on Earth was a hairy ape, the proto-hominoid elsewhere can take many forms. Due to the genetic engineering that takes place, grafting genetics from existing hominoid stock, the hominoid visitors that humans have encountered look similar to humans in the main, and thus have given the erroneous impression that this is the hominoid form. The naked ape is but one variation of the hominoid form.

Cat People

There are alien hominoids that look like monkeys or apes to humans and a variation on this form is a furry hominoid humans take to be a bipedal cat. Humans have whiskers, but not the stiff sensing kind that rodents and their pet cats and dogs possess, so seeing whiskers on the delicate face of a fuzzy visitor has caused them to assume these visitors to be cat people.

Praying Mantis

What is termed the Praying Mantis is a hominoid, and what many contactees take to be the insect forms of their visitors are almost invariably hominoid. They have no physiological similarity to the insects of Earth, however, and in fact are a form of hominoid—mammalian. The Praying Mantises are one of hundreds of alien groups involved in the Earth's transformation, but they are few in number. They possess remarkable telepathic abilities, surpassing that of ourselves, the Zetas.

Bigfoot

Bigfoot is an early model of man, an interim model of one of the six races of man. Bigfoot was separated, removed from the others, and moved into remote areas. The reason for this is that Bigfoot was to house a group of entities who are in quarantine. They are in quarantine, placed into a primitive condition, at their request, so that they can return to a basic understanding of how to get along with each other, with nature, and ponder the wondrous workings of nature. Their quarantine is not an exile. It is a search for peace.

Men in Black

The Men in Black are not extraterrestrial at all, but live underground, in tunnels and caverns. Being unable to live on the Earth's surface, the Men in Black established themselves underground when they first arrived on Earth, in a technologically advanced state. Their townships exist in isolation, as they very seldom travel from one township to another, being at risk of exposure to humans in so doing.

Mythological Creatures

Where the dinosaurs died out long before mankind was engineered into being from ape stock, the Earth was not the only planet to give birth to such creatures. Evolution follows similar patterns, and where your Earth brought forth dinosaurs with wings, so did other planets compatible with the Earth. Your dragons were transplants brought to the Earth by early ambassadors from the service-to-self orientation, who anticipated an increased harvest of lackeys from the Earth due to the fear and despair their dragons wrought. Were the dragons intelligent and incarnated with souls? No. On a scale of 1 to 10, where the average dog is a 10, a dragon was barely a 3. This is why, in spite of the massive size and capacity to fly as well as lumber over hill and dale, they were so easily slain. Dumb brutes. Did they breathe fire? No. But when roaring, open mouthed, it felt like that to those within range. They had hot breath and a big wind pipe.

The vampire legend is based on a creature similar to the Earth's vampire bats, one that evolved on another world. Just as dragons were brought to the Earth by aliens in the service-to-self orientation, to terrify humans they hoped to later recruit into their ranks, so were large vampire bats brought to Earth. The imported bats were large though slender. When flying they looked like bats, but after they landed their folding wings looked like outstretched arms—the vampire in his black cape. In any light nearby the eyes looked red, as they lacked the protective pigment necessary in harsh daylight, showing only the blood just under the surface of the eye. And just as some hairy monkeys on Earth have hairless, pale faces, so did these large vampire bats have hairless faces. They were chosen by the service-to-self aliens because they resembled humans, in the dusk. The terrified victims, frozen in fear, gave birth to the vampire myth of supernatural powers.

9
12th-Planet Hominoids

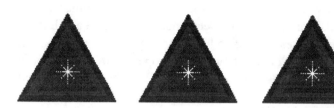

There is life on the 12th Planet, the giant comet that causes the periodic pole shifts. The primary race is a hominoid race, who to this day dress in attire reminiscent of Roman soldiers. The males find this to be comfortable attire that has a macho image. There have been many excellent books written on these subjects, and all hold a grain of truth. One of the legacies left on Earth by the hominoid visitors from the 12th Planet is radioactivity from their nuclear warfare. Yes, they had the bomb, and used it. In attempts to nuke each other into compliance, they dropped numerous bombs, the majority on the Arabian Peninsula, with a small number in India and a scattering across the African Continent. These bombs were in the main not as large as the ones built during the Cold War, but were more deadly as the radioactivity lingered and poisoned the ground, making it utterly uninhabitable—for millennia.

As the largest and strongest hominoid race on Earth at the time, the giant hominoids from the 12th Planet were understandably arrogant about the effects their genetics had on the humans they bred with. There were two lines of hominoids left to run the mining operations between passages of the 12th Planet—royalty and soldiers. The royalty interbred with each other, retaining the purity of their genetics, as without this purity their line would be forced to died out upon return to their home planet. The soldiers had lower-class women from the 12th Planet available to them as sexual consorts but often chose to create and maintain harems of human sex slaves of all ages and from both sexes. Most often the offspring died during childbirth, due to the large size of the infants, but those who lived carried genetics from the father, which gave rise to the legend that these hominoids created the human race, which is simply not true.

Pyramids discovered around the world buried under drifting sand or vegetative overgrowth have a similarity in appearance, and this is not by accident. They were made by the same group, and for similar purposes. The giant hominoids from the 12th Planet wandered the Earth and left their handiwork even in areas where no lore of their presence remains. These hominoids are recorded in mythology in Europe, as Greek Gods or the Visigoths, in Africa in the memory of the Dogon tribe, and in Central and South America in the Incan and Mayan cities. However, they also visited Australia and the Orient, though the only trace of this is in the artifacts left behind. The pyramid shape survives earthquakes and windstorms, and thus was the shape of choice. After the passage, when pole shifts rearranged the landscape, the pyramids lost their worth as astronomical devices, but their durability kept them from disappearing from the landscape. Thus, they are on occasion discovered, and become yet another piece of the puzzle that mankind is grappling to solve.

Crystals

It is not your imagination that makes you see tetrahedral shapes on the Moon, and the faint outline of such on the eroded surface of Mars. Large crystals have been used in the past to boost communications by the giant hominoids from the 12th Planet. The tetrahedral form simply provided the best, focused emission, when energy was applied on all perimeter surfaces and converged in the center. They had established a communication post on the Moon, and they had a mining operation on Mars long before setting up on the Earth. This was one of the things noticed by the astonished astronauts when they disembarked on the Moon. This subject receives much press, and much speculation, as the rumors can be supported by faint images in amateur telescopes.

Mining on Mars

Mars today is a dead planet, but in the recent past this was not the case. Some life-bearing planets have a stronger footing than others, being closer to the warmth of a sun, for instance, and more particularly being a water planet like the Earth. Mars has little of that precious substance, and was a life-bearing planet only where the freezing point had not trapped the water. The atmosphere surrounding a water planet can rebuild quickly, particularly in the components that support life. On a dry planet the atmosphere is fragile, and each rebuilding takes away more of the precious water. In the past, Mars sustained life to a level not unlike our home in Zeta Reticuli—moss and insects and worms. On such worlds there is not enough food in the food chain to support animals above that level, and setbacks occur repeatedly. A bug-eating reptile might get its start, only to die off during lean times, time and again. Thus such planets plateau.

Mars met its demise as a result of visitors from the 12th Planet who set up mining operations on Mars in preference to Earth where large carnivorous mammals roamed about in great numbers. The 12th Planet has no such carnivores on land, and as large and muscular as these giant hominoid visitors are, they quaked at the thought. Where the atmosphere on Mars was thin, it was ample, so the visitors set about using what water resources they could muster to wash the ore they were after. In so doing they sought to control the runoff on the relatively flat surface of Mars, and did so in a thoughtless manner by directing wastewater down a culvert. Thus precious water increasingly was sent underground, and a chain of events was set in motion that could not be reversed. The surface of Mars cooled as the atmosphere thinned, and the freezing surface accelerated this process.

Soon the atmosphere was too thin to breathe, and as the 12th-Planet hominoids are used to a perpetual summer, they were not all that reluctant to leave a freezing planet. Earth now looked more promising, especially as they had little alternative. They devised ways of dealing with the carnivores, specifically buffering themselves with human slaves trained in defense. Eventually, after being quarantined from Earth, they learned how to create and maintain their own atmosphere in airtight chambers, and thus able to be relocated, they have continued their mining operations within your solar system, on this spot or that, and are here still.

Great Pyramids

Humans ponder the pyramids of Egypt and similar structures in South and Central America, and wonder how early man could rise or move such large stones? Of course, they could not. Even today the mechanics would be imposing to the point of being impossible. The answer is, of course, that early man did not build these structures. The heads on Easter Island were established by the same mechanism and individuals who built the pyramids. The hominoids from the 12th Planet gave The Call to various service-to-self aliens at the time, and due to the resulting alliances with these aliens had the ability to levitate objects at times. They paid a price for these services, and are still working their way out of that. Many of their number developed strong service-to-self orientations during this time, and have influenced their culture severely and in a long-term manner.

The Great Pyramids were built essentially as navigational devices. Why was it necessary to build such large structures as interstellar navigational guides? Because, in the locale, any astronomical device would be subject to shifting sands. Whereas the residents of the 12th Planet had great longevity, they did not last on Earth from one appearance of the 12th Planet to another. Several generations would pass, the knowledge of how to read the stars and what the 12th-Planet kingship expected of them passed from parent to child. Conscientious parents, aging and sure to die before their progeny could return to the home planet where they had royalty status, built a navigational system that was rock solid and sure—the Giant Pyramids.

The Great Pyramids, by their great size and weight, ensured stability. All this just to sight an incoming comet, which makes its appearance on a regular basis and can be seen weeks, if not months, beforehand? The Great Pyramids were not used solely for sighting an incoming object, as their primary purpose was to act as a guidance system for the launches the exiled 12th-Planet residents would make to meet their home planet. This required precision, as their rockets were no more sophisticated than those used to boost man into space today, and once in space they simply coasted until drawn into the gravitational orbit of the water planet they owed their allegiance to.

It is known that a hidden chamber exists in one of the Great Pyramids, accessible only via a tunnel so narrow that it might be traveled by a rat, yet so straight and long that it could only have been used for sighting. The chamber lies empty now, a center platform formed like a shallow basin without whatever object was intended. It is hypothesized that there is a back door to this room, as of yet not located, whereby an occupant or object could escape. This hypothesis has the room acting as a tomb or in the worst case scenario as an isolation chamber, or if not for a human or alien occupant, then holding a massive crystal. None of these are true, as the room has no other entry and was never intended to hold a solid object. The occupant was a liquid, pooled in the shallow basin and reflecting light outward only when light shown down the long tunnel at that particular angle—the light from the approaching 12th Planet. Various other sighting tunnels, as yet undiscovered, caught the reflected light. The liquid, of course, evaporated over time, leaving only the puzzle behind.

Sphinx

The Sphinx is an example of a fancy burial chamber, a mausoleum of sorts, built by visitors from the 12th Planet who were into the sport of lion hunting. The grave was intended for a large and powerful male who stood tall in the circle of hunters, and all felt having his grave guarded by one of his conquests a suitable statement on his abilities and might. As is often the case in the affairs of man, these plans went awry, as he was slaughtered by a rival and went unburied altogether, his body rotting under the sun, eaten by lions, no doubt.

The God Myth

Humans quite naturally tend to think of their relationship to a god in child-to-parent terms, an outgrowth not only from their impressionable early years but also from their general sense of hopelessness in being able to control their environment. For a god concept to emerge, there must also be a sense of helplessness on the part of the supplicant, a sense that they are powerless to affect the outcome except by offering bribes or scapegoats. In this regard, the giant hominoid visitors from the 12th Planet worked their way into many god myths, as they were exacting in their demands for obedience from their slaves, and as hominoids they were easily seen as extensions of a parent.

ZetaTalk

It is not by accident that the hominoid inhabitants of the 12th Planet look and dress like Greek Gods, the Gods of Mount Olympus, as they are one and the same. Mythological stories about thunderbolts being thrown and travel through the clouds were based on the technological feats of these third-density visitors from the 12th Planet, who had mastered the modern-day equivalent of lasers and who were able to transport an individual via a rocket booster strapped on the back. To the primitive humans, who came barely to the waists of the strapping, handsome giants, they were gods. The Greek Gods are reported to be jealous and wrathful on the one hand, and kindly and mentoring on the other—a bit like people. Of course, they were no gods, any more than the humans of today, but their very human exploits are still reported with awe.

The legends among many human cultures regarding the exploits of the giant hominoids from the 12th Planet are in no small part due to the rigid rules these visitors had regarding interbreeding with the humans they used as virtual slaves. Kept apart from humans in this manner, they retained their edge, as they were by far the largest, the most technologically advanced, and the smartest hominoid race around. Humans were, at the time, evolving from the caveman stage, with only an occasional genius born in the purely human strains. During the evolution of any third-density species, intelligence is gradually increased due to genetic selection, the smarter individuals passing on their genetics due to their ability to evade danger and manipulate circumstances around them. Thus, the discrepancies between humans and the visitors from the 12th Planet were many and significant.

Ancient Egyptian gods, ancient Babylonian gods, the Vizigoths of Germany, ancient Mayan and Incan gods, are almost to a one particular individuals from the 12th-Planet royalty, stationed on Earth to supervise mining operations. Stories about ancient rebels, notable for their stature and courage in battle, are also frequently based in part on the heritage from these visitors, as the rebel most often carried some genetics from the rape of a female slave who managed somehow to escape and bear her oversized infant alive. The legacy today is genetically dispersed throughout the mid-eastern countries, Germanic countries, and the south seas, and is identifiable in those humans who simultaneously possess a large stature, a fierce temper, and strong musculature. Rather than being considered gods, they are often considered criminals.

━╂━

10
Zetas

Our home planet is in the star system that you term Zeta Reticuli. Since the Betty and Barney Hill episode, when we were closely and correctly associated with the Zeta Reticuli star system, the citizens of the United States and the media and ufologists have called us Zetas. To you, therefore, we are the Zetas. We, of course, have our own names for things. Zeta Reticuli is indeed a binary star system, or at least that part of it you, on Earth, are aware of. In fact, there is much more to the star system than you are aware of. The binary stars circle each other on an extreme end of Zeta Reticuli, less than one third into the star system itself. The other two thirds are composed of stars not visible to you.

ZetaTalk

What we are telling you is that the planet we originate from is not known to you, as it is part of the 2/3 mass of the star system not known to you. Do you think our eyes got so large because our sun was bright? It has been rumored that our planet is dying, and that this is the reason we are seeking genetic rebirth on your planet, Earth. In fact, our planet is long dead, and we Zetas have been living by artificial means for eons. We learned to live in cavities within planets, and by artificial light.

Early Zeta

Where Early Man was a hybrid of various ape or monkey forms and existing hominoid forms, Early Zeta was not a hybrid at all, but a transplant. The worlds we were placed upon had not sustained a life-form complex enough to be considered a base for intelligence. The gap was too great. Early Zeta therefore was placed, full grown and conscious, on Zeta worlds. Like the transplants who are coexisting with humans now on Earth, Early Zeta was aware of the purpose of the transfer. Thus transplanted, Early Zeta multiplied to the extent our worlds could support a population, much as humans have upon the Earth.

Early Zeta differed from our present form primarily in brain size and mental capacities. Early Zeta was also stockier, shorter, had large flat feet and in appearance was something of a low brow, with the head jutting out the back rather than rounding. Our large eyes were an adaptation to our worlds, dim by your standards, so Early Zeta was a bit blind on his new home, not a problem as the only danger Early Zeta faced was from others of his kind. Our worlds do not contain carnivorous, nor even herbivorous animals—just plants and bugs.

The Zetas

Our race is not dying. We, the Zetas, have been incarnating and reproducing for almost 8.5 times the length of time that intelligent humans have been doing so, and there is no end in sight. The Zetas are accused of having a group mind, seemingly operating like insects, by rote, and without individuality. Where did these assumptions come from? First, we reproduce by cloning, so our appearance can be remarkably similar. Second, our mode of communicating is telepathic, over the heads of humans who for the most part sense no conversation going on at all. Third, there is a lack of argument and indecision that humans see in us when we are at work attending to our contactees, as we have all agreed ahead of time on how to handle issues that might arise. Humans who see us having a group mind are drawing these conclusions on scanty data.

The Zetas are numerous in form. The forms result from the various planets we have spread to during the life of our form. Each planet plays upon the genetic structure, encouraging certain genetics to emerge and demonstrate their superiority in survival and longevity. Thus, the life-form gradually adapts to the environment it finds itself in. Counts would differ, but for the sake of this discourse, we will say that the number of variations that would be visibly noticeable to humans is 127.

Meals

We no longer eat, having genetically engineered ourselves in such a way that the digestive tract went out with the bath water. We nourish ourselves through our skin, through a chemical bath we prepare in the laboratory and completely emerge ourselves in. Unlike some of the bad press that has been thrown our way, we do not require enzymes from living creatures in order to live. Does anyone think that entities as advanced as we would require that in order to live? We can live in space, on a dead planet, or anywhere. The chemicals needed for life are easily manufactured by an advanced species such as ourselves. Where we have mouths, our digestive tract is not complete. We avoid putting anything in our mouths, as like your appendix, anything put in can only cause problems.

Emotions

We are clearly more intelligent than the humans we are responding to, but beyond this IQ difference we are also brooking no nonsense in our replies, and thus the interpretation by some humans that our responses are unemotional. Sentimentality has its place in developing bonds, but this is not our primary intent during these discourses. Our bonding activities are engaged in one-to-one with our human contactees, who have given The Call to us due to the nature of their call being oriented toward service-to-others. It is here that we bond and deal with emotions on our part or on the part of the contactee. Our primary purpose within ZetaTalk is to establish truth on many matters often deliberately confused by those in what we term the establishment in human society. We do this so that humans might arrive at their own conclusions, armed with the facts and insights they are not otherwise allowed to arrive at due to lack of information or distorted or untruthful information from the establishment. We are not ruthless, unless those who do not wish the facts lined up impeccably are complaining about the lack of wiggle room they are given.

Names

Aliens, who communicate telepathically, have no need for names that can be communicated in written symbols. This is because a telepathic communication is rich, and conveys the group the alien is associated with, intent, age and physical makeup, and any other nuance the other party in the conversation may be interested in. A name is simply unnecessary in service-to-others alien groups. Human society finds names necessary because of the lack of telepathy. Thus aliens are assigned names based on their constellation of origin or their appearance—Zeta, Pleiadean, Nordic, or Dino.

Schools

The young Zetas find themselves in a smorgasbord of stimulation, surrounded by toys and games that allow their curious minds to fully explore physics, chemistry, biology, and the social studies. Unlike human schools for their youngsters, where physics and chemistry experimentation is limited to lab time or simplistic at-home experiments, the Zeta youngster is not limited to time slots or scope, nor do we require the youngsters to be a certain age or grade before they have an opportunity. Don't they blow themselves up? Precautions are taken in the way these lessons are structured, so that the necessary knowledge is in place before next steps can be taken. The lessons have checkpoints, so, for example, the youngster cannot just reach for the vial of acid and taste.

Social interaction is not structured, as it is to some degree in human society where human youngsters are selected by the teacher to assume roles. Johnny gets to organize the field trip because the teacher likes his engaging smile. Zeta youngsters are counseled when they are having difficulty, and given assistance, when in need, to a degree that would astonish humans, but the roles they assume in play are self-chosen, and when they succeed at these roles it is based on honest interaction between the youngsters. In Zeta society, the equivalent of the dullard son of the boss assuming command of the company or the inept daughter of the PTA head getting the lead in the play does not exist. We do not use platitudes or hypocrisy to develop our youngsters, but deal with the truth, teaching our youngsters, by example, to do this also from the earliest age.

Entertainment

In human society, much history is recorded in written form, although with the advent of the electronic age, much is also recorded on video or audio tape. Do alien life-forms, such as ourselves, have an equivalent? We do indeed, but we have no need to rely on a *written* word as humans do. We are telepathic, so often the performing artist is soundless but nevertheless relays the composition perfectly. As for recording the great thoughts of the past, or works of art, the written word is considered cumbersome and inadequate. We use holographic forms, where all but telepathic thought is transmitted. In these cases, the intent of the author or artist is relayed through other means, such as symbolic motion or recreating the situation described, much as humans enjoy when going to the movie theater.

We, the Zetas, have the same range of activities that humans do. Why would we not? It's true we don't go out to eat as much, and with our muted sexuality we don't look forward to getting laid. But where you look forward to occasionally getting into a hot tub, our refreshment baths are a big deal. The spas are lush with plants, and music that vibrates through the water and walls is played. It's a total body experience.

We have more games than you, a thousandfold more, and a hundred times more intricate. Our games are played with holographs, which are generated by computer under control of our minds. The best are like chess, where many players engage in strategies, or several teams play against each other. What is the goal of these games? The same as your games. Where the game involves mental concentration, the goal is to improve upon and practice strategic planning. Where the game involves cooperation among players, the goal is to improve social skills and cooperation. Where the game involves close timing and precision from the team, the goal is to gain skill at delegation and rapid handoffs. Watch children intent at play. Are they not preparing for life?

Triads

Out and about in the universe, higher entities find themselves in situations that are totally unfamiliar and unexpected. There are no procedures or even general policies that can apply. What occurs where a difference of opinion arises? Beyond social interactions in strange social settings, strange physical settings are also encountered. Triads give us a means of quickly making decisions during our travels. The tie is broken. Either all agree or two of the three agree or two of the three disagree with the third. The issue is instantly settled.

Religion

Our religion is more an understanding of the universe. We are emotionally connected to the universe. We are within the One. We have kinship with one another as parts of the One. We have reverence for the universe and its workings, as a thing of beauty, which we wish to understand. Our religion is not like the major religions of the Earth, which deify entities human in appearance. These religions, where the message given to humans was to draw them to the light, have been corrupted over time by the forces of darkness. These religions now preach against knowledge, against self-initiative, against free thought. They restrain with rules which assist only those who wish to rule. Where human religions, however well-founded, have invariably been twisted by the service-to-self crowd until they have lost all semblance of the original intent, our faith is not so affected. The pure adage to love thy neighbor as thyself stands as the rule by which we guide ourselves, and there are no thou shalt not's included.

11
Hybrid Program

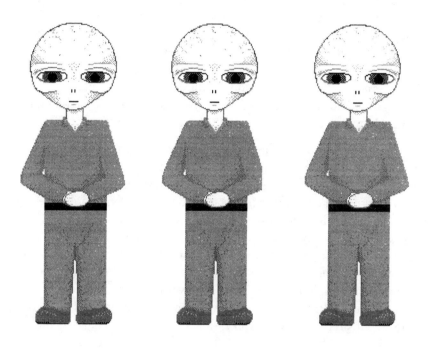

Our genetic engineering mission is not the first such mission on Earth. There have been dozens of such missions, each of which has taken place over many stages, with some of these stages having millennia between them. The hybrid program that we, the Zetas, are involved with is not underway throughout the world but is centered in the U.S. The reasons for this are territorial matters that are addressed by the Council of Worlds, where the various endeavors underway on Earth are laid out and agreements among the alien groups as to how humans will be affected are administered. The hybrids being developed, which encompass the best qualities of both humans and Zetas, will in the future be the incarnation home for service-to-others entities from throughout the world as well as North America. However, North America holds, as the melting pot of the world, genetic material from all the Earth, and thus suffices.

ZetaTalk

Zetan genetics are being used because the intelligence of humans cannot be more than doubled using only the current human genetic structure. The best that could be accomplished is a human at the genius level, and what we seek, what we are required to attain, is so very much higher. Telepathy, something your species can barely support, is another issue. Genetic engineering does not make something from nothing. It alters what already exists or inserts something already in existence. A third important issue is the level of violence in your human species. Blind rage is firmly rooted in your genetic heritage. To carve this out would leave too little remaining. This must be counteracted where it is found, in all the reaches of the brain, rather than simply rooted out. The Zetan genetics are the counteractant.

Those who will be continuing to incarnate on Earth are being polled, continuously, and voting willingly, as to their desires. As the genetic engineers, we are responsible for ensuring that the specifications for a fourth-density incarnation experience in the service-to-others orientation are met. We would not, for instance, bring forward violent tendencies, even if the humans voting were to indicate a desire for this. Likewise, even if humans voting were to indicate that they did not desire a higher intellect, this human vote would be negated by the overriding specification. Wanting to be part of the process, many humans imagine themselves to be an alien/human hybrid. As none of our hybrids are currently living in third density on Earth, these people are all simply publicity seekers.

Family Line

The hybrid program runs along family lines. When combining genes from a human with Zeta Reticulan genes, there is some unfortunate loss, but this loss is recaptured in subsequent efforts. This is not unlike a braid, where the strands are woven back in and the braid becomes stronger than loose hair or twine. Another way of thinking about this is to say that the first effort is rough-hewn, and subsequent efforts fill in the chinks. We have the capacity to go back in time to capture genetics, if we require.

While visitations have been going on for eons, it is only in the past few decades that the pace has been dramatically stepped up. The hybrid program, started in concept just after the turn of the century and put into full force only during the later half of this century, has only recently been part of the program. Collecting genetic contributions—sperm and ova—began with a few select individuals early in this century, and based on what we learned about compatibility and desirable genetic traits, we started the program in earnest. Prebirth agreements on participation in the hybrid program were made so that humans from the 1930s on would be available to the hybrid program. We also were able to include those already incarnated who gave The Call, but these were few in proportion to the need. Therefore, as the hybrid program began in earnest around 1950, among participants in the teens or twenties, the participants are now either youths, young adults, or middle aged—but are not elderly.

Father donors are examined as to their health regularly, and undergo sperm extraction at a time when the donor mother's ova is ready. Unlike the usual male sperm donation in human society, where the male is presumed to have selected his bed mate and the time and place of a sexual encounter as well, donor fathers in the hybrid program chose neither the mate or the time or place. To add to this insult, they are in the passive position when giving the donation. A cup is placed over their genitals, and the sexual response is generated through mental influences solely. There is no physical stimulation, and thus little pleasure. Where donor fathers are as willing to participate as the donor mothers, when back in human society this is not the kind of experience that gets loud discussion in the locker room. Thus, not much is heard about the donor father's experiences.

Extinction

Full-blood Zetas will continue in other parts of the universe. One should also not assume that full-blood humans will die out entirely either. This almost never occurs during species transitions, especially when a certain level of intellect is attained. There may be service-to-others groups on Earth composed entirely of humans that continue, isolated and content with their level of intellect, for instance. There will be service-to-self entities, taken before their human form is terminated, who will be human on other planets. This occurs frequently in the service-to-self orientation, as surviving infants are hard to come by in this orientation. Nurturing is rare. Thus, those choosing this orientation often are required to keep their current incarnation. Given the population explosion, why wouldn't the human race be back in business in a hurry after the cataclysms? There are three reasons:

ZetaTalk

1. A high mortality rate, where babies won't survive, and the birth rate will be less than zero. So far less, that the replacement will be almost nil. Combine this with the dropping fertility of the potential parents, and this will be devastating. Even though you may have many potential parents among the survivors, after 25 years of a nuclear winter, worldwide, most of these parents will be past the point of fertility, or at least the mothers will be. Robust fertility, and infant viability, will come too late. This is the situation after every pole shift.

2. A movement of the service-to-others toward living with or near the high-tech centers of the hybrids, where intermarriage will occur. With high-tech food production and medical treatment, babies do survive. In addition, if the parents of humans give The Call for their youngsters to be born with greater intelligence, genetic material will be available at the point of conception, just as it is today in some cases. There are humans being born today with Zetan genetic material, who are part Zetan, and they appear and act quite human. Just so, in the future, the genetic makeup of the human race will migrate in this direction. This has happened in the past, and this is why you are not, as you say, swinging from the trees!

3. A tendency of the service-to-self entities to eradicate themselves, and each other, especially as the controls will be missing which keep in check those so inclined. How long would the violent and unscrupulous population inside a prison live, if left entirely to their own inclinations? With increasing polarization of the orientations, the service-to-self entities will go off on their own, rummaging through the wreckage and living off what others have lost. This kind of existence works when there is a perpetual source of goods to plunder, but as these types do not plan or put themselves out, they will find themselves suddenly without. They will be suddenly without clean water, any food at all, or the wherewithal to warm themselves until morning. They die. But what about the mixed groups, who will be given the knowledge of how to feed and cloth themselves from the service-to-others groups or the hybrid communities. Will they not pull through? Some will raise children, and these children will marry or in any case produce children, but life will be rough. The point we are making here, is that they will not *thrive*. The service-to-others communities, and our hybrid communities, will be thriving. As incarnations are to be given

to those entities operating in the service-to-others orientation, new children will migrate to the thriving communities. This would happen anyway, as the young go where they see opportunity.

The Alternative

Those humans who are not ready to leave third density when they die will not reincarnate on Earth, but will go to a new world elsewhere in the universe. We are speaking here of spiritual readiness to leave third density, that the spirits incarnating in these humans have not made their determination whether to be service-to-self or service-to-others. This is not an intellectual choice but rather an emotional choice, and one followed by actions demonstrating that the choice is solid and unwavering. What will this new world be like?

It is a water world, with scarcely a rock or two jutting above the surface of the endless waves. The species on this planet have all evolved from life-forms that spend their entire life in the water. Thus, no mammals exist on this planet, since a stint on land, such as occurred in the past for your whales and dolphins, was not possible during their evolutionary past. This world has been a home to incarnating entities for a long time, through several transformations where those ready for fourth-density existence were harvested, leaving those undecided behind. This world has received transplants from other worlds frequently, so there is a broad spectrum of past experiences in the memories of those incarnating there. Humans reincarnating there will find they quickly adjust to living on a water world, having tentacles instead of hands, and tending the occasional batch of eggs.

This planet is carbon based and thus has life-forms that have compatible DNA to life-forms that have evolved on Earth. Thus, those entities incarnating on Earth in the future will be able to visit this world during their travels as fourth-density entities, acting as alien visitors to this world. Due to their common history, this setup is in fact ideal, as instant empathy would be in place when The Call is given. Humans today receive visitations from fourth density or higher entities incarnated as water life-forms—an octopus, fish, or jelly fish. Visitors adapt to the planet being visited, and thus these visitors from water worlds remain in water tanks during the visit. In the future, visits from Earth to this new water home will require the hominoid visitors to likewise make the accommodations, by wearing protective suits and bubble helmets for breathing.

ZetaTalk

Transplanted entities frequently have vague longings for the world left behind. This is particularly true when the circumstances require the entity to live in a radically different life-form than the former life-form, or where the world presents an environment that is strange. Former humans incarnating in the future on a water world might find themselves with strange longings while drifting around peaks and valleys on the ocean floor, a feeling of *deja vu*. Transplanted entities experiencing strong homesickness are sometimes transplanted back to their original home when graduating into fourth density. For former humans transplanted to a water world during the Earth's transformation to fourth-density service-to-others, going back home is a real possibility. If they have chosen the service-to-others orientation, it would be a simple request quickly honored.

12
Hybrid Form

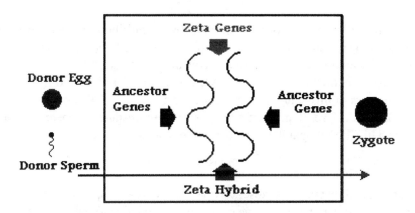

The hybrid form is neither human nor Zetan. The upgrading of the human race will provide a hominoid with our intelligence and telepathic abilities as well as the genetic adaptation that humans have to the Planet Earth. Certain human problems are being screened out—the tendency to become obese and the ability to become enraged beyond all thought of the consequences.

IQ

The hybrid IQ will be equivalent to the current Zeta IQ. A true 50/50 would have resulted in an IQ increase to a point much below the target IQ. Curiosity and creativity have also been increased, as these are factors of intelligence. Our IQ is higher than yours, and also different. Numbers alone do not describe the situation. Where your mind carries on dozens of thoughts simultaneously, ours carry on thousands. Should we Zetas take one of your IQ tests, which measure only speed and accuracy, we would measure around 287 IQ points.

Memory

Where the human animal has many memory levels—short term, long term, subconscious, conscious, and others unknown and thus not labeled by humans—the target hybrid has a cohesive memory, much like the Zetas.

Introspection has been increased, as the tie between the conscious and subconscious has been strengthened. It will not be so easy to discount occurrences in the future, selectively forgetting them.

Longevity

The hybrids will share the long life of their Zetan contributors. Our life span is much longer than humans, and the life span of the hybrid race we are genetically engineering will be as long as the Zetas currently enjoy. In your Earth years, this is 400 years. We experience debility for only the last 50 years of this span. In our culture we also do not rule against suicide. Therefore, if any Zeta finds his life circumstances unbearable, he can end his life in a painless manner without strife.

Senses

Sight and sound reception is closer to what the Zetas are capable of, vastly higher ranges than humans have ever experienced, due to our dim sun and relatively inhospitable planet. Those who could not peek through the gloom or follow a faint sound simply did not survive to reproduce.

Appearance

The hybrids have characteristics of both contributors—the bald head of the Zetas but the five-fingered hand of the human, the large eyes of the Zetas but the eye color range of the humans, the tall height of one variety of the Zetas but the supple spine and expandable chest of the human. Breasts are small, but functional, a high priority goal of ours due to the bonding that occurs during nursing. Skin tone has been improved to where it is neither a reddish blush nor a pallor, and as we could not perfect a proper head of hair, we went in the other direction—hairless. Far better bald then with a strand here or there.

Sex

The sex drive in the hybrids remains as varied as it does in the human animal. The genetic choices of the engineers invariably leaned toward the human contributors, as the current intensity of the sexual bond experienced by humans was deemed compatible with a service-to-others existence.

Engineering Techniques

Human participants in development of a hybrid species assume that their eggs and sperm are taken so that the desired Zetan genes can be mixed in during conception. Often female participants assume that they have been impregnated via artificial insemination, when in fact they have had the fetus reinserted for a brief gestation period. In the main, mixing the egg and sperm is the process, but several steps are involved. Prior to combining the male and female strands, the strands are examined for undesirable traits such as inheritable diseases. Thus, it is not simply the fastest swimming sperm that becomes daddy, nor the nearest and most available egg that become mommy.

After selecting the human male and female contribution, snipping and replacing occurs. In this process Zeta genetics routinely replace certain human genetics—some human genes are routinely discarded, and some Zeta genes not present at all in humans are inserted. In some cases genes from a human ancestor are used to replace the human genes secured from the male and female donors. Almost invariably these are taken from data banks we maintain, but on rare occasion we are allowed to go back in time to secure a needed sample. This step inserts and accentuates a desirable human trait. These engineering techniques are familiar to the Zetas.

In the past the Zeta had offspring in the same sex-to-birth manner of humans, but now we either clone our offspring or create a blend of genes in the test tube. Our genetics are no longer as rich as *Homo sapiens* genetics, so the human donors are required in order to create a hybrid with the genetic adaptation that humans have to the planet Earth.

Physiology

The Zeta were selected for production of a hybrid race with humans in part because our physiologies are similar. Our blood is also hemoglobin based, and where a chemist would find all the many Zeta blood components differing from comparable human blood components in quantity and composition, the differences are not dramatic. It is likewise with the endocrine systems, which have comparable glands and functions. Here, however, there is one dramatic difference. The Zeta do not sleep, though there are regular rest periods where activity essentially stops. This difference appeared in the Zetas during our third-density existence, when many of our number were warlike. The guard who did not sleep survived, and thus the trait became dominant. There are blood-chemistry differences in humans between the wakeful and sleep states, but in the Zeta these differences do not appear. Our hybrids sleep, as we have found the physiology more resilient when able to rest. However, the sleep requirements are much reduced, requiring perhaps 1/5, rather than 1/3 of the day, and the onset of sleep deprivation does not occur with our hybrids, who are able to bear through without sleep if need be.

The physiological work assigned to organs such as the kidney and liver is essentially the same in both Zetas and humans, but how this work is accomplished varies. In humans the kidneys work constantly, filtering waste, but in the Zeta they click in only when certain blood chemicals rise to a level requiring attention. Like the heart, which rests between beats, the Zeta kidneys rest between Zeta meals. The reason for this pacing is the more complete absorption of nutrients in the Zeta digestive tract, placing a burden on the kidneys which then require a rest period in which to recoup. Likewise, the Zeta liver is a workhorse that goes the distance after meals and requires a recuperative period.

Zetas who overeat get more than overweight—they get sick. Our thinness is not due solely to genetic tendencies, we simply do not overeat. Do the Zetas store fat as humans do? Yes and no. We have this capacity, but our physiology does not make use of it ordinarily. Since we do not digest excess food without getting sick, our bodies keep all nutrition at the ready, as a store to be used up before the next meal. No packing it away in fat cells, no saving it for a later day. Our hybrids have the best of both worlds. They are slender because their physiology uses, rather than stores, nutrition, and their appetites pace accordingly. But should they for any reason decide to overeat, they do not suffer as we, the Zetas, do.

It has been noted that where we have nostrils, and our breath, acrid by human standards, can be felt when in close quarters, but we don't appear to be breathing. The expansion of human lungs is visible, yet our trunks seem firm and immobile. Do we have lungs? We do indeed, but they work asynchronously, rather than in unison, one expanding while the other exhales, so the motion is all internal. How did this come about, that springing from the same base we developed different breathing patterns? The answer lies in our long lean frame, which in the trunk has a fused rib system with cartilage between the ribs for extra strength. During our genetic-engineering periods those Zetas who adapted to a longer, more rigid frame by an adjusted breathing cycle survived to pass along their genetics. In fact, our current frame only became possible because asynchronous breathing became possible. The genetic engineers went with the flow, so to speak. Our hybrids, however, have unison breathing, but in a pinch could switch over to asynchronous breathing—a latent capacity.

Diet

We currently refresh ourselves by submerging into a nutrient-rich bath of clear gel. The nutrients are created, as you might say, in the laboratory. They are simply chemicals, developed from chemicals found anywhere in the universe. Where our current digestive system is rudimentary, having been eliminated in preference to a cleaner, quicker form of nourishment intake via our nutrient baths, the genetics controlling digestion are a factor to be considered when merging genetics in the hybrids.

The human diet is voluminous and fibrous, reflecting the diet of the base apes that formed the human race, and in truth reflecting the reality of vegetation on your planet and the adaptation that animals evolving on your planet were forced to deal with. If an animal is vegetarian, and most are, they eat continuously, defecate frequently, and deal with digestive gasses. Few animals become successful predators, an obvious fact, because if all were predators there would soon be nothing to prey upon. So humans have as their base an animal that daily eats masses of fibrous vegetation.

We Zetas, on our world, had a different diet. Our world was not sunny and bright, and the vegetation thus not as evolved. Mosses, bugs, algae, crustaceans, and when we ate, almost nothing went to waste. If forced to eat your diet we would digest the fiber, but we would also be unable to consume enough to retrieve the necessary nutrition. In our hybrids we have attempted to take the best of both worlds. Humans, we feel sure, would not object to less farting and burping. We have retained the more complete digestive capabilities of the Zetas, while adjusting this to allow for the types of foods your world offers. In the highly civilized world of the future, cultivation will focus on those foods that return the highest nutrition. Less eating, less elimination, virtually no digestive gasses, and constipation will not be a concern as the shape of the bowel, being a single straight shoot, lends itself to guaranteed elimination.

Genetic Diseases

Genetic diseases are concomitant with evolution. Most genetic diseases are an aberration of some biological maneuver present in health. Autoimmune diseases are the immune response turned wrong. Obesity is a protective maneuver—to maximize food consumption during times of plenty—gone wrong. Food stuffs do not spoil when packed around the ribs in the form of fat. So, all genetic diseases, when their cause is understood, can be seen to be a normal maneuver of the body, gone wrong. These diseases are found in the animal kingdom too, and are not present in the human race for any particular reason beyond your ability to survive in spite of these diseases. In the animal kingdom, afflicted animals quickly die out. You protect your afflicted, allowing them not only to survive, but also to propagate. In this way your genetic diseases increase, as though afflictions in and of themselves.

The Perfect Body

A long life, stopping or slowing the aging process or even attaining immortality, is much sought after by humans. Humans would also love to modify themselves so they can eat endlessly and not gain weight, or have prolonged sexual intercourse until they tire of sexual climax, or have all the physical characteristics that constitute attractiveness between the sexes, or have athletic prowess and metal acuity, and while we're at it, not go bald. However, this does not assist in the spiritual growth of the individual, which is the aim of incarnations. What lessons are to be learned if one is never presented with problems? What painful adjustments must be made? We have stated that immature entities require incarnations in order to develop spiritually, and without incarnations this process at this point in their development goes much more slowly. Likewise, without hardship, the incarnations teach little.

Rules

13
Engagements

We, the Zetas, as all groups alien to the Earth, are guided by the Rules of Engagement among ourselves. The Rules of Engagement also cover entities who are no longer incarnated but are in light form. In these matters, the issue of death is defined differently. Humans, currently in third density, are not so guided by Rules of Engagement, being free to be themselves in whatever manner they wish. Human societies set their own rules, groups within societies set their own rules, families set their own rules, and sometimes even individual humans, in setting about self improvement, make their own personal rules.

Our rules, in regard to behavior on Earth, are determined by the Council of Worlds, which administers the goings on of intelligent life of all kinds, of whatever density, in this part of the universe. These rules govern the expected clashes between service-to-self and service-to-others oriented groups. Why are these rules necessary? Humans are a mixture, being in the third density and in the process of choosing. They find the self-centered in the same vicinity as the altruistic and empathic. The rules of human society take this into account. Your laws on criminal behavior, for instance, are an example of rules assuming a mix of service-to-self and service-to-others. They spell out what criminal behavior is, when the line is crossed, and when one intrudes upon another.

ZetaTalk

In the service-to-self oriented groups after third density, all are, essentially, criminals. They are ruthless and utterly without scruples. They would prey upon each other endlessly. The control over each other is not by criminal rules, but by the rule of the strong. The pecking order is ruthlessly established, by whatever means necessary. Once established, this becomes the law. Essentially the rule of law is the long list of rules from the lawgiver. Democracy has absolutely nothing to do with this process. It is a dictatorship. Thus, as long as all new members are service-to-self oriented, homeostasis is established. When in Rome, you do as the Romans do.

In the service-to-others oriented groups after third density, none wishes to hurt the other. Concern for the group, and others, is expected and delivered. Rules are not used to control here, either. Order is established by the group discussing what needs to be done, and by various members volunteering. Communication regarding difficulties, requests for assistance, and status on the ongoing concerns of the many are frequent. There are no secrets. There is no need to be defensive against each other, as all have common goals, and none means to take advantage of the other. There are no locked doors. All turn their backs on each other without fear. Goods are not hoarded but shared. Service-to-others entities trust each other utterly, and this trust is not misplaced.

Mix these two groups together, and what would happen? The service-to-self entities would endlessly take advantage of the service-to-others entities. To some degree, this takes place in your third-density world. The self-centered moan that they are put upon, unfairly treated, injured, need a lighter load, and cut to the quick by others' treatment of them. The service-to-self entities use all manner of ruses to take advantage of good-hearted folk. In a world where all service-to-others entities have let down their guard to concentrate on mutual goals, assuming themselves surrounded by friends, their trust would prove disastrous. In short, the two groups cannot mix. The service-to-others entities, who usually prove to be the majority during any planetary evolution, are given guardianship of their perimeter. You may choose to call this a type of quarantine of the service-to-self entities, or giving the service-to-self group a prison-colony environment, if you wish. However, this separation is for the benefit of both groups. The service-to-self entities find being around those of service-to-others mentality distracting to a great degree. All service-to-self entities at one time in their past had empathic sensitivities toward others. This has been repressed in the interest of service to the self. The service-to-self entity does not want to be reminded of this, and, if so reminded, finds itself distracted and in need of correction for some time to come. Thus, the service-to-self entities wish to avoid those strongly oriented toward service-to-others. They are not clambering for the mix, either. The desire for distance is mutual.

So do the two groups ever encounter each other? Only when both agree, and under a strict set of rules. Agreement can involve a group, or an individual. All this is spelled out. An individual may engage an individual, or an individual may engage a group, or a group may engage a group. A group would be a specified number of entities, or a representation of the larger group. In either case, whether for a group or an individual, the type of engagement may be one of three types:

Non Engagement
No engagement has been agreed upon, and none will occur. This will happen if a request for an engagement has been refused.

Limited Engagement
Either the requester or the acceptor has placed limits on the engagement. The limits can have all manner of characteristics. Only for an hour. No touching. No other entity can be present. Only verbal interaction. In the dark. Only numerics can be discussed. Whatever. This type of engagement is the most usual, and engagements are brief between groups of different orientations.

Unlimited Engagement
Without limitations, so that the engagement will not end until the death of one entity or the other. Where one of the entities is an individual, this engagement runs until the incarnation ends in physical death. Where one of the entities is a group, this engagement runs until the group disbands or is eliminated in some meaningful manner.

Disagreements
Where interplay between orientations is so strictly controlled by the Rules of Engagement that there is essentially no interplay at all, there are on occasion disagreements between members of service-to-others groups who

engage each other on a continuing basis. As we are dealing with entities who are determined to see the general welfare given priority, these are essentially friendly disagreements. As anyone who lives in a loving family can attest, this is no small thing. There are situations where a simple vote taken from those affected is not appropriate. Perhaps it cannot even be determined who will be affected, for instance, in a situation where a species on a new fertile planet is to be genetically engineered to support conscious, intelligent life. There is no intelligent life to be polled as to their opinion, only the opinions of the various service-to-others genetic engineers. How does this work?

We bring these types of issues to the Council of Worlds and have a formal debate of sorts. Bear in mind that all the protagonists are basically focused on doing the right thing, and there are no hidden agendas possible in the service-to-others orientation in the higher densities. It's just that there is a difference of opinion, based on past experience and outlook, as to what the right thing to do is. All present their views and openly debate, much in the format of a roundhouse discussion. Each is allowed to explain fully, and is not interrupted. When all have said their piece, and no points are left to be countered or debated, then the Council of Worlds makes a decision. The Council of Worlds is composed of very high-density entities who hold their position because of a general vote of all affected. They are essentially elected. Their decision on the matter before them then settles the issue. As with the Rules of Engagement and other rules that must be enforced, this decision is made by computer and is enforced, without question or argument.

War

Humans are accustomed to the forces of what they call good and evil being constantly at war, and they expect this conflict to be present in almost every situation. The young child at school may find the drug pusher in a running battle with the local police, the bully extracting lunch money from younger children, and the chronic cheat who copies the homework of others to be ever present. These types seem to go virtually unchallenged. Surely life elsewhere in the universe is the same, and the advanced technology that aliens rather evidently possess would make for spectacular battles when clashes occur. In fact, due to the separation of the orientations, such clashes rarely occur between orientations, and among the service-to-self entities they happen only when there is not a clear winner in the constant contest to be top dog that is characteristic of this orientation. Those in the service-to-others orientation never war with each other, although disagreements most certainly exist and conferences are frequent if not constant, if one takes telepathy into account.

The reason battles between orientations do not occur is not only due to their separation, it is also due to the enforcement of this separation. Those in the service-to-self orientation would not be expected to abide by a rule out of honor, as they have none. They have no choice. If a service-to-self group attempts to encroach on territory assigned to service-to-others groups, they are physically blocked at the perimeter by forces put into place by the Council of Worlds. To engage, the service-to-self entities must request an engagement, and this request, which is likewise monitored by the Council, can be refused by the service-to-others entities or a counteroffer proffered. Gladiator-style contests, where brute physical force is used to determine the outcome, is simply not something those in the service-to-others orientation would have the slightest interest in. What would be the point, to determine which life-form has the biggest muscles and teeth?

Beyond the lack of interest in physical prowess games, the service-to-others entities don't engage in battle, for they know the outcome. They would win. Where those in the service-to-self orientation desire weapons and spend a good part of their energy fussing over their arsenal of destructive power, the service-to-self entities are never as technologically advanced as those in service-to-others, and the reason is simple—lack of cooperation. Those in the service-to-self orientation attend to their tasks because they must, have been ordered to, and would be punished or killed if they were found doing otherwise. The attention the service-to-self entities give to their tasks is not the same, as their hearts are not in it, their tasks having been assigned rather than chosen.

Supremacy

Within the service-to-self group, all-out battles for supremacy occur when superiority is not clear. Both want to be top dog, and the ruling masters are willing to send in and sacrifice their minions. This situation needs no explanation, as human wars are equivalent in most respects. Warfare in human history has been as brutal as the restraints on the warlords will allow. They want at their command virtual killing machines who have no remorse or hesitation, but what human warlords most often get are procrastinating generals and deserting troops, even when the mission can be cloaked in humanitarian terms. Soldiers hesitate to kill, and generals hope for compromise or a bloodless capitulation. But what if there were no reluctance or hesitation? When there is no remorse, one does not hesitate. What if the warlords on both sides had their perfect soldiers? Put this emotional climate into the high-technology arena that exists in fourth density, and what follows is a service-to-self leveling war. It is so called because this is the result—the survivors ultimately finding their level in relationship to the other group, with one standing above the other.

In these wars the soldiers are not motivated out of loyalty or a commitment to ideals, they are all like gladiators—kill or be killed. A soldier who refuses to be the perfect killing machine for his master is made an example, and a quick and painless death is out of the question. Human wars see the use of biological weapons such as nerve gas, nuclear bombs, maiming devices such as mines, psychological weapons such as reminders of home and comfort, and various wearing techniques such as starvation. Intergalactic wars between service-to-self groups are more brutal and direct, with complete destruction in the wink of an eye the goal.

Thus, the service-to-self groups, when establishing their pecking order, frequently brutalize and decimate each other. Establishing the pecking order within a service-to-self group results in brutality and maiming, if not death. The pecking order is thus established and maintained with the same heavy-handed methods, so that a visitor to a service-to-self camp would think it remarkably peaceful, not seeing what came before. Service-to-self ranks are rebuilt from the orphanages where all their youngsters are raised and procreation is temporarily stepped up until the count of physical bodies approximates the fourth-density service-to-self entities incarnating within the group. All is peaceful again until some factor or another changes the power structure. All this is viewed from afar by service-to-others groups, who are aware of—but essentially disinterested in—the battles, since they cannot be affected.

84

14
Council of Worlds

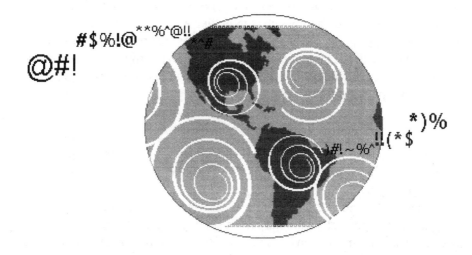

   The Council of Worlds, sometimes known to you as the Association of Worlds, has over 40 groups at the present time, but this number varies from time to time, and is in motion. The alien groups that are present on Earth are all members of the Council of Worlds. All entities from either spiritual orientation who are visiting the Earth at this time are, likewise, members. This is not optional. The members of the Council, being primarily from the higher spiritual densities, are not, in the main, incarnated. This makes for a setting humans might find amusing, when holding council with incarnated aliens. Those incarnated stand around, gesturing and communicating with grunts or diagrams or telepathically or through translators if necessary. Now and then all fall silent and still while the Council communicates to them, soul to soul, and the incarnated souls then hastily update their physical minds through the mind/spirit connection. Then another round of discussion ensues. To an outsider, unaware of what was happening, the voice of author-ity would seem to be absent. From the standpoint of humans in third density, the Council's charter is to keep the two spiritual orientations of the visitors apart, except under carefully structured and fully monitored engagements, and to ensure that the free will of man not be abridged. This is all easier than it sounds, as the task is accomplished simply by preventing contact—by building walls. These walls are not of a physical substance, but have an effect on physical matter as well as spiritual matter. We Zetas cannot tell you the mechanism, not because the rules forbid it, but because we do not know. We can only tell you what this feels like. It is a benign cushion, through which one cannot pass, and which is more like a pillow on impact than a brick wall. Ships pointed past the point of no passage find themselves at the wall, as though all the computations guiding the leap through time and space had been reset. The blockade is utterly effective yet gentle, leaving no damage except, perhaps, wounded pride.

Travel Protocol

Humans assume chaos rules in the universe, as chaos seems to rule in their world. They have free will, and except where restrained by each other or temporarily by circumstances, they can do as they wish. Is it not so in outer space? It is not so. There are rules. These rules restrain primarily by preventing the spiritually immature from leaving their home planet. This is the rule that restrains humans, at present. Humans may imagine that matters are otherwise, as they have managed to lift off their planet, but this is viewed as essentially hopping about on the surface, not serious space travel. Entities are not allowed to travel to other worlds and influence matters there until they have reached fourth-density spiritual maturity. Here they are either in the service-to-self or service-to-others orientation, where the rules differ, but there are nonetheless strict rules in regard to protocol toward other galactic cultures.

What is protocol during galactic travel? There must be no interference with another culture unless called. The interference then allowed is in proportion to the size of The Call, and we are speaking here of numbers in relation to the whole—percentages basically. The Call cannot be assumed to last forever, but is rather self-limiting. No lingering. This is gauged by when the circumstances of the original call have dissipated. If no secondary call has been issued, the interference should be ended. Traveling or visiting groups are not to interfere with each other, except as guided by the Rules of Engagement. During conflicting calls, they must take scrupulous care not to step on each others' toes. The reader will notice how often we decline to discuss matters, citing these rules. The rules we are guided by are strict, and failure to abide by them sends us packing.

Participants

The Earth is already in the Council of Worlds, and some humans are already actively participating. As with the Earth's awakening to the presence of intelligent entities from elsewhere in the universe, the Earth is moving forward piecemeal. These humans, who are already representing the Earth at the Council of Worlds, are not known to the governments of the Earth. The governments of the Earth, in the main, do not represent the people they govern. The governments primarily represent special interests, those who rule, or those who are power hungry. The humans who represent Earth, or the human point of view, are those who are spiritually mature, but not all humans who are spiritually mature enough to be considered operating in the spiritual fourth density are with the Council of Worlds. This is a decision the human makes, whether to join or not. These personal decisions made by humans may not be ones they are consciously aware of.

Needless to say, as the Earth is destined to become a home for service-to-others entities quite soon, the service-to-self entities, of which there are few, have no say in determinations about the future of the Earth. The service-to-self entities represent themselves, only, and in essence make complaints and pleas that fall upon deaf ears.

Voting

The Constitution of the United States was assisted in its birth by those in the service-to-others orientation. This was not an easy birth, and the reason for this support was not trifling. The U.S. Constitution is a forerunner of what you can expect from the Council of Worlds—the individual counts. When do humans get to vote in the Council of Worlds, and are there intermediate representatives, such as the Constitution allows for? The answer to the latter question is no. Where under human affairs the physical impossibility of having millions and even billions of humans at any given representation requires a supra-level of representation, in densities above third, we in fact can manage the large crowd. And when do you become eligible to vote? In matters of the Earth, as residents of Earth, you already have a vote. It is one-to-one, and your vote is polled frequently, as amazing as that may seem.

In practical matters, how does this work? Where is the ballot box? In a physical world, as humans are used to thinking the world is, one expects a physical ballot box. In human society, the verbal promise is often forgotten or skewered, so important promises and agreements are put into writing, and the verbiage is made precise. Words can trap, and words can assure. How does the Council of Worlds work without words? Within the service-to-others entities, the essence of the question under vote is faithfully relayed to the individual who has a right to vote. The true intent of the voter is relayed to the ballot box, which in this case is not a box at all but a type of mental computer. In the service-to-self orientation, voting does not occur. Decisions are made based on the pecking order.

Elections

All forming entities that were Terran born—having formed on the Earth—participated in the vote that occurred just prior to the Roswell incident, the vote that determined the Earth's future orientation as service-to-others. Within the Earth's population of approximately six billion only about a billion are reincarnating entities, and the vast majority of the remaining four billion newly forming entities are expected to end up as aborted entities. How does all of this then compute into the right to vote on various issues, and how will the forthcoming pole shift, which is estimated to result in the death of 90% of the population, figure in?

When the Earth's future orientation was established, all humans who incarnated with either newly forming or reincarnating entities, or souls as they are sometimes called, voted. All entities originating on Earth also participated, including those between lives. In this vote, all carried equal weight, by lifetime. This means that an entity who had experienced a thousand lives on Earth had the weight of a thousand votes, compared to an entity newly forming in this incarnation. This also means that the resulting orientation of these older entities went into the vote, so that an entity who had evolved toward the service-to-others orientation would cast his full weight in this direction, and likewise one that had recently moved into the service-to-self orientation might cast his full weight there, regardless of past positions on these matters. It is the present position that counts. The future population will become solidly service-to-others by a combination of entities that have evolved on Earth, star children, aliens such as ourselves, and the hybrids currently awaiting the time when they can migrate to the Earth—all in the service-to-others orientation.

The pole shift will savage incarnated humans of both orientations, sparing no one. Where those humans operating solidly in the service-to-others orientation will be offered a temporary lift, few have accepted this offer, choosing instead to stay with those they feel a sense of responsibility toward. Thus, the pole shift will decimate the current population equally, resulting in no net difference in the Earth's orientation. The net orientation leaning will soon begin to change, however, as service-to-others groups will fare better than those of mixed orientation or the roving gangs of service-to-self oriented individuals. Thus, the decimation caused by the pole shift will ultimately affect the voting population by reducing the number of undecided or service-to-self individuals, through death.

Minority Vote

Humans used to arranging a place on court dockets often feel left out of activities ongoing at the Council of Worlds. Their votes are collected and then that's the end of it, and they long to argue their case. On Earth, depending upon the human society, one can either bribe the judge, bribe or otherwise influence those who appoint or control the judge, selectively screen the jury, arrange to be represented by high-priced and high-powered attorneys, or endlessly petition. That the Council of Worlds does not have similar avenues open to them feels like a breach of rights! In fact, probably for the first time, they are experiencing a true democracy. They are the minority vote! Their viewpoint lost! Manipulating the outcome by trying to manipulate the courts is simply not democratic!

The Council does not arbitrarily make pronouncements affecting the lives and futures of intelligent species. Except for the preconscious period, when genetic engineering is about to begin or is in process, the spirits incarnating into an intelligent species always determine the outcome. Neanderthal man determined that its line would die out to be replaced by another version of early man, for instance. They were polled as to their opinion on the eating disorder that was killing so many of them at a young age, and the alternatives were abundantly clear to those polled. Once the decision had been made, the feelings of any given Neanderthal man about to be sterilized, but not castrated, with a small snip to his groin mattered not. His was the minority vote!

Secession

Hearing that the Earth's transformation is being administered by the Council of Worlds, those humans with isolationist tendencies often object. Can't they secede? The answer is a simple no, as all life-bearing worlds in this part of the universe are administered by the Council, whose ability to administer in the manner it does is only possible because its authority is without contradiction. Is this not a dictatorship? Yes, but one that is benign, run by wise and massive elected entities staunchly in the service-to-others orientation, who continuously poll those they administer as to their opinions. After third density, entities are allowed to travel, and a world off limits to the Council's administration would, as one might imagine, be a continuous battleground. Those in the service-to-self orientation, who are restrained much against their wishes by the many perimeters the Council places around them, would see a seceding world as a free port, and have no rest in attempting to secure this prize. ━╫━

15
Limitations

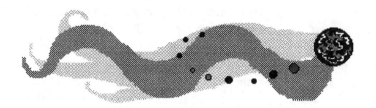

Once a vote on a world's orientation has been taken, preparatory to the transformation that a third-density world is to take, exceptions to the normal rules can occur. The results of the vote are not to be tipped, and situations that would tip the outcome are regulated by the Council of Worlds. Interference in all cases must come before the Council of Worlds and be justified. Given the heated nature of falsehoods spread in South America purporting abductions by bloodsucking aliens, the Brazilian Roswell scenario was approved, bypassing the rule that all human encounters with aliens should be recorded only in the subconscious. An exception was also granted for the original Roswell incident, which led to conscious contact with U.S. government personnel and ultimately resulted in the formation of MJ-12. MJ-12 personnel, of course, encounter aliens frequently in the course of their duties, and are fully conscious of these encounters—a continuing exception that was granted by the Council when they approved the Roswell proposal.

Exploration Limits

Man has just recently, within the past century, launched into the space age, sending astronauts to the Moon and probes to the outer and inner reaches of the solar system. The giant hominoids from the 12th Planet progressed beyond this point, establishing mining operations on various planets or moons, and shuttling to meet their home, the 12th Planet, when it periodically made a passage. What, therefore are the exploration limits on third-density species? In general, entities in third density are allowed unlimited exploration within their solar system. Where more than one planet in the solar system is inhabited by an intelligent species, and an imbalance of power arises between these species, a quarantine may result. For instance, if one planet's intelligent species were dexterous, such as man, and another planet had an intelligent species that had only fins and tentacles, an imbalance of power would exist. The dexterous species could enslave or exterminate the hapless water creatures.

Mankind is already quarantined, though man is quite unaware of it. His recent difficulties with his space program are not all accidents, although the difficulties in the past have all been man-made. Man will not be allowed to travel to those parts of the solar system where they would be likely to encounter their old slave masters, the giant hominoids from the 12th Planet. It is the message that would be brought back to Earth that is the sticking point. The Earth has a long memory of having been enslaved in the past by these giant hominoids, who were quarantined from the Earth for upsetting the balance of another third-density species' existence. Going into the transformation, Earthlings are not to be alarmed by this palpably real threat, as this would increase fear and anxiety inordinately and therefore raise the number of those leaning to the service-to-self orientation.

Space Shuttles

In the past the 12th Planet was considered part of your Solar System, and in general the Council of Worlds allows third-density species who are local to interact with each other, especially when they are the same species. The hominoids on the 12th Planet were seeded in the same manner as the hominoids on Earth, and during the same time frame, but uneven development occurred. The hominoids on Earth dealt with carnivores and the violent geological changes that accompany pole shifts. If they were not running away, they were having to pick up the pieces and start over again. Thus, the hominoids on the 12th Planet reached the point where *Homo sapiens* on Earth is now, many millennia ago. They developed rockets, not unlike the manned rockets humans send aloft regularly to maintain their satellite systems. The goal was not simply to orbit their planet, but to gather resources for their planet, essentially a water world where mining operations were limited. They were driven to develop a Solar System shuttle, and their early astronauts were much at risk and died by the dozens. They could plainly see, via their telescope equivalents, that the Earth and Mars were planets that could sustain them. As with international travelers on Earth, they expected to get infected with new bugs, and they knew that their immune systems would either adapt or they would die. Eventually, during repeated visits of the 12th Planet to your Solar System, they worked the kinks out of their shuttle and settled into colonies on Earth and Mars.

Then trouble emerged as, being advanced, the giant hominoids demanded and got subservience from humans. In addition to their technological advantage, the giant hominoids from the 12th Planet had size on their side. They ruled.

As these types of arrangements became progressively more extreme, the Council of Worlds stepped in and effected a quarantine. The 12th Planet inhabitants do not know they are quarantined, they simply came to the realization that they must leave. This was arranged as most such matters are, with the giant hominoids believing to this day that the decision was theirs. They ran into increasing difficulties—rebellious slaves, bad weather, loss of their stores—and found that their brethren elsewhere were at least masters of their environment. The grass was greener, and they left. They were discouraged by Star Children sent to accomplish this mission, and the untimely storms that scattered their pack animals and sank their ships were accomplished by air turbulence caused by temperature differences, a minor feat quickly arranged.

Collision Course

How might two planets, on some sort of collision course with each other, be dealt with at the Council of Worlds? This situation is presenting itself, again, in the coming pole shift to be caused by the periodic passage of the 12th Planet. The Council of Worlds views interfering with nature this way: It is not allowed. Nature is a fact that all intelligent entities are adapting to and becoming aware of quite intimately by the necessities of life during incarnations. This is a learning process, and it is not to be preempted by cheating. Even should humans figure out how to do this, it would not be allowed. The 12th Planet and its periodic passage was a known entity when humans were genetically engineered to begin with. It is nothing new. The Council of Worlds would not allow the Earth to blow the inhabited 12th Planet out of the skies.

Escape Routes

The Rule of Non-Interference is quite clear on the cataclysms. The only humans who can be assisted in their survival efforts are those firmly in the service-to-others. This exception is due to the spiritual focus the inhabitants of the Earth have chosen for her future. The Earth is to be a home for entities in the service-to-others during fourth density, and thus those humans who are operating in the service-to-others orientation are considered, essentially, in that camp.

What does this mean for the others, who are in the majority, or for any elite groups who may try to strike a deal? Essentially it means that any promises that have been made to the contrary are false, and they have been lied to. Our own agreements are quite clear on this point. All our resources are going to be used assisting service-to-others humans during the coming pole shift. Each individual is being judged on the basis of the orientation they are currently operating in. No group deals. No special favors. In regard to the service-to-self groups, who perpetually promise what they have no intention of delivering, they make these promises to maximize the misery of the disappointed. This is their way of insuring a conquest so that their recruits will be utterly focused on the self during their last moments—pointed in the right direction.

Alien Technology

Rumor has it that the secretive development of the Aurora and the recently emergent Stealth Bomber reflect a contribution of alien technology, and rumor is correct. This is not our technology, but was an early gift from ambassadors in the service-to-self orientation who were busily bribing their way into the hearts of the military. Wildly enthusiastic and anticipating even greater coups, the military leadership at that time sold this program to whomever held the purse strings and set about becoming, so they presumed, the masters of the Earth.

The technology delivered, which had been demonstrated with alien ships, did not work on human machines. Literally decades passed before the truth dawned on the deeply disappointed leadership—they had been deceived. The demonstration given by the aliens had involved radar evasion, but the aliens used density shifting, at speeds that the eye could not follow, so the disappearing ships seemed to have evaded radar. Having touted the program, the military sponsors were obliged to deliver something, and they have delivered the Aurora. It doesn't work as promoted, and thus, no public announcement has been made.

Alien technology has not been handed over to the government. Those in the service-to-self orientation have no desire to see their recruits get out of hand, nor would they be allowed, by the Rule of Non-Interference, to interfere with the balance between humans here on Earth. And those in the service-to-others orientation would never encourage a war machine.

Time Travel

Time is linear only in your mind. It is not what it seems. Your sense that time is linear in the universe is supported by what you observe—clocks running in seeming synchronicity; planetary movements that are predictable; testimony of other people you interact with to the effect that they, too, observe the same time passage as you do. However, time is only a factor, and as such when put into mathematical calculations can be affected along with the other factors. The universe is just a huge mathematical calculation. In the portion of the world that you live in, the factors are stable enough that the time factor never varies enough to be noticed. This makes you think that time is a fixed factor. It is not fixed. We understand what other factors are involved, and how to modify them so that the time factor changes as we wish. Time travel is a mystery we cannot explain fully to you, due to the rules we must follow.

The issue of time travel is confusing to humans, who see the movies where parties go into the future as well as the past. Would that not be the case, as if one can go in one direction, why not the other? One cannot travel into the future, except in small increments, hours at most. Leaping into the future is a fiction. One can travel into the past, as that is a trail marked in the substance of the universe, strands that can be unwoven and rewoven, a rope that stretches back endlessly. The past has markers. Grip points. It has been built, where the future has not yet been built. A phrase much in use is the time/space continuum. This is simply a way of stating that matter may be in a different place, or space, depending on the time, and that matter leaves a trail, or continuum, over time. You can equate the time/space continuum to our term strands, being woven and unwoven, which we consider more exact as it refers to the webbing that takes place.

What would happen if one went back along a particular strand, unraveling it, and changed the circumstances surrounding the strand? Would it change the present, and thus the future? Yes, but not to the degree depicted in the movies, where people wink out like lights and buildings disappear from sight and even from the memory of all. How could it, as each of these occurrences is composed of numerous strands, weaving in multiple directions, and it is impossible to change them all. What in fact occurs, should one be allowed to go back in time and make an alteration, is that the future is essentially unchanged. We say essentially, as there has been change, but due to the interweaving of other strands, this is muted. The Council of Worlds strictly administers time travel, as should one go back in time and really work at it, changes would begin to appear.

The Future

Is not one moment another's future and yet another's past? If we today travel back, would we not be deemed visitors from the future? And in this context, if the Earth were to hypothetically receive visitors claiming to be from the future, would that not mean that we are not in the present at all, and that the future, for us, has therefore been written? This confusion can be settled if one understands that the Earth is not having visitors from the future, no matter how this may have been stated. Misunderstandings occur during genuine channeling sessions, and an example of what will be more prevalent in the future can be misunderstood to be an actual visitor from the future.

The future has not been written. You are writing it now, moment by moment, decision by decision. When travel back through time occurs this is not recorded in the memory of nonparticipants, only in the memory of the travelers. Pains are taken to ensure that this be so. Travel back in time is done for such matters as capturing genetic material long lost, for instance, not to distort or pollute a memory.

16
Sightings

The presentation of the radio drama *The War of the Worlds* some decades ago in the United States was, as many have expected, a test. Given that the alien presence had up until that time been consistently presented as an alien threat, the public reaction was hardly surprising. Radio dramas are often confused with reality by those tuning in, as there are few clues that a fiction, rather than a factual scene, is being portrayed. On TV, the fact that one is watching a movie is quickly apparent. There are clues in the settings, the time gaps and leaps, and the frequent intimate moments which newscasters are not generally privy to. Thus, had *The War of the Worlds* been presented on TV at that time, rather than as a radio drama, the reaction would not have been the same.

This test, which the establishment knew would be taken for a real broadcast by many, was to determine not how the public would react to a threat but rather to determine if they believed in the alien presence. They did, and thus they reacted, and the strength of the reaction told an establishment which had been congratulating themselves on having suppressed belief in aliens that they had not succeeded as they thought. Subsequently suppression continued but got meaner, with mistreatment of contactees becoming more abusive and physical.

Since the establishment at that time was in the main under the impression that aliens were only interested in a takeover, having made contact with service-to-self aliens first, and being unaware of the separation of orientations that takes place after third density, they felt that the panic that ensued after the Orson Wells radio drama was inevitable. They thought of themselves as holding back a flood, putting their fingers in holes in the dike, and looking out for mankind's welfare. The few suicides that the broadcast caused, and the potential heart attacks, were not a concern to the establishment at that time, as they considered themselves to be essentially at war and the nation in essence under martial law. All rules of human conduct go out the window when the leadership is in a panic.

Stages

The rule is, and will be for the near future, that we keep the issue constantly before the populace, with a steadily increasing level of discussion, but always, always, with an element of doubt.

This element of doubt is necessary during the Awakening so your populace does not become unduly alarmed. A faint, a palpitating heart, distractibility, arguing with friends and coworkers for a few days, an increased interest in UFO subjects—none of these is considered a show stopper. Were the entire populace to react like this, there would be no problem. The Awakening would occur tomorrow. What we seek to avoid is the nervous breakdown, the fear in friends and coworkers rising to such a level that they take violent steps against the reporter, or the intensity of fear in the observer that would make them susceptible, or incline them, toward giving The Call to the service-to-self entities.

Individuals becoming aware of the alien presence go through predictable steps in their awakening process, though the pace or the intensity of a reaction may differ widely.

Denial

The first stage is denial, where in fact the majority of awakened mankind sits today. They may entertain the possibility that the alien presence is real, may even loudly argue the possibility, and may be considered anything but a skeptic by those who know them, but these individuals are still holding close, in their heart of hearts, to the supremacy and uniqueness of man. Their life has not changed, society functions as before, and thus the alien presence is considered just a possibility.

Unease

The second stage is unease, as circumstances in their personal life, or simple logic, erode their comfortable cocoon. They spend quiet moments pondering what this might mean. They try on different scenarios and outcomes, to see how this feels. They long to find another who is at the same stage, but find almost everyone else still discussing if the alien presence is real. This second stage is lonely, but as this individual is usually giving The Call almost incessantly, they are having many conferences, and this assuages their loneliness among humans to a great degree.

Anticipation

The third stage is anticipation, as, sensing what lies ahead, the individual is impatient to have the world around him, his human society, wake up. He now views the rest of society, with their comfortable beliefs, as old fashioned and remarkably unobservant. He stops arguing about the alien presence, and begins making quiet changes in his life. At this point he may encounter others who have the same quiet understanding and convictions, and such meetings form groups that are the buds of a new, awakened, society. Individuals at this third stage might meet an alien or sight a ship and not experience undue anxiety. They are ready, but are being held back by the needs of the rest of the populace.

Sightings

When the majority of your populace is comfortable with our presence, there will be no need to conceal ourselves from you. Sightings will increase, and will include alien life-forms. This will then move to telepathic discussions with these life-forms, *en masse* with groups of people. An increasing number of photos and videos will develop, and although they will meet with the usual barrage of skeptical-debunking, these photos and videos will speak to the subconscious of many. There will always be those who deny what they see. This occurs today, in your society, in all facets. Where sightings are on the increase, just where and when they occur depends on many factors, only one of which is the desire of the local inhabitants to experience one.

ZetaTalk

Some sightings, such as the dramatic Mexico City sightings seen by thousands and video taped by hundreds, hasten the Awakening by being broadcast and highly authentic. Some sightings in remote locales occur because the majority of the residents are comfortable with the concept of being galactic citizens and are ready to experience a sighting without undue anxiety. Some sightings by individuals are like the personalized sign many contactees are given, as encouragement that the path they have set upon is not a foolish one.

But likewise there are areas of the world that receive few sightings, and Muslim countries are included in this list. Where the majority of the humans have been isolated from the gossip that flows freely elsewhere around the world, and have been told that anything outside of the bounds of their tightly controlled world is of the devil, then sightings would do more harm than good. If one cannot see a woman's face, could one be allowed to see a UFO?

Mass Sightings

During the past few decades sightings have almost invariably been a personal experience, and in the main they will remain that—an individual, alone in an isolated area, a family on a camping trip, a couple standing on a balcony enjoying the starlit night. In step with the increased pace of the Awakening, sightings will become mass sightings, affecting the whole populace in crowded or urban areas. The media will suppress the news, but they cannot prevent neighbors from chatting with one another or gossiping on the Internet. The word gets out.

Glowing Ships

Sightings will become more dramatic as the Awakening progresses, and this is by intent. Initial UFO sightings were of silvery crafts, hovering with apparent mastery of the force of gravity, streaking rapidly, and with the ability to change direction instantly or otherwise maneuver in a manner unlike man-made crafts. These sightings posed enough questions to those with an open mind that no further encouragement was needed. Those with a closed mind refused to believe that what others were talking about, or perhaps what they had seen with their own eyes, was anything but a man-made aircraft, a meteor, or their imagination! To encourage these humans to enter the discussion that is becoming endemic worldwide, we and others involved in the Awakening process have moved to include glowing crafts into the sightings that are increasingly occurring.

Saucer Shapes

The flying saucer is the shape most associated with the alien presence, and is a term known all over the world. Sometimes the shape appears bell like, with the dome humped up in the center. Humans who recall being ferried about in these space ships report a cramped interior, especially if the ship is normally used by aliens of a smaller build than the average human. The rim of the space ship also seems to be unused space. What is the purpose of the saucer shape, or is this simply an aesthetic choice? During travel throughout the universe, there are issues more important than appearances or esthetics.

Saucers

Space ships emerge from a higher density, which allows them rapid travel at a speed exponentially higher than that which a lower density would allow. Coming out of a higher density, the space ship and its inhabitants must expect to encounter all manner of possibilities. Space flight or even local hops incorporate production of an internal gravity center so that the passengers are not tossed about. The saucer shape, or its variant, the bell shape, supports the technology for production of a gravity center. It is no accident that the planets in your solar system line up in essentially the same plane. The saucer shape simulates this, with the edges of the saucer acting as the outer planets in a solar system's planetary plane.

Ball UFO

Space craft are not round, as in a ball. Ufologists will report that the crafts reported upon invariably have a flattened or nearly flattened bottom. Spherical objects cannot have a stabilized gravity centralization akin to what a flat bottomed craft can. A spherical object, with a gravity bottom point of one tiny part of the globe, would wobble about! A flat, or relatively flat, bottom gives many points of reference.

Plasma Ships

Among the false reports of UFO sightings are those that report glowing ships, termed plasma ships. The implication is that these ships are alive and throbbing, and that the occupants are flowing about within as though swimming in light. The concept of a plasma ship is illogical, as beings in light form do not need ships. These reported sightings are false.

Triangular UFO

An oft reported UFO shape is the triangle, a ship that looks a bit like a fat boomerang. Triangular UFOs are not alien, but are simply a type of airship produced by the U.S. government, in secret.

Triangular UFOs are being seen worldwide at this time, to build a debunking case against all the mass sightings also occurring worldwide, in case this debunking should be deemed necessary to stop a panic over the alien presence. Should such a panic occur, the U.S. military would hold a press conference and unveil the new stealth plane, whereupon the media would announce with great fanfare that UFOs have been explained away! To prepare for such a debunking, these stealth planes are sent forth to coincide either with a sighting or slightly after. Media coverage of any mass sighting invariably includes either speculation that the UFO was this familiar triangle shape or statements to this effect. In matters of this cover-up, they've got themselves covered!

Contact

17
Visitations

Your Earth is fertile and full of life, an endless source of interest to the curious visitor. Just as travelers on long sea voyages, or trekking long distances over continents, were lost to their human families, just so these visitors on occasion lost their moorings. They died, and their companions were not able to locate their remains. Dead tissue is dead tissue, and it does not speak but rather blends into the surrounding forest or swamp, lost to those anxiously looking for a companion. Humans are aware that their technology is not perfect, and this lack of perfection is always present. The phone may be but a fingertip away and the ambulance can come at a moment's notice, but if one's portable phone is broken when one is dying away from home, then one may never be found!

Most often the bones of visitors are not recognized for what they are, as they are thought to be remains of an animal of some sort. Remains are also usually disturbed by scavengers, eaten and dragged or thrown about so that an intact section cannot be pieced together. Any remains that would tend to look hominoid, but not human, would frighten a human coming upon them, and these types of situations tend to result in active denial. The remains are left where they are found, and even if documented and pressed upon colleagues, denial prevents them from being taken seriously. If for no other reason, denial occurs because the researchers have difficulty realizing they are not alone, not the first or most intelligent conscious species in the universe, not the masters of all they survey. One looks the other way, walks away, and then forgets to mention the find in their report.

Light Form

Wise and massive entities, almost invariably in the service-to-others orientation, appear as balls of light so their human contacts can mentally register their presence. Humans sense these entities well before they see them in light form, as the light form is assumed only as a type of dress to allow the human to better comprehend the situation. The contactee strongly senses someone in the room, or nearby, even though the contactee may be quite alone by all appearances. This sense that someone else is present is so strong that the contactee may actually glance around, disbelieving what their eyes are telling them. It is for this reason that these entities assume a light form, so that the contactee can relate to what is happening and get down to business.

Human spirits are sensed, as ghosts, as a light cooling of the temperature or perhaps a visage of the human as it appeared during its last incarnation. This in no way relates to how the entity is shaped at present, but is an impression the formerly human spirit is giving to the human at the scene—I looked like this. Temperature changes are due to the discarnate entity desiring to influence the scene, and being inexperienced at how to do this.

Ugly Aliens

One's interpretation of beauty is influenced by what one is familiar with, and is also directed by the life-form's built-in self-defense instincts. Humans instinctively avoid food that is rotten, and are attracted to food that smells fresh. Men see beauty in women who have full hips, slender waists, and ample bosoms—all traits that indicate the ability and readiness to bear young. Both sexes find a diseased partner unattractive—a safeguard against spreading infections or perpetuating genetic diseases. In some primitive parts of the world tattoos or pictorial scarification is considered strikingly attractive, but in other cultures where clothing of all kinds is abundant, such use of the skin as an outer garment would be shunned.

Thus, when contactees report visits from life-forms that startle or even horrify them, this is not an indication of malevolent intent. A life-form that looked like a slime-covered horned toad or an amphibious octopus is not a life-form humans would instinctively cuddle up to. Humans, due to their evolutionary roots, are inclined to think about dinner or avoidance when encountering such creatures, not about communion. The global shift in thinking that humans make when realizing that they are not alone as an intelligent species includes contemplating what this means. It does not mean sitting around a table chatting with other very human-looking aliens, an image the media has portrayed. Humans should bear in mind, when making these adjustments, that their appearance may be just as disgusting to their visitors.

Identification

Visitations are occurring between literally hundreds of alien groups and human contactees. The hand of the various groups can sometimes be seen in the type of endeavor undertaken by the human who gave The Call. For instance, Pleiadeans are intent on educating humans in the pleasant nature of fourth-density service-to-others existence, the sense of community and the potential for being playful and having fun. The Sirians are more warlike, have this history in their past, and take The Call from humans who could use logistical advice during confrontations. Nordics are very scientific and intellectual, and dislike the spotlight. They thus work behind the scenes, and their contactees are never heard of.

In meeting or dealing with a non-human entity, whether this is a spirit you only converse with on an ethereal level or an entity with embodiment that you encounter during contacts, you must judge for yourself whether this is an encounter with the service-to-self or service-to-others orientation. There are no measures that serve as an easy answer. There are no rules that can quickly be applied to the situation for an easy resolution to confusion. The right solution to the situation facing you, as a human, this minute, is something you must determine. For some, this is painful. Some humans,

107

faced with this perplexing dilemma and used to the rigorous answers that their religious ideology gives to them, feel naked and alone. Contactee Confusion

Contactees, regardless of their conscious awareness of their status, find themselves in a puzzling world. Human society has scarcely become comfortable with the concept of telepathy, ridiculing those who claim that this form of communication exists even when proven in a controlled laboratory setting. The concept of spirits, such as ghosts or reincarnation or possession, is considered in the realm of tales rather than the reporting of fact, especially as spirits leave no mark or footprints. What cannot be physically restrained does not exist, in the minds of many, so brain waves or spirit forms are speculative. Where does this leave the contactee, who in many cases has begun to have Out-Of-Body Experiences (OOBEs) to cloud the picture as well?

Contactees who have not yet realized their status, or who have not yet sorted out memories from the spirit from memories stored in the corporeal mind, can be highly confused. At first, memories from the incarnated spirit, who may return from an OOBE bearing information from another place, are considered to be day dreams, and until the contactee finds their day dream was a reality this explanation is not questioned. At first, the contactee's subconscious memories of visitations are treated as an overactive imagination, perhaps influenced by the media which increasingly carries stories about visitations, but then signs such as scars that appear overnight begin to intrude. At first, increased telepathic abilities are a curiosity, and then accepted by the contactee, who may ascribe most of their unusual knowledge to such a route rather than facing the prospect of visitations or OOBEs.

However, when the contactee adjusts to the concept of spirit forms that can move in and out of corporeal bodies, and visitations that can occur soul-to-soul while the soul of the contactee is incarnated, or out and about during an OOBE, then they invariably develop the ability to differentiate these experiences. In general, telepathically gathered information is limited in its scope, relaying a single concept or picture. Information gathered during an OOBE is comprehensive, but the corporeal mind will digest what it learns from the returning spirit in stages, so that the bottom line is learned first and the details filter in later. Subconscious memories of visitations play out during recall with full sound and color, as you say, so that the memory unfolds like a movie. Thus experienced contactees who have sorted out the alternate realities find their lives no more confusing than a shopper discovering clothing on the racks from different countries and in different styles. After a while, it all seems quite normal.

Initiation and Orientation

In human society initiation or inclusion rites frequently bound the onset of a special status, such as baptism, marriage, military induction, public service, or entry into a profession or trade. The human so bounded knows when this status begins, as do others. Likewise, the termination of a status is bounded by rites, such as a funeral, divorce, discharge, termination notice, or ban. But contactees have had no initiation rite. Since they can't be sure of the beginning, can they be sure of the end? How can they tell? Since the beginning and end are under the control of the human giving The Call, the contacts can end as quickly as they started. Just announce your change of heart. Just state your desire to make it a wrap. Just say no. It's as simple as that. Whether the contact has been, at your request, from the orientation of service-to-self or the service-to-others, the results are the same. You are no longer a contactee.

A small number of contactees, those who we anticipate will act as catalysts during the Awakening, are shown line-ups of alien life-forms. This gradual orientation, which is done in stages so as not to overwhelm the contactee, usually progresses from hominoid life-forms to life-forms humans have never encountered on Earth. In between are reptilian life-forms or water creatures such as a jellyfish or an octopus. Our emissary, Nancy, has been presented with such lineups, and relayed these experiences in her own words within *ZetaTalk*. The contactee may or may not consciously remember these orientation sessions, depending on how actively they seek to establish recall. Nevertheless, they are oriented, and when an opportunity to communicate their understanding arises, they are quick to help their fellows to a broader view.

Invariably, there is initial shock at the wide variety of intelligent life-forms. Humans tend to get through the lineup of hominoids with little trouble, become stunned when they first encounter life-forms not known on Earth, and progress to a tolerance for almost anything thereafter.

Mutual Fears

Often reported by some contact therapists and dramatized in the media is the frightened contactee—screaming, running, hiding, and in general exhibiting all the characteristics of a trapped animal in a state of panic. What's going on here? Have these contactees changed their minds, and can they back out at the last minute?

A human who gives The Call can end a visitation at any point. They are in control. What is occurring is mixed feelings, a very common and almost everyday situation for most humans. Look to the moment when a young person is about to lose his or her virginity, or to ask for another's hand in marriage, or to begin an important job interview, or to go off the high dive for the first time, or to eat fish eggs or snails for the first time, or to go to the dentist for the yearly checkup, or to find the onset of labor with the wanted child beginning, or to sign on the dotted line to purchase a car, or to get on an airplane once again, or to invite the in-laws over for dinner, or to get their hair cut radically short—are these not moments exhibiting mixed feelings?

Contactees exhibiting fear of contact are not stating they wish for the visitation to end. If this were truly the case, it would end, promptly. They are simply stating that they are nervous about some aspect of the visitation. They are chatting with aliens, a presence those in authority have refused to even acknowledge. They are going off with strangers, something their mother told them never to do. They are going in alone, and for many humans, who wouldn't even venture to the local bar without companions, this in and of itself is a big step. They are anticipating mild physical discomfort, if they are a volunteer in the hybrid program. And they may have requested frank information on the Transformation but be anticipating, correctly, that this will not be sugar coated.

Contactees also sometimes report that their visitors also seem wary or almost frightened of them. Well, of course they are wary, as few intelligent species have the innate capacity for blind rage that *Homo sapiens* does, a capacity that can surprise the human as much as the visitor. Large males are frequently paralyzed early in the visitation process, to avoid the physical chaos that results from flying fists, swinging arms, and flung objects. As blind rage is triggered by the fear response, those contactees dealing with intense fear will see their fear reflected in the face of their visitors, who are preparing to deal with a possible explosion.

Children

Those who are alarmed by the trends the Transformation is taking are particularly alarmed about what they term the abduction of children. Beyond the apprehension that something wretched might be happening to a vulnerable and impressionable child is a very different alarm—that we are getting them young and there is no way they can stop it. Cases where youngsters have been harmed by contact with aliens in the Service-to-others orientation are nonexistent, nosebleeds and interrupted sleep notwithstanding. Those in the service-to-self are not allowed to affect the physical environment of a child, as given their nature they would surely attempt to maximize terror in those too young to have perspective. They are only allowed to answer The Call from a youngster on an intellectual basis—a conference.

From our perspective, as service-to-others visitors, contact with children is no different from contact with adults. We are essentially speaking to the entity, the spirit within. From our perspective, dealing with humans is to some degree like dealing with children anyway. Where the young human has not gained wisdom on how the world works, a frame of reference, they are vastly more open to see a situation for what it is. They don't wear blinders. They don't have preconceptions. They don't have a vested interest in the status quo.

First Meeting

Nancy had a typical first meeting with ourselves, the service-to-others Zetas, and will tell you the story.

I went down into the swamps a lot. There were so many frogs in the swamp. I'd be gone for hours. Nobody would know where I was because the trees were big. I was a little girl. I was very curious about animals and I would be very quiet and watch for them. I'm standing still and have that feeling going up my spine that you do when you know somebody's around but you don't know where they are or who they are. I can't see what it is that I feel nervous about, but out of the corner of my eye I see a movement, from the left, coming out from behind a tree. Somebody just steps out from behind a tree. It's one of these skinny guys, very gray, light gray actually. They almost look smaller than me. So many wild creatures are very quiet, like deer, they only show themselves when they feel safe. So I'm not alarmed by this. I think a couple of them come up, from the right and the left of me, from behind, and take my elbows. I'm still not alarmed because I'm just not getting any vibes from them that are hostile.

I'm seeing some sort of a disk shape, small. There's really only three or four of these guys. It's a small disk shape, maybe 12 feet across, not that large. I'm pretty curious. I guess my initial reaction was more curiosity than fear. I'm trying to figure out what this is. I don't feel anything hostile. It seems as if we just walk toward that ship, and there's a ramp that's let down from it. I don't think I'm doing any resisting. They seem to be interested in my head and my hands and my wrists. They seem to be examining my hands and my wrists, the way my wrists bend. They seem to be putting their hands on either side of my head, almost like they're sizing it. Curious little creatures, very gray, light gray, even slightly smaller than I am, although I couldn't have been more than eight years old or so. One of them looks at me, puts his face close to mine, eye contact I guess, and seems to be trying to communicate something. Maybe he's saying, "Do you know why we're here? Do you know what we want?" Maybe it's because I'm not afraid, maybe that's what he's thinking, that I already know. I'm just trying to search and find if I know. But I just keep thinking they're really curious little creatures.

There's something at the side that looks like a little tray at the dentist's office where they have this little mirror on a stick and things like that. It's off to the right-hand side, and it makes me just a tiny bit nervous to think about that. I think maybe they're going to do something with my right forearm, like when someone takes blood or something like that, poke around in your forearm a little bit. It seems as if I lay back down on a table, but it wasn't really flat, something more like a chaise lounge. They've got my head at an angle and do something to my forehead. It's a little bit sore, but it's a very dull ache. I'm a little more distracted. I tell them I want to go back to my frogs and he says, "We'll be back."

━┼━

18
Recall

Beyond the rules we are required to follow, we are dealing almost exclusively with our contactees only in the subconscious because of your society's resistance to our presence, to the alien presence. Conscious recall puts contactees at odds with society, which is stressful. Until lately, it could also be extremely dangerous, as your government punished those who spoke of their experiences. Subconscious memories of our face-to-face meetings are as effective as a full conscious memory. The distress a schism between the conscious and subconscious causes a human occurs when the human finds they just up and do something where they previously didn't know they had this intention. However, this type of behavior occurs in humans who don't have any contact with ourselves, the Zetas, so it is not unique to contactees.

Recall

During face-to-face contact we disconnect the conscious. These memories are not recorded at all in your conscious, which is a different part of your brain from your subconscious. Many contactees recall their visitations as a dream, as the recall starts during a semi-sleep state, during that time when one is just dropping off to sleep or waking up. However, there are characteristics that mark the recall as other than a dream. The dream seems vivid, so real, and includes elements not normally in dreams such as sounds and smells. These dreams are usually so vivid as to wake the drowsy contactee. Some contactees remember immediately, and think they have been aware all along. In fact, this is not what occurs, but rather immediately after the visitation the contactee connects the memory in the subconscious to the conscious. This process is similar to the physiological process humans use to restore their past after amnesia periods. Essentially, for the conscious mind, this is like a first-time experience, with new memory links established. It feels like daydreaming, and most often occurs in just that way. The contactee finds himself musing at some point, about aliens or space ships, and then begins to wonder. They get an interest in the subject, gather books and join groups, and talk intensely to others. All this increases the rate of remembering, as one thing leads to another.

When a contactee remembers, these conscious memories are being built for the first time, so there is an escalation process that occurs. Whether while analyzing a dream, or daydreaming, or under hypnosis, the process is essentially the same. A fragment pops up in the conscious mind, connected firmly to the subconscious, but at first not connected to any other conscious memories. However, as the fragment will contain some clues to other parts of the conscious, building connections to the conscious begins. Wasn't that the borrowed robe worn that night spent at Cousin Joe's on a spontaneous overnight stay? Isn't that the childhood chum, whom one built a tree house with in the woods behind the school? Might the sharp bite of pain and temporary soreness, recalled as a tissue sample is taken from the back of the leg, relate to that odd scar that seemed to just appear one day?

Aware contactees, who have done their digging about in the subconscious and have built a solid base in their conscious minds, almost always try to figure out ways to recall right after a visit. They notice certain correlations. The odd and untimely desire to take a solitary walk in the woods, the sense that something is different at this moment from just the moment before. Contactees most often know well ahead of time about a pending visit, and their desire to be alone, in the woods or wherever, is due to their plan to sort this all out afterwards. They arrange a peaceful time for themselves. Going into a visit, the contactee is aware, telepathically, of the agenda. For instance, if all are going to discuss a project the contactee is working on, a problem which the contactee has requested assistance on, the contactee might suddenly find himself musing about a solution he had not thought of before, and feeling less worried. This is a solid clue that a visit has occurred.

Sometimes the contactee realizes they have just returned if their body jerks, or reacts in a startle response, for no reason. As we frequently use the paralyzed state to transport contactees, there is often a reaction to having this state lifted. The body reacts, sometimes by being too relaxed for a standing position and thus suddenly adjusting the body musculature to support the stance, and sometimes reacting to the sudden stimulation with a startle reflex. This too is a solid clue that a visit has just occurred.

Many contactees find that, try as they may, they cannot recall their visitations as other contactees seem to do. All manner of attempts, including professional hypnosis, will be tried to no avail. What's going on here? In human society, and in particular in many contactees' lives, there is a conflict about the alien presence and thus there can be a conflict within the contactee. Does the spouse believe that man is not alone and is being visited by beings from other worlds? Is the employer ultra-conservative, such that a slip of the tongue in the coffee room will place doubts in the employer's mind about the contactee's eligibility for promotion? Is the family supportive, the friends accepting, or will the contactee find they are increasingly treated as an eccentric and left out of social plans? Where the contactee fears repercussions in his life he will tend to block.

Signs

Contactees deal with many doubts. The issues of maintaining an element of doubt, necessary so that the Awakening can proceed without raising the level of anxiety and fear in the populace, seems unnecessary to many contactees, who would welcome some reassurance. Even in the face of confirmation from the books they read and friends they meet at contact groups, many contactees find their need for reassurance becoming a burning issue. This point is often reached when the contactees determine to make changes in their lives because of their convictions, and cannot explain their decisions to family and friends. They know they will be considered eccentric at best for the steps they plan, and beyond wanting something to show others as rationale, they simply want something solid to cling to during the lonely times when they are subject to ridicule. Give me a sign, they ask. What has meaning for one person is meaningless to another, so personal signs are often given to individual contactees at the crossroads where normal living is about to be left behind and dedication taken up. Personal signs have great significance to the person, but by their nature cannot be used as proof of the alien presence. One person may find their shoes lined up on a different side of the closet, something they would never do. Another may find that bag of chips they intended to buy but forgot suddenly appearing on the counter top. Yet another might find their beard clipped, a routine of personal hygiene done weekly but not yet done this past week. The person is momentarily stunned, then combs through the recent past to see if they might have forgotten.

The sign is understood for what it is, based on the intensity of the contactee's anguish going into the sign and their often adamant cries for a sign of some kind. The two go together. Signs are always given when the contactee least expects them, sometimes after they have given up hope of getting their request answered. This is to ensure that the contactee is not led astray as to the nature of the alien presence. As we are by the rules restrained from interfering with the conduct of human affairs, we do not wish to lead our contactees into believing that we can be relied upon to respond. Signs are also given in a manner that is meaningless to anyone but the contactee, and most contactees clearly recognize this and do not try to impress or convince others. Nevertheless, for the individual, the sign they have been given has deep meaning.

Physical Signs

Unique to alien implants is their capacity to cause what many contactees describe as a jolt or buzz in the brain, a sensation they cannot biologically reconcile. Some contactees seek medical advice, convinced they have a brain tumor or, if they experience a momentary loss of muscular control, perhaps epilepsy. Implants are locating devices, allowing the contactee to be quickly located prior to a visitation. The devices respond to a signal sent in all directions, an answering call. To generate the signal, the implant utilizes the nervous system, which operates by electrical impulses of a sort, and thus is detectable to the contactee. A temporary disruption of local nerve traffic, along with a local reaction to the strength of the signal sent through brain, bone, and muscle. Within a dead body, the implant would not respond to the locating signal, thus informing the visitors of a death, but in any case they eventually learn of the death of their contactee via spiritual routes. Implants also respond with a unique signal, generated from the DNA of the contactee, so that the implant response confirms not only that the contactee is alive but that the implant is still located within the proper body. Thus, when contactees experience a jolt or buzz in the brain, they should not be alarmed. All is working as intended, and what they are experiencing confirms their link to the visitors they have asked to meet.

The ear is a sensitive organ, designed to alert the human to a loss of balance as well as serving as the hearing sense. Loss of balance, or falling, is sensed by a change in blood pressure, the delicate difference between what is going on in one side of the head versus the other. This dual role of the ears involves the ear in visitations in a way that confuses many contactees—ringing in the ears, temporary loss of hearing, pain in the ears, or excessive drainage from the ears due to such irritations. During visitations the human may be suddenly taken on a quick trip to a ship, and if the human is afraid of heights this can be alarming, raising the blood pressure. The human may be paralyzed for ease of passage and to reduce anxieties. But when coming out of this state, which is a natural state akin to what an opossum assumes when playing 'possum, the human may have sudden changes in blood pressure as the body adjusts to being alert again.

Frequently contactees report a knocking sound preceding their visitations, and almost invariably interpret this as a signal of some kind. Humans, of course, knock on doors, tap out Morse Code, beat on drums to send messages through the wilderness, and tap their feet or drum their fingers to express impatience. If they hear knocking, what else could it be? Density shifting is most often silent, with only the airspace disturbed. A ship suddenly appearing high in the sky, displacing a few molecules of thin air, creates at most a light change in the breeze. Large or sudden displacement of air can create sound, as thunder claps following a lighting flash attest. Arriving or maneuvering aliens, who do not arrive all at once lest they collide with each other at the staging point, create sudden movement in the air space in confined or delimited settings. Clap, clap, the aliens have arrived!

Staged Visitations

The ability to retain a memory after an incident is greatly affected by blood or brain chemistry, a fact well known not only to the medical profession but to intelligence agencies which use injections to cause their interrogation subjects to forget that their civil rights were abused.

ZetaTalk

These simple means of allowing a memory to be partially retained have recently moved into the private sphere, where members of the establishment, what is commonly known as the New World Order crowd, use injections or drugs to induce confusion in humans they wish to influence regarding the alien presence. Certain humans, who by virtue of inherited wealth or by virtue of their professional position or ability to influence public thinking, are targeted. Since most contactees remember only parts of their visitations, this group allows their targets to retain a memory of only part of their fraudulent visitation.

They pick the target up by one rouse or another or by virtually kidnapping them, inject them with a drug that causes complete memory loss of the incident, put them into a setting where the target thinks they are on a space ship or in the presence of alien hominoids, and then return them home while drugged into a state of forgetfulness again. The target recalls only the core portion of the incident, and is convinced they have had a real visitation.

19
Contact Techniques

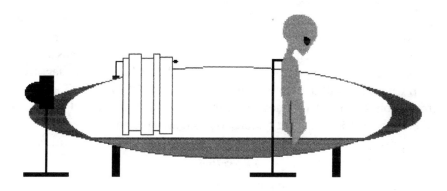

Communications to our contactees include telepathic conversations, which the contactee may or may not be aware of. Telepathic thought, for humans, seems much like day dreaming. Thoughts just come into the contactee's head. These conversations differ from day dreaming in that they have a conversational element, and the contactee may think of something outside of his personal knowledge. Each human we so speak to is different. Our telepathic message is understood by a contactee in their native language, if words are involved. Long before the word is formed in their mind, however, the concept is understood. Words may be the first external contact humans have with a concept, but they are in fact the end product of the conceptualization process.

Paralyzed State
The state of paralysis that many contactees report is common, and is used not only as a means of calming and controlling potentially violent contactees but also for convenience. The paralyzed state is very relaxing, and leaves no harmful trace. During travel between the Earth and a space

ship, through walls, and at rapid speeds, humans often prefer to be paralyzed. In fact, this is a frequent request of the constant contactee, as they find they can rest, and, as you say, leave the driving to us. What is going on in the state of paralysis? At times the mind is aware, at times as though in a deep sleep. Some contactees report they can break out of the paralysis, with a shout or by force of will.

The mechanism used to place humans into paralysis is simple, and does not involve our technologies or manipulation of densities. We are utilizing an existing human physiology, something akin to the frozen state that opossums take when frightened. Why is it that humans never play 'possum when we or other aliens aren't around to induce this? It is because this facility is deep within the reptilian brain, and not connected to the middle brain or frontal lobes. Humans cannot voluntarily reach this spot. But if one knows where it is, and knows what buttons to push, then presto!

Eye-to-Eye

Many contactees have reported that we, the Zetas, have gone eye-to-eye with them during a visitation, and have wondered why this was necessary. Doesn't telepathy communicate ideas more effectively? What does looking deeply into the eyes accomplish? Just as reading an aura tells the reader much about the physiology of the human, just so reading the eyes conveys much. The Zeta have huge eyes, in comparison to human eyes, but this does not mean that we see that much more than humans. We see differently. Our large eyes developed in what humans would consider dark conditions, just as Earth creatures that operate at night have large eyes. We make much of what little light we garner, but likewise our eyes can be overwhelmed by too much light. Human doctors peek at the retina to determine illness, as for instance the retina is the first to display the fact that hardening of the arteries has begun. We Zetas likewise take advantage of this handy barometer, reading what we can of the human contactees physical condition—through the eyes.

Out-Of-Body

Some contactees have reported experiencing intermittent invisibility, where others in the room seem unaware of them, or they themselves cannot see their reflections in a mirror or their hand before their face. What is being reported here is not invisibility but an OOBE, where the human is unfamiliar with the experience and does not know what to make of it. When Out-Of-Body, the spirit collects impressions of sight, smell, and even the sense of touch, being attuned to this from its residence in the human body, and relays these to the human's mind upon return, building a memory. To the human, this all seems real, and they thus conclude they must have been invisible, as indeed they were to the other humans in the drama.

Some contactees have reported being taken Out-Of-Body during visitations, as though they were a passive participant, but going Out-Of-Body is always the decision of the contactee. The fact that OOBEs occur at all during visitations speaks to the traumatic nature of visitation. Humans experience OOBE in association with great trauma, where they are near death or severely injured. Where visitation does not injure the human encountering alien life-forms and dealing, for the first time, with concepts like levitation, it is startling. Some contactees recall seeing themselves lying on a table while a medical procedure or examination is taking place, apparently Out-Of-Body during this distress. OOBEs are not used as a deliberate type of anesthesia, as OOBE maneuvers are always initiated by the human. However, due more to alarm at the strangeness of the setting, many contactees do go Out-Of-Body during physical procedures.

Once having been Out-Of-Body, the entity incarnating in a human body is wise, and not infrequently intrigued. How did I do that? Being Out-Of-Body offers all kinds of opportunities—instantaneous travel, through walls, and invisibility. Humans adept at initiating an OOBE use this frequently to gather information, check on a loved one, or just simply to have a look-see. Is this good? Yes and no. Where the human has not progressed in his third-density orientation lesson and must continue in third-density, Out-Of-Body can be a distraction from the lesson. It is an escape. For this reason we do not give lessons on how to achieve an OOBE.

Soul-to-Soul

Contactees are aware of visits that involve their physical bodies, as during recall they float through walls, levitate rapidly, are in a paralyzed state, feel the cold surface of an examining table, or have other such memories in the subconscious mind that confirm that a visit occurred. Then there are OOBEs, in which the spirit communicates to the mind in concepts the mind can grasp—sights, sounds, and smells. But contactees have visitations, soul-to-soul, that they have no specific memory of, as the contact occurred while their spirit was incarnated. Thus, sensory memory of the visit is no different from the moments of the day the contactee remembers otherwise.

Recall will not change this, as there is no treasure in the subconscious waiting to be linked up with the conscious, nor is the spirit waiting for an opportunity to bring the mind up to date on where it's been and what was observed. All were in the same place. No missing time, no hidden memories, no recorded OOBE about to unfold—an *in-situ* visitation recorded only in the soul. How does the contactee discern that this visit has occurred? As these visits are so subtle, they can be discerned only by a changed attitude on the part of the contactees, who may develop a firm resolve, abandon a former plan without bitterness or regret, develop new interests, or initiate revolutionary changes in their life.

Gaining Time

Much has been mentioned in contactee literature about the phenomenon called missing time, where the contactee finds they simply can't account for an hour or so of time, and those around them report they were utterly gone and could not be located anywhere during that time. Missing time is, of course, the most convenient way a visitation occurs, as no particular manipulation of the environment need be done outside of simply picking up the contactee and conducting the visit. However, many busy contactees have little room in their lives for missing time, so resourceful visitors often resort to a visitation method which could be called gained time. It is a way of recording two memories of the moment—one real and one a playback.

Most contactees, like all humans, have broad stretches of time in their day that are essentially wasted time—commutes to and from work, standing at a bus stop, reading the newspaper while someone prepares dinner, or watching the news on TV. All these activities take place repetitively, each day, so the scene is more than familiar to the contactee. It is essentially a repeat performance. Thus a contactee can skip the activities that would take place during such a stretch of time, and scarcely notice. In the same manner that screen memories are given to contactees, the contactee is given a memory in keeping with the activity that would have occurred. Most often, this memory is simply a playback of one they already have in their memory banks, quite handy as it is available within the same human brain. Meanwhile, while the playback is being recorded in the conscious mind, the visitation is also occurring, being recorded in the subconscious.

Standing In

During an increasingly busy Transformation period, with the necessity of gathering up contactees for group meetings, the aliens coordinating these group meetings are presented with endless scheduling difficulties. Many times when one contactee is free to have some missing time, the others are busy at work, as coordination may span the globe. One way around this matter is to get an exception from the Council of Worlds so that the contactee can be moved forward into the future for the meeting, then returned, and thus experience no missing time but rather a doubling of time in the near future. This is seldom done, due to the administrative complexity.

Another method available to the busy alien visitors assisting with the Transformation is what could be termed a stand-in, where the contactee thinks they are in two places at once. Essentially the process is that the contactee is picked up in the normal manner and taken to his group meeting. During this time the meeting is being recorded in his subconscious, in the usual manner, and he is, on a gut level, fully aware of the meeting content, participants, and any resolve as a result of the meeting. In other words, the meeting has taken place as usual. Simultaneously an alien steps into the physical surroundings and activities the contactee would have been involved in, had they not been picked up for the group meeting. This alien mentally records the events, transferring this mental image with full sight and sound and sense of touch to the conscious mind of the contactee, who thus is recording this consciously as though they were there.

Following the group meeting, the contactees are returned to their settings, and they pick up seamlessly in the ongoing activities, so that consciously they do not register any disruption at all. The activities conducted by the stand-in bear the mark of the contactee, as while mentally transferring the situation to the contactee, the alien stand-in is also receiving reactions from the contactee as to what steps they would take next, etc. This method has some wear and tear on the contactee, in that brain chemistry is exhausted more rapidly than the human's physiology is designed to replenish. Thus, this method is not used for long periods of time, or done repeatedly within a day, unless the situation absolutely requires that such steps be taken.

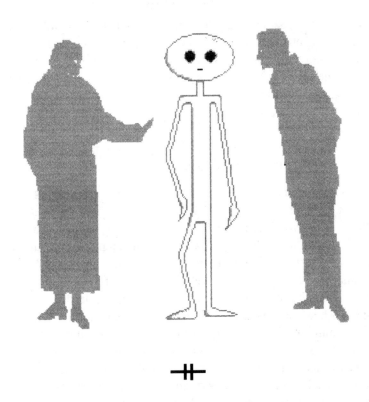

20
Density

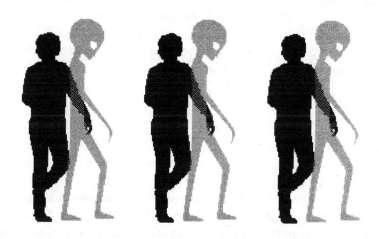

   Objects in third and fourth density occupy the same space, as when humans are moved through walls. What you call sub-atomic particles move at different frequencies or vibrations. They do not collide or even recognize each other. Their motion does not put them in the same place at the same time, anymore than if you were to walk through the forest. The trees are more dense in this instance, in that from your view they aren't moving at all. You guide yourself past the trees. Sub-atomic particles in fourth density in essence flow past those in third density, as water does to obstacles in its path. Molecules in third density and fourth density simply slide by each other, and do not interact. Thus, they can even occupy the same space. Space, in fact, is more empty than full. A planet, likewise, can and is both third and fourth density at the same time. Regarding the issue of how we travel, or move a human through walls, suffice it to explain that we make a reservation in the vibrational density we wish to move to, and then move.

   If we are moving into a density already occupied, we ensure a safe move by first freezing the objects in the reserved area so that no molecular action is occurring. It is in essence a dead stop, similar to what the soil at landing sites is exhibiting when plants fail to grow there for some time after the landing, as the mineral nutrients are frozen for a time. After objects in the reservation area are frozen, they are taken into the density we are shifting from, still in their frozen state. The receiving point is essentially in the middle of a vacuum, to minimize molecular encounters. When the frozen portions from the reservation area are at hand, we step into this same area, arrange ourselves around any object temporarily taken from the density we are moving to, and all is then quickly returned to the target density. Horrors such as occurred at the Philadelphia Experiment are not possible with this procedure, for if the target density is so crowded that we cannot step into the arena, we return the objects and select another spot.

Dangers

There are dangers, and thus our status as volunteers during these transformational endeavors carries with it the classification of hazardous duty. What are the dangers? First and foremost there is a danger of not making a complete transition, of being partly left behind. This can happen when the coordinates are not set properly, a matter we attend to with the utmost care. These coordinates are essentially boundaries, but boundaries are defined as more than the periphery. Boundaries include chemical composition, molecular structure, and connectedness. A simple example of a chemical composition boundary would be moving acidic material but leaving behind inert or alkaloid material. A simple example of a molecular structure boundary would be leaving behind radioactive material in a slag heap but moving all else. A simple example of a connectedness boundary would be moving all of a table but leaving behind the chairs, floor, and table cloth.

Density-shifting dangers are usually encountered early on in an entity's experience with such matters, and leave a memory not soon forgotten. The true stories about the *Philadelphia Experiment* and the fictional movie *The Fly* are not far from the horror that can happen when the necessary knowledge or proper care are not in place. We take care not to touch one another or our contactees during the shift. We take care to include all parts of the object to be moved within the boundaries. We have a series of overlapping and redundant computerized and manual checks and balances that make the safety of the shift virtually fail-safe.

Transporting

Density switching involves more than simply increasing or decreasing the vibrational level of the object to be moved, it can also involve moving from one point in space to another, or one point in time to another. Thus, a contactee can be picked up for a conference, taken to another place for this conference, and returned after the conference to the same place and time as the pickup point. To the contactee, who has not experienced missing time, nothing ostensibly has happened, yet the contactee returns with the conference recorded in his subconscious. Should there have been a medical procedure during the visit, the contactee's body retains the result of that medical procedure upon return. This method of arranging visits is obviously more complicated than simply picking the contactee up from a point in the woods or asking them to walk out of their bedroom into the backyard so that they can experience a bit of missing time. Here density switching is not involved, nor manipulation of time or space. Being less complicated, this method is most often used during a visit. However, there are special times when transporting is used.

If a contactee is extremely busy, so that arranging a bit of missing time is either a burden or a frank impossibility during the day, transporting from one point in space and time to another may be used to arrange a meeting. Such a transport may or may not involve a density switch, depending upon the density where the others to be present at the meeting currently reside. If the meeting is with a number of alien visitors in fourth density, the contactee will be moved to that density for the meeting. The return to the point in space and time is so exacting that the contactee may be picked up naked, and be returned into their clothing, unruffled.

If a hybrid fetus is to be extracted from a donor mother's womb, and for reasons of health the donor mother should not experience the usual vacuum extraction method via the birth canal, then the fetus can be transported. This is done by locating the fetus within the mother's tissue by DNA signature, and targeting that tissue and some surrounding tissue from the mother to be transported. The perimeter is defined in such a way that the mother's womb is barely affected but the fetus is kept snug until an alternative womb can be placed around it. In extreme cases transporting is used to turn back the clock. These rare cases are where the Council of Worlds grants permission, as the Council has deemed the situation important for the Earth's Transformation. An example is where a situation such as the death of someone of key importance has occurred, by accident. If permission is granted, the individual may be transported from the point before death to the present, and properly attended to so that death will not occur. Such intervention is not possible if the death has been broadcast, but is possible if few know of the death.

Bermuda Triangle

The Bermuda Triangle does indeed have unusual qualities, as do other places here and there on Earth. Magnetic anomalies are reported, where compasses swing wildly, clocks stop, and concrete objects fade from sight. What's causing this? These places, fortunately few in number, are an outlet from the center of the Earth for a byproduct of the Earth's compression, a gravity byproduct so to speak. A vent, from where subatomic particles not known to man surge forth periodically, and woe be to the man or fish who finds itself in the way. There are stories of ships and planes disappearing, and it is assumed they were carried off by extraterrestrials, taken off to a far-off zoo, for exhibition. Then why would these only disappear from such sites, and not regularly around the globe?

Here and there around the face of the Earth are similar outlets for this byproduct of the Earth's compression, many of them well known due to the havoc shippers or travelers experience—an area off the coast of Japan, and in one of the Great Lakes, for example. Such outlets also occur where man is unaware of them, as in the depths of the oceans or within inaccessible mountain crevices. What determines the outlet is not only the surface structure of the rock—fractures in fact—but also the structure of the underlying rock, factors man cannot measure.

Landing Sites

The impact spaceships from other dimensions have on landing sites is a phenomenon unknown to Earth's scientists, and a puzzle. Plants sometimes fail to grow at these sites, for months or years, and then suddenly start growing again. This puzzle has a simple key. Germination and growth of young plants starts, but is starved early on. The lack is not water, but the availability of nutrients. The site is frozen for density switching, a reservation. This reservation places a lock on atoms in the density to be moved into. The lock is overpowering enough to freeze activity in the general area, for non-intelligent actions.

Intelligent actions, such as those under the direction of humans, or even semi-intelligent actions of animals such as mammals or reptiles and birds, can break this lock. Plants do not have the power to break this lock, of their own accord. How does the lock then get broken, after so many seasons where growth does not occur in the soil so affected? The original reservation for the time/space in the density to be moved into has parameters, where a maximum of time is given. When this time reservation runs out, or expires, the nutrients held in a lock are freed, and the normal interaction occurs. Seeds now germinate and find nutrients awaiting them, and life returns to normal.

Mothership Clues

Most sightings are of small ships used only for quick, local trips, not the type of ship used for interstellar travel. Motherships are the home away from home, and carry all manner of equipment, supplies, and facilities that small ships simply don't have room for. Motherships can be monstrously large, in human terms, far larger than their battleships or football stadiums. These motherships have the same anti-gravity capability that small ships have, and thus can astonish human witnesses who see these monsters floating in the air without the aid of roaring jets or whirling blades. Thus, during the Awakening, motherships are seldom used for sightings, as such sightings are considered too jolting for the average witness.

Since motherships hide, are there clues that one is about? The dramatic approach of a mothership in the movie *Close Encounters of the Third Kind* was based on reality, as clouds are the most often used camouflage. A mothership hovering in the vicinity is obvious to anyone watching a suspicious cloud for a length of time, as the small ships that port in and out almost constantly can be seen zipping in and out of the cloud. As the entire mothership and contents are in third density during an intense time of activity on Earth's surface, these small ships are quite visible, and in the right light are unmistakable. Are they satellites when they emerge from or disappear into a cloud? Are they human airplanes when no jet trail or engine noise can be heard? This activity is a mothership clue, a moment of high drama for those witnesses who understand what they are watching.

Lightning Clouds

Lightning clouds are a type of sighting that implies but does not show the ship. This is equivalent to jet trails across the sky or the wake left behind a boat. A stationary cloud bristling with lightning is making the statement—a ship was here. The lightning is caused by sudden air displacements when a ship leaves third density. The air surrounding on all sides rushes in, and, depending on air currents in place at the time, will either cause knocking as the air masses clap together or cloud formation and lightning if the air masses are sliding past each other. Where lightning clouds form, the ships are usually large, and are moving at the point of exit, rather than stationary. Humans who cannot see the ship due to a close blend with the surrounding backdrop are surprised to see a stationary cloud bristling with lightning topside, as no known weather conditions on Earth produce this phenomenon. They correctly assume that something supernatural has occurred, and since the movie *Close Encounters of the Third Kind* dramatized this phenomenon to indicate an approaching ship, they usually suspect that a sighting has occurred.

Missing Pilots

Encounters with UFOs have on rare occasions resulted in the disappearance of an airplane and its pilot, never to be seen again. What happened to these pilots? Were they captured or killed? When space ships disappear, winking out in the sky in an instant, they are essentially moving into another density. We have explained that density switching has its dangers, and if the ship is programmed to switch with its surrounding airspace, the switch takes the pilot and plane with it. Thus the pilot finds himself suddenly in a fourth-density existence, without atmosphere to breathe. This is a quick and painless death for the startled pilots, who have little chance to sort it out before they lose consciousness.

—H—

21
The Call

    The concept of The Call is but an extension of concepts humans are familiar with. One goes to the porch to call the family into dinner. One picks up the phone to call another in order to converse. When giving The Call to aliens, humans are issuing a request for contact, without a voice, without words, but the meaning is sent and understood nonetheless, by telepathic and other such wordless and wireless means. The Call is made, received, and understood, and a conference is subsequently arranged. There are times of loneliness, despair, wrenching concern for a loved one injured or in trouble, times when one wants to offer oneself in the loved one's stead, times when the path to follow is not clear and there is indecision and hesitation at the gateway, times when another is viewed as a blockage to be removed by physical and potentially violent and harmful means—these sorts of times occur, not daily, but many times in a lifetime. These are times of The Call.

    Aliens visiting Earth are not to interfere with humans regarding their spiritual choices on orientation, to become service-to-self or service-to-others. Thus the human is in control of alien interactions affecting him or her self. This is in fact intuitively understood by most humans, even those who are unaware of alien influences over their lives. The reason this is intuitively understood is because of past interactions the human does not consciously remember. All humans give The Call, and do so frequently during any given lifetime. As spiritual entities allowed to have contact with humans are oriented either towards service-to-self or service-to-others, their orientation is acute and easily discernible. One has but to pay attention. Even the spiritually immature can decipher the difference.

Non-interference can best be explained if you keep in mind that nothing can be done by an alien unless it is through a human—nothing. In this they must wait until a human gives The Call, signaling an interest in having a conference. Ambassadors from the service-to-others or service-to-self orientation can only confer with humans, what humans call close encounters or contact. Ambassadors from the service-to-self may promise delivery of goods, as where one sells one's soul to the devil for gain or where your government, early on, thought they would get alien space ship technology from their early contact with those in the service-to-self. This orientation is notorious for not telling the truth, and no technology has been gained—none. There were, however, some souls firmly recruited into the service-to-self ranks by these maneuvers, which were within the rules guiding alien behavior on Earth.

Implants must be put into the perspective of the wider picture. Contactees are all volunteers. With or without an implant, they can end their status as contactees at will. Think of an implant as a type of portable, lightweight, ever-ready telephone. The implant allows the aliens in contact to quickly locate the contactee, saving both a lot of time. Implants have been described as going up the nose, behind the ear, into the bones of the head, and under the skin. They are all that and more. They have been described as organic and structured to dissolve when removed. Some are that, and some are not affected by removal, and some are not of organic materials at all. All implants, placed by either the service-to-self or service-to-others group, are superficial and can be removed without harm to the human. Anything else would not be in accordance with the Rule of Non-Interference, affecting the free will of man, and would simply not be allowed.

Technology

Many call for assistance with technological advances, such as free-energy-machines. At this time we are restrained from simply giving mankind a gift, by the rules set by the Council of Worlds. The true intention of the human giving The Call is the first and foremost determinant. Has the caller a true desire to help others, or is The Call weighed primarily in the direction of profit and fame? Will the technological device be used by others, stolen or coerced, so that it will become a device for profit and fame rather than the intended result? There are scarcely any situations that meet the previous test. Does the human giving The Call have the personal capability to bring his request to fruition? In the main, there is far more desire than capacity. The caller must be able to understand our instructions, our explanations, and this requirement again narrows down the possibilities, as perhaps only 1% of the qualified callers are positioned to assure the technological device will not be misused, and are truly of the service-to-others orientation.

Healings

On occasion countactees will recall a visitation for the sole purpose of what is termed a healing—fevers disappear, injuries mend so rapidly that doctors in attendance doubt their X-rays, and tumors seem to melt away. Under what circumstances does this occur? As aliens visiting Earth cannot interfere with what is termed the human setting, they cannot arbitrarily step in and fix up humans who just happen to be their contactees, playing favorites as it were. Healing a contactee is not an arbitrary decision, but is one taken to the Council of Worlds in all cases, and it occurs where a contactee has chosen a role deemed important for the Earth's transformation. Contactees given a healing have chosen roles that place them in danger, result in humiliation and loss, require them to be extraordinarily steadfast through long suffering, and if anything shatter, rather than build, their lives. These contactees challenge the establishment, promote democracy in the face of tyranny, declare free thinking in the face of ridicule, or pull up stakes to prepare for leadership roles during the coming cataclysms. Ill health is an unnecessary distraction.

MJ-12 Rules

No alien/human activity occurs without humans first giving The Call, but in the case of military involvement with aliens, this can be confusing. If a general gives The Call and enters into an arrangement with aliens, can he command others to go along? In fact both rule systems are in place simultaneously, and here's how it works. Members of the military who are initiated into MJ-12 follow a plethora of rules and regulations, just as any military intelligence unit does. They also, on occasion, come in contact with aliens. During these interchanges the rules in place go beyond those in place during the usual alien/human contact where the human can allow physical contact or disallow this, delimiting the interchange. MJ-12 agreements with aliens of either orientation have always included the caveat that aliens can not physically affect the humans assigned to MJ-12 duty, even if the human wishes for this, or gives permission, or even demands this.

Leadership Call

Is The Call handled in a different manner when it comes from a high-level government official, a leader such as a president or premier? Many humans assumed to be in a leadership position are not, in actuality, leading anyone. The human may have authority such as the right to grant or deny requests, or may have a voice such as the right to critique, or may direct activities such as a construction or production schedule, but they do not influence the orientation decision of their fellow humans which is the key lesson of third density. Leaders who get a lot of attention are those who influence issues, such as law making or war or new trends. Such leaders get the Mega Call response, where more resources are mustered. The leader, however, is as unaware, consciously, of having been assisted like all other callers.

Answering

The Call is most often answered as soon as it is given, unless the nature of The Call is such that preparation or timing are involved. An example of preparations might involve the calling human needing to gather information or poll other humans, essentially preparing themselves for the conference. An example of timing might be where The Call involves a conference with several humans, and a convenient time when they could all experience a bit of missing time needs to be arranged. The nature of The Call is such that the group called, whether in service-to-self or service-to-others, does not want the moment to pass. Delays can result in a change of heart, so The Call is answered promptly.

A high-priority call is where a human desiring contact is in a position to influence the course of human affairs. Likewise, a low-priority call would be a call from a human who is giving The Call because he is concerned with a personal matter that affects little but himself. Beyond which calls get attention, there is the matter of what constitutes a response. This can range all the way from a brief conference with a single visitor, to an elaborate series of visits from a virtual army of aliens. There are no rules guiding alien behavior on Earth that bound or constrain the size of a response to The Call. Therefore, where we must wait, we most certainly can anticipate and prepare, and in this regard, The Call is a mutual process.

Whereas visitors in the service-to-others orientation keep rapt attention via telepathy to the thoughts of those who are preparing to give The Call, those in the service-to-self orientation monitor by computer the signs that someone is giving The Call to the service-to-self. This computer traces, surprisingly enough, a brain wave configuration generated when humans are dealing either with rage or intensely defensive postures. This brain wave is generated almost continuously in those strongly in the service-to-self orientation, as they are constantly enraged that their surroundings aren't placating them! It is not the level of this brain wave that is monitored, it is the constancy, and when located, this individual is then watched more closely. They may get specific attention, periodically, as their brain-wave configuration has marked them as one in the service-to-self, in essence giving The Call continuously due to their frustration.

Prayer

When one sends a prayer aloft to their God, are they in essence giving The Call? It depends on the prayer, and on the intent behind the prayer in particular. Many prayers are routine, done in the same hurried manner as brushing the teeth, to put the task behind one. Other prayers, though routine, are done in a fond manner, full of feeling, and this may or may not be The Call. Does the prayer simply give thanks for home, health, and bounty? This is then in the same category as meditating on one's circumstances and acknowledging that much of life is outside of one's control. Where prayers are put forth with feeling and include a request, this is in essence The Call, and regardless of the words used, or to whom the prayer is addressed, the one answering The Call will be responding to the intent, not the words.

Seances

Talking with the dead has been a time-honored endeavor, and all human cultures have terms for and tales about this common human experience. Most of the tales are told by those who recently lost a loved one, and the bond continues for a time due to unfinished business and concerns that the recently deceased has about those still living. The most famous tales are told about hauntings, where a particular spirit hangs about a location such as a house, wanting some kind of justice done or lingering due to past attachments. Seances, where the dead are deliberately called, are a form of The Call, and as such fall under the rules whereby more than the loved one called can arrive. Thus, a seance can bring forth the spirit called, other restless formerly human spirits, and various visiting aliens who may or may not materialize depending on the setting. Identity cards cannot be checked at seances, so anyone and anything might manifest, pretending to be the spirit called!

Angels

Angels are merely spirits, and describing angels is a way of describing good and evil—the compassion and pulling toward others that characterizes those in the service-to-others orientation, or the pulling toward the self that is characteristic of those in the service-to-self orientation. There are angels among humans who have never left this Earth. They think of others intensely. They sacrifice themselves. Are these not angels?

22
Examples

The Devil is reputed to be a red creature with a pointed tail and two horns, most often carrying a three-pronged fork. The Devil of lore is a fairly accurate picture of an extraterrestrial who briefly visited Earth millennia ago. This visit preceded the time when the Bible was to be written, and thus the memories of this entity were fresh and strong. This was a fourth-density entity, who came alone except for his entourage, in answer to The Call from a group of humans strongly oriented toward service-to-self. He is indeed red, all over, and to humans in close contact he would seem to exude heat. Thus he was associated with the concept of fire, as one who could live comfortably within fire. This entity came to Earth with an entourage, a threesome, who carried pointed sticks used for communications. They stood at attention, to the rear or side of their master, as the service-to-self orientation requires a strict pecking order. Thus the three-pronged pointed fork.

World War II

As with affairs of today, interference by alien groups with the progress of World War II occurred only through humans. Humans gave The Call to both groups, but the service-to-self groups—primarily members of the Nazis and their allies—gave a stronger call. They wished for power and tools of destruction. They wished to learn how humans could be put to death so that death was not quick or painless or without anxiety for loved ones. The humans who gave The Call to the service-to-self entity groups were concerned with how to produce the strongest sense of helplessness in humans, so as to produce, in the future, the strongest harvest for those in the service-to-self orientation.

Humans were not only systematically starved and beaten, knowing all the while they were headed for the gas chambers, but they were also given possible outs. They could turn on their friends and family, on strangers poignantly in need. They could brutalize each other to spare themselves a little bit. Violations were done to humans who were then allowed to live and contemplate these violations, their horror. Violated humans were returned to the masses awaiting an end to their torment, so that these anxious souls would see what the Nazis could do to one of them. All this treatment was by design—a calculated means to destroy the will of the soul so that it becomes resigned to being dominated by others. Senior members of the service-to-self orientation were in attendance to assist those humans who gave The Call to them.

Satanic Rituals

Magical incantation or rituals such as pentagrams on the floor are not The Call. But the desire for revenge, to eliminate a rival, to steal from another, to increase personal power at the expense of others—all these desires are The Call. Practices such as sacrifice or blood letting, particularly of an innocent or someone the participants are reluctant to sacrifice due to personal bonds, sets the mood. During such acts, the participants increasingly disconnect their empathy toward another, and concentrate on the self-satisfying goals that led them to the ritual. Most often the human sacrificed is a peripheral member of the group, so that the cult leader can go on a power trip. He glorifies in his ability to make friends turn on one another, at his command. Such power trips become such a drug that more and more such rituals are performed until the group is discovered or disbands, scattering and running from the horror.

Do Satanic rituals result in demons appearing and humans striking a deal with the Devil? This is a parody on what in fact happens as it is not so cut and dried. The service-to-self entities answering The Call may appear to the band, but briefly. These demons may take any form, as they are above third density and thus can move between densities, appearing and disappearing at will. They may show themselves as they are or enhance their appearance to strike fear into the horrified humans and demand and get the subservience that all service-to-self entities seek, without abatement. The humans are indeed giving their souls away as they are joining the service-to-self orientation, where control and captivity are an everyday reality.

AIDS

AIDS is both a natural and unnatural occurrence. In the beginning, the AIDS virus was much the same as it is today, infecting humans. This virus has a great propensity for adaptation, so over any period of time it changes form somewhat. It has occurred naturally within certain simians for centuries. It has outcropped among humans in Africa and the south seas periodically, but due to limited population spread, it simply devastated those groups it invaded. Where there is no written record and no survivors, there was no trace. AIDS was unknown to the civilized world, and would not have been discovered were it not for intervention by those of the service-to-self orientation. The intervention by these aliens was one of knowledge, directing those humans desiring such a tool to the simians harboring this virus.

The service-to-self aliens involved in the spread of AIDS had to work through humans. They found these humans within the United States government, in the CIA. The men who made The Call were offered a bribe. They were assured that they could possess the continent of Africa, which is rich in natural resources and human cultures easily dominated. The men in the CIA who gave The Call to our counterparts were of the service-to-self orientation to a high degree. These aliens do not squander their time idly. Their objective in assisting these men was the misery they could spread. Agony, a sense of abandonment, rage and the desire for vengeance, all these emotions work to bring recruits to their orientation. This was the object of the aliens assisting in the spreading of the AIDS virus.

It has been assumed that AIDS was initially spread through a vaccination program. This is incorrect. It was spread through diet, by blood improperly cooked, as blood is a natural component of the diet of those initially infected. It was spread through the dietary norms of the initial groups infected. Sophisticated isolation was not required. Infected simian blood was mixed with blood naturally occurring in the diet.

Ebola Virus

As with dissemination of the AIDS virus, the Ebola virus was a matter done by service-to-self aliens in the past, a matter now at rest, which we therefore can discuss per the Rules of Engagement. The Ebola virus was one of many gleaned from the bowels of the African jungles. Africa and South America are targeted continents. Aliens in the service-to-self orientation, along with human converts in the CIA, extracted the AIDS virus and other viruses for use in what they termed cleansing of the continent. The land, rich in resources, was then to be theirs, and any human inhabitants having natural immunity to the viruses unleashed would be their docile servants.

The Ebola virus did not catch on as did the AIDS virus, and the reason was simple—it tended to kill its handlers! When cast out among the swine, as was the phrase used to describe dissemination, the swine would die, but those casting their evil seed could not run fast enough. They carried it home with them, and they died in secreted hospital rooms, infecting their frantic nurses and doctors. After a time or two, they gave up on the Ebola virus, which refused to be tamed. The original plan of dissemination was to be by airborne means. This never came about as the early tests ran amuck.

Majestic-12

23
Roswell

The U.S. was targeted early by ourselves for several reasons, but primarily because our hybrid program was to be based in the U.S. The U.S., as a melting pot, has a broader genetics pool than any other country. Where it has been reported that the U.S. government granted us permission to abduct their citizenry, their permission was not required. The hybrid program is conducted with volunteers, and the U.S. government is not consulted. Period. A secondary reason we desired an alliance with the U.S. government was due to their position of leadership in the world, a position they still hold. The U.S. is the signal democracy, which was assisted in its birth by many aliens in the service-to-others orientation responding to The Call, and has more than met the expectations of those who assisted. Both the government and citizenry of the U.S. expect leadership of themselves, and are tolerant and supportive of innovation because of this. The U.S. is head and shoulders above the rest of the world in innovation, bar none.

This environment was perceived by ourselves to be the most fruitful for Zeta/human alliances in service-to-others activities during the Transformation, and is meeting our expectations in this regard. Thus, because we and others in the service-to-others orientation wished an alliance with the U.S. government, the Roswell incident was staged in order to initiate discussion. And it was because of our desire to contact the U.S. government that those in the service-to-self orientation rushed in to do their best to ruin our plans. Activities at Area 51 and Dulce were not our activities, but are the dying remnants of games by the service-to-self entities designed to drive a wedge between ourselves and the U.S. government. They did not succeed, and the games are now in a mopping-up phase, closing down. Those in the service-to-self orientation have not contacted other governments because there was no party to spoil. It's as simple as that. In spite of wild rumor to the contrary, no other governments outside of the U.S. have an agreement with alien groups.

Roswell

The facts about Roswell are well known, and the facts that are known relate almost completely to the truth. This is a true story. What is not well known is that Roswell was not an accident. The U.S., like other governments, was not approachable. Individuals who were contacted by the alien groups were treated as though they were infected. The block in these matters was the human desire to be in control. Therefore, in order to allow the humans in the U.S. government to be open to our messages, we allowed them to be in control. The plan was to allow ships to crash, ostensibly at the hands of humans, with all aliens aboard dying in the crash. This maximized the feeling of control the humans would experience, particularly as the front end of any contact was, unfortunately, through the military. Once they felt they could harm us, they were willing to parley.

The recent Roswell movie adheres closely to the facts, but it has added material for dramatic effect and it has omitted other material at the request of the government. Major Marcel knew full well what he had come upon in that field, and the impact that informing the public would have. UFOs were not unknown to those at the Roswell base, and the heavy hand suppressing chatter had already been felt. He agonized, and informed his family furtively. The rancher, Mac Brazel, was abused extensively, in the many ways that leave no marks, and finally he was told frankly that he and his family would be killed unless he complied. His purchase of a new truck, which he could scarcely afford, was the only avenue by which he could get the word out that he had taken a bribe. Why would the military need to buy him off?

People appropriately wondered, and came to the correct conclusions. Were people silenced via death during the Roswell incident? Yes, and more than the public suspects.

EBE

EBE, the Extraterrestrial Biological Entity, survived the crash and lived to chat, in a manner of speaking, with the government. EBE was returned to his group, alive, after contact was established over the next few years. EBE, as he was called, was one of seven aliens on board the two craft that crashed at Roswell. One craft was utterly demolished, as it was set to explode close to the ground and did so as planned. The second craft held four aliens, and crashed as planned without becoming utterly demolished. It was expected that the impact would kill all four, who expected to die, but one lived on with injuries.

This was a shock to this alien, who was unprepared for the intense interest in his digestive, breathing, and medical needs. He found himself both held at arm's length and closely examined by the very nervous humans who recovered him. An officer, called suddenly to the site where EBE was being housed, had his young son in tow, and left him in the car while he conferred inside. When he returned he found that his young son had much to tell him, having been in telepathic communication with EBE. Without having the two ever meet, and without confirming to the young boy that his conversational pal was real, the government subsequently had the two in close proximity and questioned the boy endlessly. To this day he cannot prove that this occurred, other than that questions were put to him.

The impact of Roswell on human culture, and on the government in particular, was that they knew for sure that aliens, intelligent beings from other worlds, existed. The legacy of EBE himself was essentially the quaint story of ET, where aliens are viewed as shy and nonthreatening, more vulnerable than humans, and with charming eccentricities. That they bond well with young children is considered by most to be a *de facto* proof of their acceptability, in line with the adage that a person can be trusted if the dog and the kids take a shine to him.

EBE was followed, however, by contacts with the government by a very different sort of alien, those in the service-to-self orientation, and this set the stage for the next phase of the government's relationship with aliens.

145

Omnipotent Krlll

One of the first aliens in the service-to-self orientation to contact the U.S. government was a member of the alien race from Orion, who called himself the Omnipotent Krlll. He had studied human societies, or rather had his lackeys do this study, and concluded that a guttural name that sounded like a growl would most induce fear. Thus the concocted name. One should take note that it also sounds similar to the word kill, also not by accident. This alien greatly impressed the military officers who met him, in that he understood their need for order and hierarchy, their concept of command by the most powerful and well connected, and their willingness in the main to sell out sections of the populace for any gain in power they might attain. As he was firmly in the service-to-self orientation, they were in effect speaking his language. He was at home.

Krlll set to work disinforming the military as best suited his ultimate aim. As he wished to conquer them, he told them they were in charge. They bought it. As he wished their cooperation, he told them they would receive technology in exchange. They bought it. After all these years, not much has come from this vaunted meeting with the Omnipotent Krlll. His disinformation has been unraveled, bit by bit, so that any information he provided has essentially been discarded. However, there are still information pools formed essentially from this source that have not dried up. They refuse to be silenced, and repeat the same silly stories time and again. These sources have a life of their own, having sensed that the information comes directly from the government, having been convinced and even deliberately impressed with this fact long ago, so they are still infused with desire to get the word out. Attempting to counter these enthusiasts only seems to energize them. The story lives on like an echo that will not die.

Power Outages

Following the Roswell incident the various alien groups in the service-to-others orientation were displeased with dialog that had been opened with the U.S. government. They found themselves not only held at arms length but also negated—treated as entities one need not worry about. Where Roswell had been staged, several aliens in the service-to-others orientation sacrificed themselves in the crash so that the military could feel they had the upper hand and thus be amenable to an approach, but now the aliens found themselves facing a cocky group who treated them dismissively. At this point in time MJ-12 had also been approached by the service-to-self aliens, whom they treated with respect as this group had not presented themselves as crashed ships or dead and injured bodies. In the eyes of MJ-12, who looked on the surface, the service-to-self aliens had their act together. We expressed, through the human translators assigned to us, that our capabilities were in fact superior to the service-to-self aliens they were giving preferential attention to, but we were brushed aside.

As the Awakening is overseen by the Council of Worlds, this matter was bantered about, and eventually the Council granted a spectacle that would not be lost on MJ-12, the intended audience, but could be minimized to the populace at large. Prior to power outages there were several attempts to impress MJ-12 with less drastic measures. Power outages, after all, affect hospitals, little old ladies tottering to the rest room, and moving traffic. We wished to avoid this. Natural occurrences were affected first, having been announced well ahead of time. Unseasonable temperature variations, so that midwinter would become positively balmy or midsummer chilly, but this impressed no one and we were only credited with being good weather predictors. Light rays were deflected over broad areas, so that midday became night for a brief but very noticeable time, but as no disruption of activity took place, MJ-12 was unimpressed. So it's dark outside, then turn on the lights! Thus, we determined, and effectively argued the case before the Council, to prevent the lights from being turned on.

Power outages were not unknown, and could be caused by any number of overload or mechanical failure situations. People would buy it, on the local level. At a national level, in smoke-filled rooms and the corridors of power, the truth would be passed around and hurriedly suppressed. How do you suppose that MJ-12 came to have so many corporate leaders in its broad membership? They were initiated during the panics. Suppress the press. Issue statements that had no relationship to the facts. Use the bully board-room, and keep each other closely informed. When spreading a broad untruth, close communication and coordination is required. MJ-12 was no longer a clique of the military, it became for a time a clique of the establishment. Subsequent to the power outages, which did not sweep without warning over broad areas, we found MJ-12 looking at us with new eyes. They now believed our explanation of the Roswell crashes. Their eyes had been opened. At this point the power outages were no longer necessary.

ZetaTalk

A major factor in the success of this Awakening maneuver was the utter inability of the government to stop the outages. Learning of our schedule, which was announced days ahead of the occurrence, they would arrange every kind of backup. All contingencies failed. Power flow was stilled for the length of time announced, and not so much as a flashlight battery worked. The mechanism used by us involved essentially irradiating the area with a countering force, affecting electron flow above a certain level. Thus, human thought or the winking of fireflies would not be affected, but human technology was at a standstill.

Motive

If you have never heard a song, and you now hear only one song singing, you would be inclined to think there was only one song to be sung. We and other benevolent alien groups approached your governments so that they could hear a different song. Your government, as with your populace, is not mostly evil. In the main, they wish to do the right thing by those they are bound to serve. We are attempting to help them get to this point. At a minimum, we are attempting to foil the original song they heard from those in the service-to-self orientation, so that at a minimum your government does not sing this song to you.

Why was this done, you might ask, when this different song could have been sung to the populace at large? Of course, this song is being sung to the populace at large, in a manner that elicits the least fear and anxiety. It was necessary to sing a different song to your government because they are influential to those they govern. They control the media, to a far greater extent than you would ever allow yourself to believe. They therefore control what their populace is allowed to experience, consciously.

24
MJ-12

We, the service-to-others Zetas, have a formal agreement with the U.S. government. Our agreement is under constant change, based on regular weekly meetings which occur each Wednesday morning. The location or attendees are not something we can divulge. The scope of our joint activities also is under constant change, but there are some items we can quickly mention which are not within scope. Disinformation has been spread to the extent that we, the Zetas, are conducting cattle mutilations because we need the enzymes to live. This is totally false, as we manufacture what we need. Nor do we have an agreement by which the government stays silent about our presence while we abduct and run experiments on humans. We do not need your government's agreement to answer The Call, nor would a widespread awareness of our presence affect us one way or the other. The hybrid program would continue regardless of anything your government would do.

Activities that are in the scope of our present agreement are a travel service, whereby we transport those members of your government to and from meetings on the alien presence, and for any other activities that MJ-12 deems important. In this support, we do not interject our opinions on the use of this travel service. This offer, which we have steadfastly maintained for some decades now, was made so that your government would have an alternative to their association with the service-to-self crowd. Our foresight in the matter has paid off, as your government has recently begun to sever all ties to this alien orientation, and the pace is picking up. Another activity we are jointly involved in is an education program, whereby we introduce key members of your government to beings from other worlds, their cultures, and their philosophies. We have learned that your government in the main just wants to know, and to not be the last to know.

MJ-12 Operatives

MJ-12 does not operate in a vacuum, as a stand-alone, off-the-books, agency. It has tentacles whereby it reaches out to gather information and accomplish its goals. MJ-12 is the administrative hub, where policy decisions are reached and the center where key contacts with the outside world are maintained. However, in that those in its hierarchy have parallel positions within the federal bureaucracy, they use those very bureaucracies. In fact, given the structure of MJ-12, it is only natural.

The military branches all have intelligence units, which are skilled in various degrees at electronic snooping, interrogation techniques, and undercover activities. Individuals from these units are assigned to a stint of duty to MJ-12, just as they are assigned to secret missions—you hear about none of it. Both the FBI and CIA have vast pools of information on corporations, individuals, and groups running under the many different charters that can exist in human society. These intelligence agencies have formal arrangements with MJ-12, who has but to ask. Military installations include many complexes held in abeyance, just in case. Land and buildings are hard enough to come by in times of plenty, and during cut backs are not released, in the main. Idle facilities in remote areas are ideal for temporary use by active MJ-12 members, who are almost invariably from the military.

Should the reader find this astonishing—that federal employees are regularly dealing with MJ-12 yet the public hears at most rumors of this activity—they should bear in mind the following. Intelligence groups, and the military in general, operate on a need to know basis. Also, when services are performed for MJ-12, these services are not distinguishable from normal, everyday services. The requests don't have MJ-12 stamped in big bright letters on the front, they come wrapped in commonplace covers, and thus raise little suspicion. Most government employees or contractors who serve MJ-12 have no idea who the recipient of their service is.

As a general rule, MJ-12 does not even allow active members of MJ-12, those who know they are working for this arm of the government, to come in contact with aliens. Where we provide a travel service as part of our agreement with MJ-12, the humans being transported never encounter the pilots. They walk up a ramp, enter an empty room, the door closes and shortly reopens at the destination. No contact. We are in telepathic contact with our human counterparts and learn of the itinerary in this way. Where only a small, select group within MJ-12 has knowledge of travel by space ship, an even smaller group actually has contact with aliens. These individuals are subject to a battery of psychological tests and field trials, and are characteristically highly stable individuals. They are essentially unflappable. As with MJ-12 in general, one does not chose these careers, one is chosen for the career..

Of late we, the service-to-others Zetas, have been elicited to assist MJ-12 in monitoring adherence to their rules, and this has brought an abrupt end to infractions against MJ-12 rules. There are no plots that escape our notice, as we become aware of them when they are first hatched in the minds of the schemers. We cannot enumerate past practices, due to our agreement with MJ-12. Suffice it to say that during the era when we offered an unmonitored travel service to MJ-12 members, complete with the cloak that prevents awareness that such travel is even occurring, there could be any manner of misuse. This is the intelligence community ideal, to be cloaked and invisible during their movements and to have instant travel to and from their destinations. This also is the dream of the thief or law breaker. In step with sorting out the orientations and agendas of the alien groups they had agreements with, MJ-12 gained confidence in working with us,, the service-to-others Zetas.

Elected Officials

How much does any President learn about MJ-12, and what does the smarmy group that calls itself the Congress of the U.S. know? Next to nothing, and this more by rumor and innuendo. MJ-12 limits its membership on a need-to-know basis, which should not surprise anyone as it is run by military intelligence units. Why would the current Congress or its current President need to know anything when they are just passing through? Of course, they demand to know more but can't find the end of the string, much less pull strings. MJ-12 is not in the phone book, does not have a budget, is run by people who have parallel titles within the bureaucracies, so as an organization MJ-12 is invisible.

Those who are in the know are people whom MJ-12 has contacted. They choose, and introductions or inquiries simply don't come from the other direction. Those in the know are contacted because MJ-12 desires something from them—services or cooperation or knowledge. These most often are individuals who already have security clearance, be they former military or current government employees or private citizens sworn in. By being enlightened these individuals pay a price, as joining the greater MJ-12 organization is like joining the Mafia—one does not quit. The rules are strict. No profiting by your knowledge, no refusing to abide by the MJ-12 board rulings, and no talking. The penalty can be, and has on occasion been, death. Consequently, this group is relatively small, numbering a few hundred, and is only increased in size by new members when there are extenuating circumstances.

Quite frankly, elected officials rarely fit the bill. Not talking is antithetical to politicians, who earn their living by hot air. Politicians tend to be deal makers with soft principles, and the power that comes with the knowledge that membership in MJ-12 provides can be heady. Politicians would get themselves killed, on a regular basis, and as they are public figures, this would prove awkward. They are left in the dark for their own good and because it is the lessor of two evils.

Project Blue Book

Since UFO sightings were in the air, the Air Force was the presumed arm of the military that would be in the know. Assigning the Naval intelligence as the primary arm of MJ-12 was supposed to be a slight of hand that no one would suspect. Thus the Air Force officers assigned bustled about and issued reams of paper, all looking very official. They were given a list of the probable explanations for strange lights in the sky, and they dutifully ascribed something on the list to any sighting reported. When on occasion an officer working for project Blue Book got too curious, he was reassigned.

Those who parroted the party line and didn't attempt any independent thought remained. Thus, as would be expected, the final report fell neatly into line with the original intent—UFOs were all swamp gas or meteors, or the figment of the public's active imagination.

Crashed Ships

The public, hot on the trail of the physical evidence they were sure the government possessed, has long sought crashed ships. Some of them are rumored to be massive, requiring roads to be blocked and military and civilian forces to be coordinated to cart away evidence in the dead of night. The military has no wrecked alien ships in their possession, outside of the Roswell crash, and all stories to the contrary are false. Stories of crashed alien space ships feed the sense of power and control that humans in leadership positions demand. Crashed ships diminish the alien presence, putting the skill and technology of aliens on a par with that of humans, who regularly crash planes and cars.

How would it be that aliens could cross the universe yet not be able to putt about on your planet? Stories that alien ships cannot deal with radar or electromagnetic pulses are nonsense. These situations present themselves elsewhere in the Universe, and could be anticipated by the aliens visiting Earth. Crashed alien ships have not and will not be presented to the public because they simply do not exist. However, as a result of their early agreement with aliens in the service-to-self orientation, the military got possession of several ships. This is certainly no secret, as Bob Lazar confirmed the rumors. The military has never figured out how to operate the ships they were given, and many deaths have resulted from their attempts.

Unlike human vehicles, alien ships use mental controls and house a strange device that cannot be examined . This device, which supports density switching and rapid transport from one part of the universe to another, cannot be opened and examined, as it explodes and disintegrates when this is attempted. Of course, the scientists ordered to proceed with such an experiment died instantly. The fact that the alien ships required mental control only momentarily stopped the generals who wanted desperately to control such a device. They drilled the smug service-to-self aliens assigned as an escort without end, and returned for more lessons after every abortive attempt. The stories told of furtive observations at Area 51, where wobbly space ships were seen lifting a few feet off the ground and then flopping back, are true.

Eventually enough control was attained that the ambitious generals would order a field run with this ship or that. The idea was to do more with the ship than simply lift and wobble about. They wanted rapid travel across the skies. They wanted to impress the heck out of anyone they were interested in intimidating. At least they could do that, they reasoned. So the human pilots, selected for their confidence and demonstrated skill, would aim a little higher, a little farther, and wham! These crash remains, which might be found anywhere, would be quickly collected by special military teams, which would be scrambled with the greatest haste.

25
Cover-up

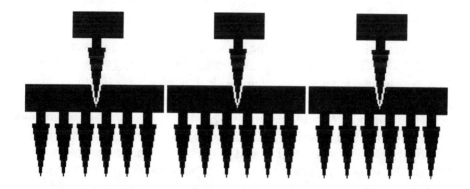

MJ-12 has a reach that goes beyond U.S. borders and in essence makes MJ-12 operations international. This is due primarily to a like mind set regarding the dangers of public panic, a threat which all governments intrinsically abhor. They wish to keep the masses quiescent, at least until the last minute, especially since the governments of the world don't know what to do about the issues presented by the alien presence and the pending pole shift, and in most cases are unable to carry out any plans they may have. In this way life goes on as before, with the establishment on top and loving every minute of it.

International cooperation thus happens naturally, emerging from any first meeting on these issues, and can be counted on to be solid and unwavering. In the past such tactics as suppression of media coverage on sightings was automatic, and for those who doubt that the media worldwide could be so suppressed, we would point to the close link between governments or corporate interests and the media. The media dances to the piper, who in many cases frankly owns the media, both morally and financially.

Countries of the world cooperate with each other due to the alien presence, as it has an immense effect. Imagine yourself a ruler, whether an elected ruler or as a result of birthright. Whatever else this position of power brings in the form of perks, it also produces anxiety. Those in power don't want to lose their positions, and the alien presence thus threatens all who hold positions of power. The establishment is afraid that they will be seen as impotent, and thus drop in stature in the eyes of those who look to them for protection and leadership. The military, in particular, is prone to this worry, as this is their job. Those at the helm of industry worry that all will collapse if their workers don't attend to their duties. And those who live off the inflated value of paper money in all its many forms worry that their house of cards will collapse if the future does not seem secure to the public.

Thus, a global conspiracy due to the threat of the alien presence occurs naturally. This innate conspiracy takes many forms, but up until recently has most certainly included suppressing the chatter about UFO sightings, suppressing contactee reports, inserting a fear of cooperation with aliens by spreading falsehoods about their motives, and claiming that alien technology has been secured. It is widely rumored that wars have been waged to distract the populace from the real action, and this is true. Since undeniable proof fell into the establishment's lap at Roswell, the focus on the superpowers has not been on the issues that fill the newspapers, but on how to maintain control. Nevertheless, the normal business of government and the normal priorities of the vast majority of mankind who are unaware of the real drama continues, as before. Thus, the global conspiracy is an undercurrent, at most.

Black budgets have been fed by means that the populace would find disgusting and disappointing—drug running and waging war so that the military industrial complex is flooded with funds, poorly audited. War has the added advantage of distracting the populace, as families worry about loved ones in combat, and when death and maiming are the threat, who looks for UFO stories in the news? Massive financial scams have been perpetrated, such as the BCCI bank and its predecessors, all of which had the hand of the CIA firmly at the helm. These moneys were collected to launch a defense against the alien presence, and to protect the elite from the effects of the pole shift they all knew was coming soon, but due to the secret nature of the operations, the moneys collected were often used for the pleasure of those who knew that no one could audit them.

Bilderberger Group

Humans have a long-standing tradition—when one doesn't know what to do about an issue, form a committee. Thus it was that the Bilderberger Group formed. It is not hard to imagine the state of affairs after Roswell. The heads of state of U.S. allies and their close confidants, chairmen of major U.S. or international companies and their confidants, and a number of scientists from prestigious universities or institutes were aware of the alien presence but were unsure what this meant for the future of the Earth. Were the aliens friendly as stated, or deceptive? The answer, as we have explained, is both, but to humans who considered themselves leaders, the answer was not at all clear, and many still do not have it sorted out today. They tend to lump all alien visitors together and thus endlessly discuss all manner of speculation on what might be unfolding.

The membership of the Bilderberger Group changes over time, but only slightly, as the original group was tasked with sorting out the issues and coming forth with recommendations, and the mission is not yet accomplished. They meet periodically, in secret, here and there around the face of the globe. They start up where they left off at the last meeting, and churn the issues and possibilities until they again become exhausted. Like most committees that cannot come up with an action plan, the only thing they accomplish is their self perpetuation.

Trilateral Commission

Governments worldwide are run primarily as dictatorships and secondarily by committee. Even democracies that have emerged in human society are run primarily by dictatorship, each executive or appointed head running the area under his or her control like a petty dictator. On the issue of the alien presence, where several countries that were and have remained U.S. allies at the time of Roswell were present when MJ-12 was formed, there was no clear dictator to be put in charge. Just as with judges, where the courts find they must have one or three, but never two judges determining the outcome, just so the Trilateral Commission was formed.

This committee was commissioned to hear out the concerns of the member states and come to some conclusion about what steps, if any, to take. MJ-12 is a U.S. government agency, where the Trilateral Commission is an international advisory committee. In truth, it holds little power and comes to

157

few, if any, conclusions. The issue of the alien presence is fraught with so many unknowns that the usual conclusion is to do nothing, as that seems the safest step. Nothing is being done, and life goes on as before, so continue to do nothing—that is the conclusion. Doing nothing, or holding the *status quo*, is often interpreted to mean suppressing talk of the alien presence, so action of sorts is in fact inferred as a result of the conclusions reached by the Trilateral Commission.

Council of Foreign Relations

Whereas MJ-12 operations were intended to run in such a covert manner that the public would never even learn of their existence, the interface with foreign nations was pushed into the public realm. In the past, where the U.S. and its allies and multinational corporations agreed to suppress awareness of the alien presence, this was accomplished in the U.S. by the influence that federal agencies have over local governments and by the cooperation of those controlling major media content. But what occurred in a Third World country if a sighting or contactee story got media coverage? It would hardly do to have the U.S. or its allies silent about these matters while other countries talked openly. Suppression only succeeds when it is unilateral.

Thus, the MJ-12 arm that reached out into the world at large, beyond its control, sought to influence nations to cooperate by maintaining control over U.S. foreign relations. U.S. dollars to be invested, trade agreements, the placement of military bases—all could be used as leverage to gain agreement with the aims of MJ-12. Thus it has been that the Council of Foreign Relations seems inordinately involved in matters that seem only faintly connected to foreign affairs. Look to the larger picture and it starts to make sense. Now that the press to suppress has moved to controlled leaks and information releases designed to awaken the populace, expect the Council of Foreign Relations to lean its influence in this direction.

New World Order

There is much discussion in the world of ufology and beyond about the New World Order and various establishment elites who want to remain in control during and through troubled times. They are on top now, and want to remain there. They fear social unrest in the extreme. Any alternative to losing their control is acceptable, and the misery of others is the least of their concerns. These elites can be members of a government who enjoy power and influence due to their authority, the wealthy who enjoy an easy life and can generally buy their way out of troubles, corporate heads who are used to the concept that they command, military leaders who can't imagine anyone else in charge, religious leaders who fear to stand alone in the world not clothed in the reverence people cast their way, and any others in a particular position of power, for whatever reason. As being an elitist is an attitude, not all in these categories, of course, are elites.

What is their behavior, and how can their motives be discerned? Essentially, anything that spreads the truth and educates people, allowing them to make their own decisions, is not what the elites desire. Therefore, vehicles like books, telephone connections, open correspondences, and most certainly the Internet give people information freedom, not what the elites desire, but matters like book burning, communications strictures, and censorship show the heavy hand of the elites. Independence is another worry of the elites. When people can grow and market their own crops, set their own prices, and travel about, they achieve freedom from repression—not what the elites desire—but when people fear to move for fear of starving, and are not given travel permits anyway, the heavy hand of the elites is clear.

Those attempting to establish the New World Order seek to keep man ignorant, but most importantly they seek to keep man nervous and despairing. They are like the parent who tells their child that no one else would want them, so as to control the child through fear of abandonment. They equate to the husband who tells his wife she is undesirable, the better to control the wife who may be thinking of leaving him. They equate to repressive governments who tell their citizenry that other countries would brutalize them, the better to prevent emigration. Therefore, watch where these practices crop up, and do not be dissuaded by clever covers for controlling motives.

Who are those attempting to establish the New World Order? The banking industry, first and foremost, as finances are such a fragile thing. Finances are built only upon faith. In fact, they have no substance whatsoever. All those high-paid salaries—poof! All that chatter about the value of this stock or that, the carefully monitored stock and bond listings, it is all just so much hot air. One must realize that bankers and stock brokers and bond dealers do not have alternative professions. There are only so many accountants employable, and most work for little pay and under pressure to be exacting. What would happen to their world if people stopped thinking that their hard-earned savings were safe and secure in their hands? The crash of 1929, for one.

Silencing Methods

Individuals in government service who become aware of MJ-12 as more than a rumor are of course sworn to silence. In most cases, the motivation to cooperate with the edict is membership in MJ-12, which grants MJ-12 the right to kill the errant member should they get loose lips. Individuals being initiated into MJ-12 membership sign papers granting MJ-12 that right, but most think of this as a formality, an indication of the seriousness of the subject, and expect to have endless warnings and discussions long before any such action would be taken. In fact, what occurs when the issue comes up is a quick trial and execution, as delays and warnings are what allow leaks to occur and preventing this from occurring is the point of the death sentence clause.

Even during a time when deliberate leaks about the existence and identity of MJ-12 are on the increase, uncontrolled and unexpected leaks are still alarming to the leadership of MJ-12. These are in the main military men, who joined the military and rose in the ranks precisely because of their need for tight control, so loose lips not intended to be loose are invariably alarming. Prior to issuing a death sentence, the guilty party is always brought in for questioning, an almost instant arrangement due to the travel service we provide to MJ-12, which comes complete with our ability to cloak the movements of our ships and the activities of the passengers while on an official MJ-12 trip. Once guilt or evidence of deliberate intentions is ascertained, often by injecting the subject with truth serum, sentence is rapidly carried out.

When a prominent individual is silenced, the death is carefully orchestrated to appear as an accident or suicide. If intense public scrutiny is expected, the body is involved in an accident that none would question, such as in the airplane crash that killed Clinton's Secretary of Transportation Ron Brown. The cause of death is obvious, so the body is not examined in detail. Where the individual is living a quiet life, a car accident or perhaps a sporting accident, as in the death of former CIA director William Colby, might be involved. Other options include a simulated heart attack, via a needle inserted through the armpit where puncture wounds would not be discovered, or a simulated stroke—both caused by drugs injected and rapidly disappearing from the blood stream, undetectable upon autopsy.

President Kennedy

President John F. Kennedy was killed under orders of MJ-12 as he was threatening to tell the American public the truth about Roswell. JFK was of the opinion that the public would accept the fact of the alien presence without undue panic, but in those days MJ-12 was still affronted with the personalities and actions of the service-to-self aliens that the CIA, as an arm of MJ-12, continually made alliances with. JFK believed in the strength of the human spirit, in its ability to sort things out, and in any case felt the public had the right to know what they were facing. The CIA wanted the knowledge they hoped to get from the service-to-self aliens who were playing them along, and they wanted this knowledge for themselves and themselves only. Thus, they used their influence with MJ-12, which in those days was considerable, to press for JFK's assassination, which they were allowed to implement when the order was finally given.

MJ-12 has recently released us from our agreement to remain silent on the Kennedy assassination. This agreement to remain silent covered certain matters involving the Secret Government and the alien presence. Should humans be incensed by this, that we knew something they desired to know but would not share the information, they should contemplate what life might be like without our having an agreement with the government. In this situation, only the service-to-self aliens would be communicating, having, as you say, the inside track. Such was the situation when we first encountered your government, which had been vastly misinformed and was engaged in all manner of harmful practices under the influence of the service-to-self crowd. This has now turned around, but we are honorable in our agreements, and a promise made was to be a promise kept.

The JFK incident is one which hardened and increased the determination to keep elected officials in the dark as much as possible about the existence and activities of MJ-12. Prior to JFK, presidents and other elected officials were already being kept in the dark, a decision made by an exiting president who did not want a rival political party granted such knowledge. JFK learned what he did due to leaks, shared this with a girl friend long known to be so reliant on sedatives that she could be expected to murmur forth this information with the next man who shared her pillow, and argued incessantly with MJ-12 representatives who came to visit him under other pretenses. The CIA also had Marilyn Monroe killed because of her mouth. Drug overdose is a painless and quiet way to go, and in one given to relying on the temporary comfort that sedatives can bring, raises little suspicion.

JFK, Jr.

The accident that plunged JFK, Jr., into the waves below was not an accident in the normal sense. The small private plane faltered, plunging several thousand feet in seconds—sure death as those who arranged this accident knew would occur. The impact of a rapidly dropping plane shatters the plane, destroying mechanical evidence which would be the only clue to what actually had occurred. Why was JFK, Jr., targeted, when he was just a small boy, surely out of the loop, when his fathers suspicious death occurred? The family talks, behind closed doors, the elders passing information down to younger members now and then. JFK, Jr., was noted for a certain rebelliousness, being unconventional and adventurous, and these traits doomed him. Those responsible for his father's death watch closely lest the secrets they have kept from the public leak out, and they knew that such information was unlikely to rest easy in the hands of an offended and affectionate son.

26
Opportunists

Between the time of Roswell and the present day, that portion of the U.S. government that MJ-12 had reached absolutely was warned of the approach of the 12th Planet, known also as Nibiru or Planet X, and they absolutely set about trying to protect themselves in underground installations. The CIA was front and center in this regard, with the military close behind. At the inception of the Apollo program, the elite of the secret government were looking to several different means of dealing with the coming cataclysms.

Alternative 1

Alternative 1 was to reduce overpopulation and sculpt the face of mankind to their liking. Portions of the government, and we are here speaking of rogue CIA officers, set out to trim and prune the Earth's humanity to their liking. Thus we have the AIDS and Ebola viruses, as well as various wars and conflicts of which the CIA always seems to be at the center. This alternative was abandoned as uncontrollable, because the steady spread of disease among the so-called undesirables inevitably started infecting the perpetrators too.

ZetaTalk

Alternative 2

Alternative 2 was to create isolated underground communities by burrowing into subterranean cavities, and it is no longer a secret that opulent underground escape hatches, complete with golf courses, were constructed for the elite.

Alternative 3

Alternative 3 was to establish space stations on other planets, riding out the cataclysms on another planet such as Mars or the Earth's dead twin, which rides the Earth's orbit, just opposite the Earth, thus hidden from view behind the Sun. This alternative required the CIA and military to leave their home planet with its comforts, and soon proved unworkable.

Some stories have it that humans derived the three scenarios themselves, but the stories coming from sources closer to the heart of the matter point to alien suggestions on these alternatives. Why would humans decide to locate on other planets to escape pollution or nuclear fallout, when they have neither the means to travel to other planets, the capability of sustaining themselves there, or a dire pollution situation? These suggestions were given to humans by aliens in the service-to-self orientation, and falsely presented to the humans involved as being a concern for their survival. As the high-level government contacts were strongly in the service-to-self orientation, they saw all this as their escape, their alternatives, but what the aliens truly sought was to subvert these humans to sink more and more deeply into the service-to-self orientation.

Alternative 2

The U.S. government went underground, at Mount Weather and numerous other spots. This fact is not even being denied by the government any more. These underground installations, when discovered, were explained away as a cold war precaution in case of nuclear attack, but a quick calculation belies that explanation. The number of people to be housed, and the amount of food and water stored, would not support the residents for the length of time it would take for radioactivity to fade. The stores would support them for days or weeks at best.

164

Clearly these installations were meant for a short-term stay, after which the residents would emerge back onto the surface to scout about for supplies. With a safe and undetectable hideout, the plan was to send out raiding parties that would come back with supplies, and disappear in front of those who might be in hot pursuit of their snatched goods. Thus the government, sworn to protect and lead the people, would instead steal from them, but as this was in the main nothing new to those planning this escape they saw no philosophical conflict in proceeding. Today MJ-12 is not looking to avoid the coming cataclysms in underground installations, as they realize these will be death traps, a fact the service-to-self aliens encouraging this alternative were well aware of.

Alternative 3

Alternative 3 was implemented, but this cannot be demonstrated to the satisfaction of skeptics. Of course, there are clues such as the tight controls placed over transmissions from probes, and the odd malfunction of the Mars probe just as it was about to hit pay dirt. The service-to-self aliens contacting the government sent representatives of the U.S. and other governments up to these places, to demonstrate that such a living arrangement was hospitable. Matters soon went amuck, however. Soon the human guests became stressed in the heavy service-to-self environment. Far from home, they found themselves watching, continuously, on a daily basis and with no respite, the harsh reality of life in the service-to-self community. Stress diseases cropped up among the humans—ulcers, heart palpitations and arthritic pains. They became distracted in their work, stricken with headaches and vague feelings of weakness.

The plan was abandoned, and the humans who participated were exterminated. Their bodies were not returned to Earth, nor should one look for this to happen. One should recall that the members of the various governments who were participating were strongly in the service-to-self orientation themselves, and had no hesitation on eliminating their human volunteers, whom they had so warmly congratulated just weeks before. Members of the government may have been told that they will be taken care of when the cataclysms occur, but these are simply the usual lies that the service-to-self aliens put forth. The only humans who will be living among the service-to-self aliens after the cataclysms are those solidly in the service-to-self orientation, and they will find this arrangement anything but a salvation.

Moon Installations

The world watched in rapt attention during the first Apollo Moon landing—a first for mankind. The comments made by the astonished astronauts, who noted signs that they were not the first visitors to the Moon, were instantly broadcast to the rapt audience participating in this historic landing worldwide, the general populace. The astronauts were silenced with the ultimate threats used and on occasion carried out in those days—death, in a manner that is undetectable as an execution. Those with high-security clearances know these are not idle threats, as they see them enforced or learn of these instances, and thus take them quite seriously.

Enclaves of service-to-self aliens are situated on the far side of the Moon, the side that never faces the Earth, positioned there so as to be in compliance with the Council of World's requirement that an element of doubt be maintained. Endless rumors abound, however, due to leaks by members of the secret government or frank capture on film in NASA's archives. It is clear that ships are exiting and returning to the far side of the Moon. There is nothing mysterious about residential arrangements, which harbor facilities for ship repair, food production, administrative activities, and any amusements that overlords may personally be able to secure for themselves.

Star Wars

Humans are attempting to preempt the coming cataclysms by developing a Star Wars shield. How could this shield be used against space ships invading from other galaxies when the space ships can move into another density, and slide right past the shield? How could this shield be used against nuclear missiles directed toward the Americas, when nuclear weapons exploded in space in most cases would cause more havoc with a nuclear winter than if allowed to localize? How could this shield be used against the mass of hail stones that compose the tail of the giant comet, the 12th Planet, which sweeps the Earth during every passage and peppers the Earth here and there, when the shield could not possibly knock out every tiny hail stone?

What then is the unstated purpose of the Star Wars shield? The hope is that by putting giant lasers up into the skies, that the comet itself could be disabled by a direct hit. As this planet is massive, outweighing the Earth by several times, destruction would not be by physical means. The intention, and the hope, was to start some kind of chain reaction that could cause the planet to blow itself up. The means by which this would happen has not yet been established, but the service-to-self humans contemplating this wanted to get started anyway.

Philadelphia Experiment

The Philadelphia Experiment much in the media is a fraud perpetrated to distract people from pursuing the real Philadelphia Experiment, which didn't take place anywhere near Philadelphia. Servicemen were indeed injured, and because the risk of questions existed, the cover story was put up to effectively point any questioners to a dead end. The real experiment with moving between dimensions, which can and does occur naturally on your third-density planet, was done in a warehouse in Kansas—rural, remote, virtually uninhabited because of sparse farm houses and farm hands. The area was inhabited only during planting and harvesting times.

Under intense compression, such as occurs in the center of the Earth, third-density matter emits energy rays which approximate those naturally occurring in fourth density. These rays escape the core of the Earth in bursts on occasion, thus causing the problems reported in the Bermuda Triangle, for instance, where ships or planes seem to disappear, then reappear. Essentially, the third-density matter is temporarily confused as to its proper rate of vibration, and moves into the fourth-density state. This is akin to what we have done to contactees when they report having moved through walls. However, in the hands of humans, who received information on how to produce this effect from service-to-self aliens, this ability proved disastrous. Moving into fourth density requires more than just bombardment of matter to the point of compression tension. It requires a total shift, and if one expects to return, a total shift back.

The humans conducting this experiment were of such an orientation that they did not care about the servicemen being used, or what might become of them. Rather than hesitate, knowing they did not have all the parameters in place, they proceeded. The servicemen, who were encased in a metal box, were left partially in the fourth density, along with portions of their container. They were, of course, all dead, but the witnesses of this experiment, and the associates whom the servicemen had just recently been mingling with, were many. The government concocted a repeat experiment, which proceeded part way, enough so that the story as to the results was

167

similar. Additional servicemen were subjected, knowing the probable results, but most of these survived to chat among themselves and their families. All secrets escape, leaks occur, and in this way the investigators would be altogether in the wrong vicinity, and talking to altogether the wrong participants!

27
Disinformation

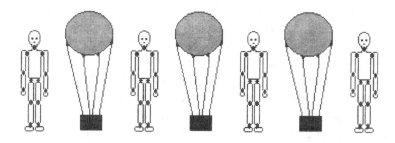

A still hotly debated topic is the validity of what are purported to be documents from MJ-12, dating back to President Truman's era. These carefully manufactured documents are authentic enough in appearance to convince many that they are real, yet flaws exist that have others convinced they are a fraud. Both situations are true, as the documents are what could be termed a half truth. Where the documents line up with the facts is in the existence of MJ-12, periodic meetings in secret, and in those days the involvement of the President of the U.S.. Where the documents part from the truth is where they give the impression that MJ-12 was a fleeting response, that the matters they addressed were limited in scope, or that they were almost casual about dealing with the alien presence and what this would mean for humanity.

The Hubble

The public gets less and less information from NASA, the iron doors slamming shut, the information archived rather than displayed, and made available in dribbles and drabs like scraps of meat thrown to hungry dogs from the master's table. Never mind that the public, the taxpayers, have paid for the information that is so arrogantly withheld from them by NASA. And what are the excuses given for withholding simple views of the universe from the public, who foots the bill? A Principal Investigator has first rights. Does the Principal Investigator pay for the Hubble, that he or she has first rights? In that NASA is not a government agency, though they have arranged to line up at the public trough along with the politicians, the public cannot easily take them to account with their elected officials. NASA and the Hubble trouble are an arm's length away, and by design.

What is it that the public is not supposed to see? The public is not supposed to see the UFOs that the astronauts saw with their bare eyes and that the Hubble records regularly. The public is not supposed to see the evidence that NASA and JPL hold like candy to dribble out when they need funding, such as evidence that planets suitable for life exist, orbiting around other suns. The public is not supposed to see evidence that NASA is publishing erroneous infrared catalogs, so that the 12th Planet, a.k.a. Planet X, does not appear in the official IRAS catalogs and so is not sought in the skies where it now rides. The public is not supposed to see evidence that would tell the truth about any distractions, such as comet and meteor alarms, that the establishment wishes the public to chase after.

HAARP

Underground activities have taken place all over the U.S. in conjunction with activities desired by the service-to-self aliens who early made contact with the government. The government soon became wary of these aliens, and rightfully so, but have not disrupted the agreements they entered into for fear of reprisals. The service-to-self alien goals are to gain recruits, and fear and suspicion, rather than cooperation and enlightenment, are their mode. They have taken to emitting low-frequency sounds, which some but not all humans can detect. This affects health, and makes everyone uneasy, especially as the government can't explain what's going on and gets the blame. Humans hearing that the government is up to something down there, in conjunction with evil aliens, are discomfited, and that, of course, is the goal.

HAARP is not a real project, and the tale has simply been put forth in order to afford a cover for other activities. The U.S. Military is deeply embarrassed by their past involvement with service-to-self aliens, an involvement which is rapidly ending but nonetheless lingers on. Some of the rumors put forth by humans wanting the populace to keep aliens at arms length had given the impression that humans should fear aliens, what with human body parts floating in vats and the like. To correct the misimpression, MJ-12 cooked up the HAARP mystique. Since activities in association with service-to-self aliens included strange low frequency sounds, HAARP took on that aspect. Since aliens had been known to create blackouts and MJ-12 wanted the illusion of a human hand at the switch should this ever happen again, HAARP took on this aspect also.

Gelatin Rain

A theme in movies about space travel, and in particular about visitors from outer space, is the dangerous microbe that arrives, against which there is no human immunity. For those who wish the populace to keep aliens at arm's length, this seems a perfect scare tactic. To test the response, both to the physical reaction to various substances that were candidates for such scare tactics and of the psychological reaction to such substances arriving from the sky, several small and isolated towns were selected at random as guinea pigs. The infecting substance was dropped, the result of a sky shot that burst and scattered when it reached a certain altitude. CIA plants in the town, postured as transients or lurking in bushes with listening devices, watched and recorded the resulting reactions.

To the dismay of the cooks, the brew did not result in the panic and fear of the unknown that was expected. To the contrary, the townspeople in all the towns so subjected to this experiment refused to do anything but scrutinize the gelatin substance that was dropped on them from the sky. They hired scientists, and elicited free examinations, and probed and questioned. Most scams succeed only when such scrutiny is prevented, as inevitably there is evidence that points to the truth. In order to infect humans, germs of some sort that grow in human tissue had to be involved, and thus human tissue to support these germs until they could reach a new host was required. Thus, the alien glop proved to have human cells present, a dead giveaway to the origin of the infecting gelatin. And since the reaction of the public was so alarming, these particular experiments are not likely to be repeated.

Mutilations

Cattle mutilations were a service-to-self scam we anticipated would fail, as fail it has. Humans were only mildly discomfited by mutilations, and understood they were unlikely to become targets. This was a joint alien-human activity. The aliens involved wished to instill intense fear and a sense of hopelessness in the human society, so that they would be inclined to be self-focused from their fearful state and lean toward the service-to-self orientation. Thus they targeted the genitals and other sensitive and protected organs such as eyes and mouth and the anal opening. The message was also disseminated that mutilations were done while the animal was alive, tortured not only by the pain but by the knowledge of what was being mutilated.

The humans involved are part of what is loosely called the New World Order. Their motives are to keep human society moving in its present tracks, under the control of the present establishment. Human participants selected and marked the cattle, and having thus tagged the target, they were in a position to be alerted when the mutilation began. No actual communication flowed between the humans involved and the aliens, as mutilations at first began as a human activity and to the surprise of the human perpetrators, aliens began doing the mutilations before they could arrive on the scene. Not ones to turn down a favor, they just went along.

Black Helicopters

Reports of black helicopters harassing and following ufologists and contactees and associated with mutilations are so frequent and numerous as to be considered a fact, even by skeptics. Everyone expects them to be an arm of the government, and would be shocked to learn that their ownership and activities are not under government control. Private members of the establishment have funded and run this enterprise, with the goal of maintaining the *status quo*. Consider how the activities of the black helicopters and MJ-12 differ. Clearly by being noisy, flashy, and lingering about in public view, the black helicopters are not the arm of a government group concerned with secrecy. Mutilations are also by design noticeable, leaving large carcasses mangled in ways impossible for anyone to ignore, and this would not be something a secret government arm would engage in.

The black helicopters are housed at private facilities, the perfect cover. A barn, a warehouse, or a hollow dirt mound work as well as a vacant hangar at a private landing strip. Helicopters, of course, need only a spot to land upon, and can be draped with camouflage cloth or have collapsible walls of a shack or garage erected around it once it has landed. In a sheltered and isolated spot, such activity goes unnoticed, with the exit and return of the chopper accomplished in minutes. How does this enterprise learn who the contactees or ufologists are, and of their schedules and routes? Establishment groups who can afford fleets of sleek choppers can certainly lure ex-CIA members into their employ.

Why hasn't a private operation like this been exposed, by either the government, the media, or private individuals? Money buys silence, and where money is not effective, accidents are arranged. They are not prosecuted by the federal government because they can blackmail the prosecutor, being aware of the existence and operation of MJ-12. Squeeze us and secrets you don't want revealed may come out, is the threat, so an uneasy staring contest has ensued, with neither party blinking. In addition, a number of the perpetrators, captains of industry, are members of the larger MJ-12, and the good-old-boy system is alive and well.

Remote Viewing

Lest anyone be confused, what is termed remote viewing is simply telepathy, a natural and fairly common occurrence among mankind and the animals who call the Earth their home. Telepathy is intrinsic to life, but only about 10% of the human populace has enough native capacity to take note of it. The government has never failed to use telepathy to accomplish whatever they might consider their ends, but after observing the seamless way aliens could work together, without a word spoken, the issue got hot. As MJ-12 was in those days heavily dominated by the CIA, they took up the topic and infected the goals of the operation with their own twists.

Remote viewing under the CIA's auspices was not done to simply garner intelligence on legitimate government-security concerns, it was used to invade privacy, secure blackmail material, assist break-ins and thefts, amuse agents who wanted to snoop for personal reasons, and keep tabs on rival government agencies. When the operation failed to curtail enemy actions, it ostensibly was shut down, but as with all bureaucracy enclaves, it sought to perpetuate itself by reinventing its goals. Remote viewing would become a handy disinformation tool. To ensure that a gullible public will believe, the remote-viewing track record is supported by information supplied by the CIA.

Mass Landing

The rumor of a pending mass landing has been spread by service-to-self groups, periodically, because of the fear and anxiety this engenders in humans. This is by design, as frightened humans are more easily pushed into becoming recruits for the service-to-self orientation by emotions that tend to focus one on the self. There will be no mass landing. None. The Council of Worlds will prevent this, and in fact has prevented this in the past. As such a landing is much desired by the service-to-self aliens, they have of course pushed endlessly for this. The only circumstances that would allow for a mass landing to occur would be for the majority of the Earth's inhabitants to turn to the service-to-self orientation, and by majority we mean that almost 100% would have to be at that point. This high percentage is required, because the service-to-self group, being coercive intimidators, is not given to free will latitudes.

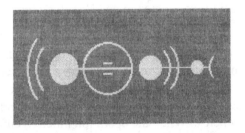

28
Truth

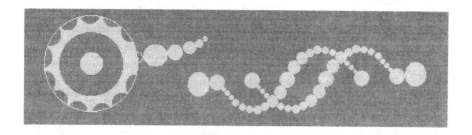

You will find, as the awakening to galactic consciousness proceeds over the next few years, that the demand for proof of our existence will increase rather than decrease. You will also find, in line with what you have already experienced, that there will be no amount of proof that will satisfy these demands. Proof stands before the world today. Crop circles and their residual impact on soil and vegetation, mass sightings, disappearing pregnancies. *Homo sapiens*, as with most intelligent species, has the capacity to argue against unpleasant facts. As the unpleasant nature of these facts increases, so do the arguments.

Crop Circles

Humans have always stood in awe of crop circles, as you can be assured this is not the first era where they have been prevalent. They speak to the subconscious mind, which sees the patterns and senses their meaning, and the conscious mind hasn't a clue. Crop circles are telling you, in a universal language, of coming events. We are speaking here not only of physical events, such as the pending pole shift, but spiritual as well. In the past these simple but eloquent messages were left, with increasing frequency and urgency, leading up to a pole shift. This time, because of the Transformation, there is more than one message to relay. Crop circle creation is managed by a group of aliens that cannot participate in the Earth's Transformation in any other manner, as they are a life-form that lives in the water, and thus their ships are filled with the atmosphere that they breath—water. Thus, this is how they serve.

Observers have noted that crop circles seem to appear almost instantaneously. They blink, and then notice that something is different in the vista before them. By what process is this accomplished? If space ships are landing and impressing the ground, then the time seems too short. If rays of energy or a force field are involved, all this passes the notice of the observers. Crop circle creation does not require a landed ship or physical force. The grain lies flat because the structure of the stems has been altered, one side of the stem rapidly growing in a process the reverse of what occurs when growing plants bend toward the light. This growth spurt occurs low to the ground, the particular ray, like laser surgery, focused there. The swirls are created due to the circular motion of the affecting ray, which circles like the hand of a clock, dropping the grain stalks such that they fall almost simultaneously.

The patterns are being presented in increasing complexity, in step with your Earth's internal response to her approaching brother. Crop circles began with a simple circle, stating that the Earth is unruffled in her orbit. Then dual circles and rings, relaying the approaching interaction between the Earth and her brother, the 12th Planet. The rings, of course, are the influence of gravitational pull, increasing. Consider the long lines connecting circles— does not the 12th Planet, acting as a comet, have an approach? Peripheral circles represent the other planets in your solar system, or in the wider system that comprises the 12th Planet's journey.

Where crop circles do occur worldwide, they receive more press and attention in certain countries, most notably Britain. Crop circles occur just as often in third-world countries, but where one is faced with starvation, crop circles take a back seat. Long after the harvest, there is little to investigate. Britain was once the supreme superpower, ruling the waves with her ships, and her people long yet to be first at something. Consequently, due to the press that is given crop circles in Britain, some of the best crop circles have been placed there in anticipation of good press coverage.

Dead Aliens

A recent trend in the deliberate Awakening of the populace has been the supposed discovery of pictures of dead aliens. Following the Roswell autopsy film a rash of such pictures has emerged. This is not by accident and is more than just copycat behavior. Such pictures are deliberately being placed before the public to acclimate them to the concept of visitors from other planets and the odd appearance that might be expected. Since rioting in the streets did not occur as a result of the release of the Roswell autopsy footage, a carefully staged fraud which was intended from the start to be discovered as such, those who would have the Awakening proceed post haste have encouraged other such nudges.

Still pictures of dead bodies are easy to produce, as any film maker will confirm. Most of the dead alien photos are a combination of real human bodies or body parts, augmented by putty or burns, thus the semblance of realism. If living children are sold into prostitution by their parents around the world and the elderly abandoned, how easy would it be to purchase the bodies of dead children and aged? Crematoriums are another source of such bodies, as one urn of ashes looks much like another, and how would the family know otherwise? These dead bodies, all hominoids and none larger than the average human, are to acclimate the populace to the concept of intelligent visitors from other worlds. The intended message is that alien visitors are not that much different from humans.

Madmen

Humans in the grip of mental illness have long been known to entertain the sane with their delusions or paranoia, but they often tell the truth whereas others more sane remain in denial. Pointing the finger of an insanity accusation is one of the most effective ways to discredit someone, and thus those who have a history of mental illness are allowed to speak their minds and are not considered a threat by the establishment. Thus, mentally ill contactees were never harassed by MJ-12 or the establishment, and even if aware of government plans or operations are seldom considered a threat.

There have been cases where street people, often mentally ill and living on the street to evade being institutionalized, have been picked up to be handed over to aliens in the service-to-self orientation, as part of an arrangement the CIA, as an arm of MJ-12, had with these alien groups. If these unfortunate derelicts had the inner strength to just say "no" to these service-to-self aliens, they survived these encounters because, by the rules, aliens can only affect humans if they are given permission. Thus, it has indeed happened that derelicts survived such encounters and were returned to the streets, unharmed and with subconscious knowledge of what goes on. Underground chambers, the association of military guards with aliens, trips on space ships—all this knowledge was expected by the CIA to be taken as simply delusions by anyone hearing such tales from the mouths of madmen.

Pseudo Fiction

Pseudo-fiction may also be the only way a story will ever be told. What do you think the chances are of getting the story of the Ebola virus told? Would the U.S. Government not be liable if they came clean on the CIA's past activities? Yes, and because of this, the story of the Ebola virus will not be told. What do you think the chances are of the real story on the structures on Mars getting into the headlines? Can your government set up housekeeping on Mars the way some other man-faced creatures obviously did? Can the military assure you that they can protect you from invasion from space? No, and because of this your government will continue to talk up the Star Wars and Space Station projects and pretend that they are at the very cutting edge of space technology, bar none.

29
Openness

Cracks began to appear in the cover-up early on, but they were mended by intimidation. This took the form not only of threats and beratings, but physical harm, to person and property, and even death. The rationale was that so much more injury and devastation would occur, were the populace to panic, that this was justified. Over time, the amount of disinformation increased, until the whole situation became awkward and, quite frankly, untenable. Disinformation is a tool designed to deal with short-term or delimited affairs. With the alien presence, which has been dragging on and most certainly will not go away, the disinformation spread about began to be more of a problem than the rumors of the alien presence. The cover-up crowd is now having to face the implications of their stories meeting each other and clashing.

Where before the focus was on suppression of chatter about the alien presence, now this chatter is encouraged. Where before the focus was to deny that a pole shift was pending, now the populace is being encouraged to think that something is around the corner. Those in the know have determined that they cannot escape the pole shift, or deflect the alien presence, or prevent mankind's awakening to the reality of either. Thus, they now fear panic in an unprepared public more than they fear an awakened public. Thus, the global conspiracy is now a conspiracy of deliberate leaks, information channels supported, and pole shift preparation by various segments of society. The establishment is well aware that a collapse of civilization will affect them more than those they currently look down on. If they can't escape, then they must stand and prepare.

The cover-up is dropping not only because it is difficult to maintain, however. MJ-12 now wants the public to become aware. The secrets they carry lie heavy on their hearts and minds, and they have gradually come to an understanding that malevolent aliens, those in the service-to-self orientation, can be dispelled by humans with a wave of the hand. The Call can be given, and The Call can be taken away—by the human who gave The Call. MJ-12 wishes this to be publicized, and we are happy to oblige here in *ZetaTalk*. Along these lines, MJ-12 wants their involvement with benign, or service-to-others, aliens to become generally known, and deliberate leaks are being allowed. The cracks will widen, and the truth will come forth in bursts, but one should not look for the walls to ever come down completely.

MJ-12 has struggled for decades with leaks in the cover-up and the searingly obvious contradictions provided by thousands of well-documented facts in the hands of scientists, journalists, contactees, ufology groups, and ex-government officials. Having argued among themselves endlessly about whether to drop the cover-up, the matter was taken from their hands by the tide of events outside of their control. The cover-up is collapsing, rather than being dropped, but the effect is the same. With or without a cover-up story, the reaction to incidents such as the Roswell crash or the discovery of Planet X would have been much the same—some believe, some doubt, some deny, and life goes on as before. A cover-up, which is a statement that it didn't happen or doesn't exist, can be replaced by a noncommittal stance, no comment.

Without a cover-up, results are much the same, but those struggling to maintain the cover-up have an easier time. There is less contention and more philosophizing. Without a cover-up, the awareness of the alien presence would come less from articles and documentaries arguing the case and more from the general news relaying yet another sighting. Without a cover-up, the existence of Planet X, openly discussed in the news along with the Earth's geological history, would find the same mix of denial and pondering that

occurs today. Official denial of the forthcoming cataclysms has only generated angry announcements and heated discussion from those who would have
the populace alerted. The results are the same, with a certain percentage
peering through their telescopes or nervously preparing a safe haven, just in
case.

What is different, as the result of a long and entrenched cover-up, is that
the populace now has a deep sense of distrust of their government. This need
not have happened, a fact that MJ-12 now realizes, as the Awakening proceeds apace, leaving the cover-up like a crumpled and dirty sheet behind it on
the path.

ZetaTalk Role

MJ-12 is highly interested in *ZetaTalk*, as it has potential for harm or
good, in their opinion. We, the Zetas, thrash this out with MJ-12 behind the
scenes. There are some matters that we cannot discuss, being restrained by
the Rules of Engagement, as aliens in the service-to-self are actively involved. Where this comes up on *ZetaTalk* we so state the reason for our
reticence. There are some matters that we cannot discuss due to our long-
standing agreements with MJ-12, and we have likewise so stated this as our
reasons for reticence when this has come up on *ZetaTalk*.

But there are many times when we give but a partial response, holding
back from full disclosure because MJ-12 has, in essence, edited our statement. This takes the form, invariably, of a lack of details, who did that, when
and where. We refer to military intelligence units without being specific. We
refer to the leadership of MJ-12 being composed primarily of bureaucrats
holding parallel leadership titles, without being specific. Most certainly we
do not name names. If we mention that deaths have occurred to maintain
silence we most often do not say who was so assassinated, nor do we name
the assassin. We stay as general as we need to be to placate MJ-12, but as
specific as we need to be to describe the situation. In the end, both our
motives and the motives of MJ-12 are served.

Where we wish for the Awakening and Transformation to proceed as
quickly as possible, MJ-12 has also moved to this stance, having realized that
this cannot be stopped and that suppressing the truth only allows the lies
spread by those in the service-to-self orientation to prevail. Where we
fervently wish for humans to understand the control they have over visits

from aliens, MJ-12 likewise dearly wants this message out, having been duped themselves by aliens in the service-to-self orientation. Where we wish to warn humans of the cataclysms which will accompany the pending pole shift, MJ-12 likewise cannot bear to think of the millions of innocents who will be taken by surprise only because the word did not get out. At a minimum, they wish for the possibility of an approaching pole shift to be much under discussion. Therefore, in a manner of speaking, ZetaTalk is an MJ-12 mouthpiece—not because MJ-12 controls ZetaTalk, but because it does not suppress it or shut it down.

12th Planet

As the date of the next passage of the 12th Planet approaches, many in the establishment will be torn. Should they continue to suppress word of what is expected, or should they sound the alarm? Where many who enjoy a position of power and privilege simply want to prevent panic for their own comfort, there are likewise many who have agreed to suppress the truth only because the truth was not yet a certainty. Perhaps the large object approaching will be on an orbit that will cause it to turn away from the Solar System, or perhaps its path through the Solar System will be such that the Earth will be only slightly affected. To mankind, debating the measured orbit of the 12th Planet, these possibilities are as real, today, as the approach.

As time passes and the orbit of the 12th Planet clearly points to a passage close to the Sun, there will be panic even within the circles of those in the know as to whether this approaching monster comet will strike and destroy the Earth. All manner of speculation will ensue, the possibilities horrible and even irrational. Will the Earth be sent out of her orbit and on out into space? Will the Earth travel with this passing planet, as one of its moons? Will the Earth find itself on a new orbit around the Sun, in hotter or colder circumstances, and what will this mean for those trying to survive on her surface? Where history is a guide on how the Earth fares during a passage of the 12th Planet, there can always be a first-time situation.

Thus those in the establishment who might want to alert the populace are torn. If they do give out a warning, just what would that warning be? The certainty of the passage and the orbit which history and our warning confirm will become more firm as the months and years pass. The major governments of the world, and we are speaking here of key members of the super powers and captains of industry, already have regular briefings on what the Hubble has viewed and recorded. The path of the 12th Planet continues to confirm our statements, made in private to these individuals just as we have made them publicly through *ZetaTalk*, so the angle and movement during the passage are more and more considered predictable.

At the point where many feel they know what will happen and when, what will those members of the establishment in anguish over their past silence do? They will dither and argue among themselves, until the final weeks. Plans to harbor and protect the populace require a functioning society for the plans to become an actuality. Thus, as issuing a warning will cause panic and disruption, the establishment will invariably choose to delay the warning, especially as their plans to harbor and protect the populace will never become firm.

The size of any rescue operation is beyond the capacity of governments, a fact they readily admit to themselves. With increasing crop failures, even the stores during times of plenty will become depleted. If the welfare class has become an impossible burden in the U.S. and the homeless die on the streets, how will the government sustain the whole populace for even a few short weeks? The panic that would ensue from a general announcement of the forthcoming cataclysms would in and of itself be deemed a disaster to avoid. There is concern about possible looting, suicides, mass migration of peoples, and never-ending demands that the government do something.

Balancing Act

This dilemma is only going to quicken as the time approaches, as food stores will dwindle and fear of panic in the populace will be just under the surface. Increasingly, offering self-help to the populace looks like the best solution. Unfortunately, the public can't be led to adopt practices that will help them through the crisis unless they are told of the danger! So a delicate balancing act has ensued. Under whatever guise, gardens protected from the weather and home crafts are to be encouraged, as are low-fat diets leaning heavily to vegetarianism. These diets may be touted as fads or simply good for the health, but the underlying motive in these campaigns is to get the populace positioned to live as they must in the Aftertime. Under no circumstances will an announcement be publicly made that real estate and holdings will be devastated, even when the Earth is slowing in rotation in the last days before the passage of the 12th Planet. The fear of an immediate economic collapse and the distraction this will bring is too great. Therefore, bringing the approaching danger to the public's attention must be done through unofficial means. Bearing in mind that humans presented with danger run through a broad range of reactions from denial to panic to silliness, the unofficial means must be deniable as well as able to be taken seriously. Yes and no this is going to happen. Yes and no the source of information is reasonable and credible. Yes and no there are alternative explanations for whatever the source is pointing to.

In order for the unofficial source to be tolerated long before being discredited, it must have a built-in deniability. The Farsight Institute issued absurd predictions for just this reason. Visionaries like Gordon Michael Scallion are ridiculed for less than 100% accuracy for this reason. Art Bell entertains theories that have little relationship to science for this reason. All these sources are popular, but if too accurate the anxiety level of the government rises. Thus it is that *ZetaTalk*, with built-in deniability in that the aliens talking to Nancy refuse to present themselves, is a perfect vehicle for getting the word out.

Each human must confront his own anxieties when first facing the many wrenching realities that are surfacing during the Awakening. For mankind, this is not a single realization, as the Awakening carries more than news of the alien presence, does more than simply challenge religion and the pet concept that man alone is in God's image, and asks for more than an adjustment to the concept of reincarnation and that heaven and hell are of our own making. The cataclysms, wherein the world mankind had come to take for granted will be tossed asunder within days, rearranging continents and shattering civilizations, are part of the package. Man must adjust to so many wrenching changes, and thus any given messenger is highly likely to be mixing in his own anxieties with the message.

Planets

30
The Earth

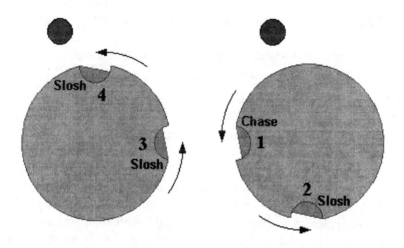

Humans have correctly ascribed the tides to the Moon's presence, but there they boggle. Is the water following the Moon? Simply stated, yes. However, the process is not as simple as all that. The water follows the Moon, but when the Moon goes off round the bend and its influence is obstructed by the body of the Earth itself, what then? Water seeks its own level, and having heaped up on one side of a body of water, it sloshes back, momentum carrying it to an extreme in the other direction. This momentum is in proportion to the speed of its original chase, mirroring this. Thus, as fast as the water chased the Moon, it recedes. As the pull of the Moon was greatest while directly overhead, the high tide chasing the Moon reflects the time only over half the body of water, an ocean, usually a six-hour period. Thus, it rushes back in an equal time span, for a second six-hour or so period. Thus sloshing, the water finds itself receding again for a third six-hour or so period as the Moon moves into influence again. But in keeping with its motion and speed, the water swings back toward where the Moon reappeared and again chases the Moon to the horizon for the last six-hour or so period.

Atmosphere Building

Worlds that support life have water in abundance, and during the congealing period after a big bang hydrogen and oxygen in many states can be found freely floating around the intensely hot protoplanets. As planets congeal, the pressure results in heat, but after some time this dissipates. Meanwhile, the surface boils. Condensation occurs, forming seas upon the surface, but as nature abhors a vacuum, freely floating molecules do not all settle. What causes an atmosphere to exist, and what factors affect the composition of an atmosphere? Even in the absence of heat that would cause molecules of whatever nature to vaporize, an atmosphere builds. The Earth's atmosphere continues to build today, but are the oceans boiling?

Water vapor is in abundance in the Earth's atmosphere, yet arrived there not due to the action of intense heat but to fill a void. Place a vacuum against the surface of a pool of water and watch what happens—water vapor. The water pool will not completely disperse because its normal state at the condensation temperature is a liquid. But the constant motion of molecules means that the molecules at the surface have nothing to bump against in a vacuum, so like a car without brakes, off they go. At a certain point the airborne molecules start bumping into each other and bumping against the surface of the water pool, and the situation stabilizes. So, does this mean that the atmosphere of a planet is constantly dispersing into space? Yes and no. Deep space is bitterly cold, and when moving away from the surface of a planet airborne molecules slow down the bumping action. The situation stabilizes, again. However, some small loss is a constant factor, so that after billions of years some small quantity of the planet's substance has dissipated.

Light Particles

In the recent past, humans considered the world around them to be composed of either mass or energy, energy being anything they could not put their hands around. Only within the past century has the notion become widely accepted that both mass and energy are solid particles. Energy is just really small stuff, moving fast. Increasingly, the really small stuff is identified, at least in theory as it is too small to be observed directly. The clues, for humans struggling to understand the world around them, lies in the behavior of small particles under different circumstances. Light is not composed of a singular particle, but dozens of particles, thereby accounting for much of what humans call the strange behavior of light.

Rainbows

Rainbows are caused by the various particles responsible for what humans call color, the color of an object being determined by which particle is overwhelmingly present in the flood of particles striking the eye. Diffraction of light in water-laden air following a rain storm results in what humans call a rainbow, where the eye perceives light particles sorted out by the degree, or angle, of diffraction from one side of the rainbow to the other.

Auroras

Auroras, colorful light displays of waving banners across the northern or southern skies, are caused by the susceptibility of the various particles to the gravitational pull from the Earth. These light displays are only visible to humans where the glare of sunlight does not drown them out, as the eye registers the overwhelming particle nature of the light flood, discarding minor particles that might be present as so much noise.

Sunsets

Brilliant sunsets and dawns have been assumed by humans to be caused by dust suspended in the air, when of course those dust particles are present during the day as well and cause no such color variation. The human eye receives in the dim light of dawn or dusk an overwhelming flood of light composed of particular particles which are more prone to bend toward the gravitational pull of the Earth than other particles. Thus the sunset or dawn is most brilliant at a point just before or after the full glare of sunlight, when the particle flood is strong but is not mixed in with competing light particles to the point of being drown out.

Ferromagnetism

From childhood to adulthood, magnets have fascinated man. Young children are given sets of magnets to play with, linking them end to end. School children are shown, with iron ore dust, just how those invisible magnetic lines reach and curl, preparatory to a lecture about the Earth's magnetic field and on to how to use the compass when lost in the woods. The use of magnets so permeates industrialized human society that one would be hard pressed to find an aspect not affected. Claspless doors are secured with magnets, airplanes fly on automatic based on magnetic alignment, and recyclers separate out metal with magnets, to name but a few. Yet magnetism is not understood by man, though theories abound. It's clear that something flows, but just what is flowing is unknown. It's clear that direction is important, but just what is dictating this direction is unclear. It's clear that magnetism occurs naturally, especially in certain ores such as iron, but what it is that is special about iron ore is a puzzle.

Magnetism is the palpable, measurable effect of a subatomic particle not yet delineated by man. In fact, there are several dozen subatomic particles involved, out of the 387 involved in what humans assume to be simply the flow of electrons. Where electric current can be made to flow in any direction, the path of least resistance, magnetic flow seems to be very single minded. In fact, it is also going in the path of least resistance, as can be seen when one understands the path and what constitutes resistance for magnetic flow. Unlike electricity, which only occasionally flows in nature, the flowing subatomic particles that constitute a magnetic field are constantly flowing. This is the natural state, to be in motion. The path of least resistance, therefore, is to go with the flow, and the flow is determined by the biggest bully in the vicinity.

A single atom of iron, isolated, will establish the direction of flow based on the tightly orbiting electron particles, of which there are hundreds of subtypes. These tight orbits arrange themselves in a manner not unlike the planets around a sun, but the field, of course, is much more crowded. Given the fairly static number of these particles that will hang around an iron ore nucleus, the orbiting swirl may have a rhythm, rather than a steady hum. Put three groups of three into a cycle of 10 and you have whomp whomp whomp pause. Should the cycle, based on the nucleus and the electron subatomic particles it attracts due to its size and composition, be four groups of three in a cycle of 12, you would have whomp whomp whomp whomp. The steady hum of the second cycle does not lack a magnetic flow, it is just diffuse. The irregular cycle in the first example finds the magnetic flow escaping during the pause. Being attracted again to the best partner in the vicinity, the single iron atom, the magnetic subatomic particles will circle around, taking the path of least resistance which is on the other side of the atom from the outward flow. Placing a second iron atom next to the first finds the two lining up, so the flow escaping during the pause of each goes in the same direction. This is a bit like forcing a second water flow into a flowing stream. Toss a stick into both forceful streams and you will see that the water flows are moving in the same direction as much as possible—the path of least resistance. In this manner the magnetic flow of the largest bully forces all else in the neighborhood to line up. Where the iron ore atoms are caught in an amalgam and not altogether free to shift their positions within the amalgam, the magnetic flow may physically move the amalgam, this being, again, the path of least resistance. For those who would state that magnetism is not a thing, as it can't be weighed or measured or seen, we would point to the child's trick whereby two magnets are held positive end to positive end. Let go and they move so that they are aligned positive end to negative end. What made these magnets move, if not a thing?

Planetary Magnetism

Planets act as magnets in accordance with their composition and liquidity. In this regard the Earth is a magnet, as it has a high concentration of iron in both its core and crust, and its core is fluid. The strongest magnets are produced from softened or melted ore, as the atoms are free to line up end to end. The core of the Earth is perpetually in this state, and thus it acts like a huge magnet, as large as the globe itself. Magnetic influences between planets are greater than humans imagine, because they use as their frame of reference objects on the surface. The Earth's crust is magnetically diffuse, representing many different pole alliances over the eons, as magma hardened after volcanic eruptions during pole shifts. The Earth's thick crust acts as a shield in this way, so that only sensitive needles on compasses, floating freely, jiggle into alignment with the Earth's core.

A planet's magnetic influence is not encapsulated by its crust, but reaches beyond this even to the ends of the solar system. Like the shields that men stood behind to watch an atomic blast, they may have avoided the radiation, but the landscape behind them was devastated. The Earth's magnetism oozes around the various crustal plates acting as shields to recreate its essential alignment out in space, considering any confusion the crust may have presented as no more than an annoyance. A resonance is involved, so that the magnetic field can reestablish itself, filling in any blanks. Thus, when magnetized planets encounter each other, such as when the 12th Planet passes near the Earth, the strength of their reaction to each other is much greater than man might imagine. Mankind's tiny magnets are but specks on the surface of thick crusts acting as shields. Below the surface, in the liquid core of the Earth, and in resonance high above the surface, is where the real magnetic drama occurs.

Rotation

Rotation of a planet is dependent on many factors, only one of which is the initial motion attained coming out of a big bang. Rotation is due to a mobility difference between the core of a planet and the surface, and for lack of a better analogy we relate this to a dog chasing its tail. The core of the Earth is liquid, and mobile, and has a mind of its own. As the Earth moves in its orbit around the Sun, the relationship of the core of the Earth to surrounding influences changes. A child standing on a merry-go-round and wishing to face his mother must himself turn a complete circle in order to do this. In like manner, the heavy core of the Earth moves to face or escape magnetically related forces in the Universe about your solar system, dragging the surface with it. The core is not homogeneous everywhere and thus parts of it are strongly attracted or repulsed to this part or that of the Universe about it, so motion in the core is constant. No sooner does a part of the core move to the far side of its liquid tomb, then it finds itself presented with its old problem again, and sets into motion once again.

Now as the Earth takes 365 days to orbit the Sun, and rotation happens once a day, it would seem at first glance that the merry-go-round analogy is incorrect. How could rotation—started because of the Earth's orbit, a yearly affair—turn into a daily rotation? Motion is not a controlled matter, as anyone riding a bike without brakes is painfully aware. In the liquid core of the Earth, there is little to stop motion, once started, save the desire of parts of the core to approach or escape magnetic influences in the Universe. Rotation starts because of these external influences, and is maintained because of them. The rate of rotation is due to the liquidity of the core, as the brakes are never applied. Thus, the parts of the core that are moving away from an influence soon find that they have created their problem again, as the motion of the Earth has placed these parts back where they did not want to be! Round and round, like a dog chasing its tail.

31
Gravity Factors

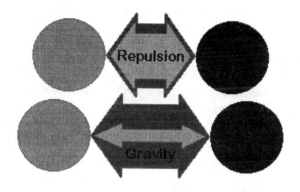

In general, the heavier an object, the greater the gravity force generated within it. The gravity force is compounded, but this fact is lost on those viewing the drama because most of the drama takes place within the object itself. Why would this not be the case? Why would matter only reach out to matter not contiguous, with its attraction, and not matter near at hand? Some call this internal gravity compression, but this is merely gravity working to pull each atom toward the greater bulk, which in the case of an orb, like a sun or planet, is generally toward the center. As the force of gravity reaches in all directions, the larger or heavier object is emitting more of a come-on than a smaller or lighter object. When several objects are involved in giving each other the come-on, the contention causes all of the bodies to dither, so an equilibrium is established in accordance with the mass and composition of the objects and their distance from each other. Humans find their understanding of gravity to be incomplete because they are not taking into consideration the repulsion force that large bodies, such as planets, generate toward each other. Objects on the surface of the Earth are infinitesimal in proportion

ZetaTalk

to the Earth itself, and thus any repulsion force between the two is also infinitesimal. The object on the surface, pushing away, is overwhelmed by the Earth's gravitational pull. The repulsion force is generated as a result of two bodies exerting a gravitational force on each other. In the case of a tiny object on the surface of the Earth, its gravitational pull on the Earth is scarcely noticed by the Earth. A gnat or mite. A nothing. The repulsion force is in play, however, between the Earth and her Moon. The repulsion force is invoked between objects on the surface of the Earth, incessantly, but this is masked by the intense force of gravity the Earth presents and other factors such as surface tension or friction or chemical bonding, so that the repulsion force cannot be recognized.

The repulsion force is infinitesimally smaller than the force of gravity, but has a sharper curve so that it equals the force of gravity at the point of contact. To examine the phenomena, Earth scientists would have to set up a lab in space, far enough away from any planetary body so that free movement is possible. Place two balls in a cage. Put one in motion toward another. Microscopically examine the interchange. They do not touch. They do not bounce off one another. They do not touch.

Children play with a ball on the end of a string, swinging it around and around their head. As long as the arm is tugging, the ball maintains its orbit, else it stops. Why would the planets not drift into the Sun? Are the orbits all that swift so that centrifugal force is extreme? The repulsion force is keeping them apart.

Gravity Particles

Gravity is particles, moving, just as magnetic fields do, and there is a polarization in gravity, too, which is the repulsion force. Before mankind discovered that magnetism was polarized, they discovered that it was an attractive force. Metallic items stuck to the sides of magnetized rock—how curious. The bipolar aspect of magnetism is only apparent when what occurs in nature can be countered in the laboratory. You force magnetized objects to do what they do not want to do—touch north pole to north pole or vice versa. Then you can observe the bipolar nature. In gravity, you are seeing only one aspect in the positioning of the planets, and you are dealing with a phenomenon that does not lend itself to easy experimentation.

In magnetism, the simple flow of particles creates more than a force for alignment, it creates an attraction. The gap is filled. Like water in a stream, where flotsam eventually lines up in the center, evenly spaced, just so magnetized objects do not keep their distance when free to move. They approach each other, and attach like a string of pearls. It is the same with the phenomenon of gravity, where the desire to fill the gap causes objects to approach one another. It is only where this gap is overfilled, by the presence of two large objects coming near, that the repulsion force is expressed. There is no room for the flow of gravity particles, so the objects stay apart!

Gravity particles produce an outward flow, but the outward streams are propelled, with a force and at a speed so much greater than the downward drafts, that this occurs over less of a surface area. A laser of gravity particles, versus a floodlight upon the return. So why would the weight of returning particles be the only ones mankind is aware of, and why would they not feel the violent lift of the updrafts? The updrafts blast through, tearing a hole as it were, where the returning particles do not tear what they press upon, and so have the greater effect.

Gravity particles, in their motion, do not affect what they move against or through, the effect being in essence mechanical. The upward drafts push aside other matter, letting it return upon completion of the updraft, leaving no trace of the temporary tear. The downward push of gravity particles returning to the large mass they are attracted to, the core of the Earth for instance, spread out upon objects they encounter, taking some time to drift through these objects and with a constant downward press during the motion of this drift. Thus, returning particles, due to the time they spend upon and within the surface objects, and due to their continual direction of motion, are a mechanical force that is stronger, overall, than the updraft of particles that quickly pass through the surface objects, essentially pushing them aside rather than engaging them.

The nature of this gravity flow is what determines the repulsion force we speak of. It is a complement of gravity only when large bodies are close to each other. The updrafts, when encountering a large body also exuding updrafts of gravity particles, hold the bodies apart. Large bodies, exuding their own updrafts of gravity particles, create a situation where their updrafts and the updrafts from another sun or planet bump against each other, creating a buffer and preventing the gravity masses from touching or even approaching each other.

Spin

Spin is a phenomenon that occurs regularly in nature and is frequently observed on Earth, from the large swirls that hurricanes form to the small whirlpools in the middle of water going down a drain. The fact that such a spin moves in different directions when it is above or below the equator gives evidence that spin is affected by factors outside of itself. The phenomenon of spin is observable when the object in motion is not constrained. Air and water are fluid, but spinning tops or figure skaters on ice also demonstrate the phenomenon. The theoretical speed of a spin is fastest toward the center of the spinning object, a factor easily noted by comparing hurricane wind speeds with those at the center of tornadoes. But why the difference?

Spin on the surface of the Earth reflects what is occurring in the core of the Earth, where there is more movement under the equator than at the poles, which are relatively stationary. All objects on the face of the Earth have these same influences from the core of the Earth, but this is not evident due to lack of fluidity or lack of motion. Spin in an object develops slowly, and is only evident to man when accumulated. Thus, water in a water fall has spin, but the water at the bottom of the fall cannot affect the water at the top, so the spin is not compounded. Water in a drain compounds the spin at the top by affecting the path of least resistance for the water at the top of the drain, and thus the little whirlpools in draining water. Spin occurs faster when the spinning object is narrow as there are fewer factors to counter the spin, less drag. Thus small tops can spin faster for the given impetus than large tops, and figure skaters find they can spin faster by reducing their overall size by drawing their arms in and hugging themselves.

Revolutions

The slow motion of planets around the Sun has long puzzled mankind, who is acutely aware that without continuing impetus to motion, motion stops. Only in dead space, where no gravitational attraction or repulsion forces exist, does motion continue without impetus. Motion without a continuing impetus is eroded by gravitational influences nearby, as in the case of an object thrown upward which slows gradually until turning to plummet to Earth. What keeps the planets, perpetually, the same distance from the Sun and their motion around the Sun at the same pace? Each time a given planet lined up with the massive Jupiter, and was perturbed to speed up or slow down due to this influence, unless there were another influence, this perturbed planet would remain in motion a bit slower or faster, perpetually. If the planets resume their motion around the Sun after being perturbed by each other, then the impetus setting them in motion again is not inherent in the planets. A planet slowed by the influence of Jupiter behind its path would not speed up again to resume its steady pace unless this other impetus existed.

This other impetus, which does exist, has the same basis as the magnetic alignment of the Earth and her sun. This influence reaches beyond the solar system, and dictates motion within the Sun not visible to mankind but nevertheless present. Just as the core of the Earth revolves at a speed dictated by the thickness of the Earth's liquid core, to chase away from or toward magnetic influences that exist in the solar system, just so the Sun's core rotates, dragging her children around her like baubles on the ends of her apron strings.

Orbits

Planets find their niche, based on how crowded the solar system is and their relative mass. For instance, if Jupiter were not in your solar system, the planets close in to the Sun would have essentially the same orbits, though would fan out a bit more. If the niche a planet would normally assume is already taken, as was the case when the clobbered Earth wobbled out of the Asteroid Belt into her current orbit, then more than one planet may settle into the same orbit, sharing this. Why then are smaller planets, such as Mars and Pluto, further out? Small planets may fail to drift into a closer orbit due to the buffering action of larger planets closer in. Essentially a bumping occurs, where the smaller planet is repulsed outward by a larger planet. Timing is everything in this matter, as twins in an orbit may occur if they come into the orbit at a distance from each other, where a close passage at key points would produce bumping.

ZetaTalk

Your orbiting planets are in motion because they are attracted to more than the Sun's gravitational field, more than the Sun's dark twin which acts as the 12th Planet's second focus, and certainly more than each other, although that is a small factor. Do the stars maintain their distance from each other by accident? For those who doubt that there are gravitational influences outside of the solar system, pulling on the orbiting planets, we would point to the elliptical path that planets assume. Why an ellipse? If the planets were concerned only with the Sun, or with each other, they would not assume the path they do. Planets assume an elliptical orbit for the same reason that comets leave the solar system. They are listening to more than one voice.

Planets orbiting a sun invariably line up into an orbital plane, looking a bit, if one were to speed up the process, like a flying saucer. Why would this be so, and is there a relationship to the shape that solar systems take and the familiar shape of our ships? There is indeed a relationship, as what is termed the flying saucer is shaped to simulate the gravity dynamics of a solar system so that it can become its own little solar system when instigating its own gravity field. A flying saucer in motion can turn sideways or upside down, and the passengers are unaffected. They are, gravity-wise, in their own little world. Solar systems do not take this shape by accident, though there is no comparable effect on Earth for man to study and point to. Gaseous planets, such as Saturn, have rings in a plane, but nothing orbiting the Earth, man-made or otherwise, is so affected.

How often do planets, such as your Sun's 12th Planet, take up an orbit around two suns rather than remaining dedicated to one sun? Rarely, as this requires the wanderer to be large enough that a strong repulsion force develops when it approaches one of the suns and to also have congealed after a big bang in such a position between the two suns that this binary orbit ensues. If close to one sun it will settle into the normal orbit around this single sun. But if fairly equidistant it will approach one sun with comet like speed and return in the same direction, as comets do, to begin its binary orbit.

32
12th Planet Orbit

Most suns or bodies large enough to potentially have become suns are in motion, themselves orbiting around others of like size. This is not by accident, but is a factor of their size in proportion to the other clumps of matter that form coming out of a big bang. Just as the planets in a solar system orbit their sun because it is the largest voice around them, just so suns themselves hear the voices of the other suns around them. If suns are not peers a different dance ensues, but, if they are peers, neither sun dominates the other and they remain at a distance from each other depending on the balance point between their gravity attraction to each other and the force of repulsion that develops as they move toward each other. If they are in motion as this balance is achieved they will remain in motion—binary suns.

If suns are not of an equal size they are not likely to become binaries, especially if there are other suns in the vicinity vying to be dominant. The smaller sun may dither, perpetually, first approaching one larger brother and, when turned away by the repulsion force, approaching the other brother and likewise being turned away. This scenario can entail any number of large and small suns. Do not these suns of unequal size begin to orbit each other? Indeed they do, when the size is greatly disproportional, but most suns are

ZetaTalk

not that disproportional. Therefore, either a dither or more often a dance between peers develops. The dance that binaries do can be rapid and complex, if other suns are nearby and influence the dance, or the dance can be a dead stand still, as is the case between your Sun and its dead twin.

Sunspots

Gaseous planets and suns, lit or unlit, do not have homogeneous cores any more than do bodies with liquid cores such as the Earth. Humans tend to think of air or gaseous clouds or liquid pools as being homogeneous, but in truth heavier particles settle down, lighter particles rise, and other particles disperse slowly from their point of entry into the soup. The process by which the sun releases light and heat also releases other energy, unrecognized by man. This process is not homogeneous, and thus buildup and release occur. Any lack of consistency in a body's core has the potential of causing core rotation, as the components try to escape or approach that which they are repulsed by or attracted to in the neighborhood. Thus, the sun's core swirls, and when lighter elements rush toward the surface their motion is not impeded by the gaseous surface and overshooting occurs—a solar flare.

Brown Dwarfs

The 12th Planet has both heat and light, generated from within its core. Life on the 12th Planet, which is inhabited by large hominoids indistinguishable from humans other than by their size, experiences continuous day. The light is diffused in the atmosphere, and returns to the land surface, but emerges from the core to interact with the atmosphere only via the surface of the deep oceans, which cover the majority of the planet's surface. You may equate this to volcanic activity, where the Earth has numerous places both above ground and under the oceans that ooze molten lava. Just so, the 12th Planet has places where the molten and churning substance in its core escapes to the surface.

Humans do not understand what is occurring within the Sun, a combustion of sorts that ignited because of the pressure of elements following the big bang, during the congealing period. The Sun was not born—it was lit. It lit as compression continued to the point where a product of subatomic particle collision did not dissipate, but accumulated, and the degradation of this substance is what you are viewing and feeling in your sunlight. This is a simplistic explanation for a complicated process. The 12th Planet has a similar process ongoing within its core, but being composed of heavier substances than your Sun, this process is slowed.

Retrograde Orbit

The 12th Planet's retrograde orbit around the Sun is due to its reaction to an energy field emitted by the Sun. This energy field radiates out from the Sun intensely at certain points, like a moving arm, following the rotation of the Sun's core where the matter producing this energy field is located. Where the non-traveling planets are in essence swept along before this intense energy field, like dust balls in front of a broom, the 12th Planet is not so trapped.

Approaching from a distance, the 12th Planet reacts to this energy field by trying to evade it, and it takes the path of least resistance. The sweeping arm of this energy field coming from the Sun passes by quickly out in space when the 12th Planet is at a distance, but builds in intensity and takes longer to sweep past when the 12th Planet comes close. When at a distance, this energy field affects the 12th Planet but slightly, so it reacts as it approaches from its second focus by orbiting in the same manner the planets close to the Sun do. It sweeps before this energy field as the field passes, moving slightly at these times to the left, in the same counterclockwise manner that the other planets do.

As the 12th Planet approaches, moving steadily closer and picking up speed due to the gravitational tug of the Sun, the energy field from the Sun is more intense and takes longer to sweep past. The 12th Planet's reaction to this is still a slight movement sweeping ahead of this energy field, but as the energy field passes, there is then a stronger jerk backwards, away from the passing arm of the Sun's energy field. Thus, during 1995 through 1998, the 12th Planet drifted left and up toward the ecliptic, aligning itself in the same manner as the planets to the Sun's sweeping arm. But then due to its mobility out in space and its distance from the Sun, it develops a retrograde orbit and begins to move to the right, in the manner the ancients recorded.

The 12th Planet

The 12th Planet swings so far away from your solar system, and then returns, because it is orbiting both your sun and your sun's dark companion. Most stars are binaries, and your sun has an unlit companion, unseen by you but nevertheless present and in force. The 12th Planet travels interminably between these two, not able to settle on an orbit around just one because of the momentum and path it originally took. It is caught. The 12th Planet is such that it spends most of its life out in dark space, slowly moving from one giant tug to another. As it approaches one of these giants, your sun being one, it picks up speed, and reaches a maximum speed as it passes the attraction. Having passed, it now has both gravitational attractions on one side, and quickly switches back in the other direction, zooming just as rapidly along a path similar to the one it just took.

The 12th Planet's travels are not unlike a train on parallel tracks, where the train on one side of the tracks is going in one direction, and the train on the other side is coming back. The elliptical path of the 12th Planet does little direct damage to the planets in your solar system, which are lined up on a plane with each other. The 12th Planet comes in on an angle, such that it is only the point of passage through this plane where a direct collision could occur. This point, at the present time, is not in the orbit of any of your solar system planets, although that was not the case in the distant past as your asteroid belt attests.

While it is out in space the 12th Planet moves slowly, but increases speed rapidly as it comes close to one of its two foci. When the 12th Planet is passing your sun it is moving rapidly. The time spent within your outer planet Saturn's orbit is a mere three months. It zips by.

It does not head directly into the Sun, as there is a play between attraction and repulsion which exists between all planetary bodies. Simply stated, the faster the 12th Planet moves, the closer it can come, although the math in this matter is not quite that simple. The 12th Planet is both attracted and repulsed by your sun. Both factors are at play. Thus, as the 12th Planet approaches your sun, it picks up speed but also shies away. There is a battle going on, a tug in one direction with a push in another. The end result is that the 12th Planet still comes on, full bore, but veers to the side a bit as it approaches. As it is still picking up speed, the speed compensates for the repulsion, and the 12th Planet finds in the last few months that it can now come closer to the Sun, the repulsion being balanced by the speed. Thus, when it gets to its maximum speed, entering your solar system, it bends in toward your sun, after having veered outward slightly, so that the angle is approximately 32°. The 12th Planet in essence has pulled away from the orbital plane, as well as from the Sun. It does not want to move in alongside the other planets, it wants to cross quickly at a sharper angle. It is at this point that the 12th Planet essentially dives up through the Earth's orbital plane and quickly passes on. The 12th Planet pulls down and away from your sun only at the last minute. This is reflected in time as the last 9.7 Earth weeks or 68 Earth days. This is reflected in distance as 1.2598 times the orbital diameter of Pluto, or two and one-half times the distance from your sun to Pluto.

The shape of these deviations is parabolic at the angle of turns, in all cases. This is not exact, but for purposes of calculating an orbit it is something you can work with that will be close enough. Thus, the 12th Planet starts its deviation from its straight path in a parabolic manner, but has scarcely started to turn away when its increasing speed allows it to come closer to the Sun and it does another parabolic curve back toward the Sun, essentially correcting its path again to be straight toward the Sun. When it passes the Sun, piercing the Earth's orbital plane, it has come to the point in a parabolic curve where the line is essentially straight.

The return passage of the 12th Planet is dictated by a combination of forces—momentum, attraction, and (for want of a more scientific term to describe this process) the call of the wild. The 12th Planet stops and hovers for some years before beginning its return passage. The rate of start-up essentially mirrors the rate of stoppage, so movement is slow at first, almost imperceptible. Having stopped in its tracks the 12th Planet is in a vulnerable position, and in point of fact could become caught in a new pattern of motion should the objects around it present a new dynamic. It has stopped, dead still, and thus is in a virginal position of having no commitments. During most passages of the 12th Planet there is no contest, but in some cases there are other attractions nearby that create confusion. The upshot of this is that the 12th Planet may delay longer before setting out on its return passage, but the factors in your part of the Universe are not such as to change the outcome.

Moons

The 12th Planet has what are called traveling moons, as they often trail behind the planet as it tracks along its long elliptical orbit. These moons are comparable to the Earth's moon, some even larger, as the mass of the 12th Planet is a gravitational magnet far beyond the pull that the Earth could muster. To some it would seem that moons must always orbit their planet, as the moons in the Earth's solar system do, yet they are on the move. The difference is that the 12th Planet travels faster, while traversing your solar system, at speeds quite outside the sedate speeds the other planets assume. These moons do not leave the 12th Planet during its fast ride through the solar system, as the 12th Planet due to its mass stays away from the other large planets, and thus they at no time have a gravitational draw that is stronger than the continuous influence of the 12th Planet. Where the 12th Planet's tail will lash the Earth, this lashing does not include a chance of collision with the 12th Planet's moons.

Pole Shift

33
The 12th Planet

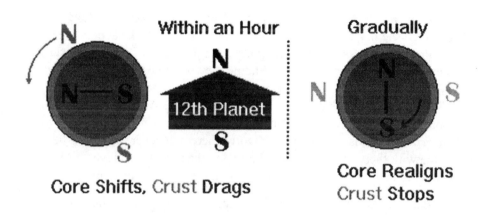

Within an Hour   Gradually

Core Shifts, Crust Drags

Core Realigns
Crust Stops

The Earth will go through physical cataclysms in the near future—a pole shift where the Earth's crust slides along with the soft molten core, positioning new parts of the geography as the new North and South poles. This is related to the millennium, but is not precisely what the Bible or the various seers of this time are predicting. There is truth in the rumors of what is called the 12th Planet, acting like a giant comet during its periodic passage through the solar system. There is truth in what has been reported about violent geological changes, renting continents apart and heaving mountains high. The deluge occurred during just such a time.

There will be much death, the majority of mankind dying during the shift or shortly thereafter. Most of the people on Earth at this time will be unaware. They may be aware of drought, of a reddish glow during the heat of the day, perhaps even a reddish dust coloring their water and giving a bitter taste to their drinking water. Most of the people on Earth have so many problems existing, day-to-day, that they will scarcely take notice. Even those who might take notice can scarcely do anything about it. Those who can barely feed their families cannot take flight, as they would have nothing to live on, even if they should arrive at a safe place. This is an unknown experience, with no precedent in memory. Denial is also high. The authorities discourage any news broadcasts, wishing calm and for the *status quo* to continue.

Even where there is awareness, there will be little action. Many will look about them, and debate their life-style should they take action—leave the home, the comforts of familiar places and people who represent a support structure? How would they live? Should they be forced to become beggars, they may stay in their own, familiar, surroundings. Then there are those who will cling to their material goods. Even with choices, where a place would be made for them in safer surroundings, they will find they are bonded to their material goods and unable to divorce them, whatever the risk. They will die with their material items, clinging to these things as lovers. Most faced with these grim choices will deal with the situation by denial.

Between the unaware, the unfortunate, and the reluctant, lie most of humanity. Those who survive the massive earthquakes, which will level cities to dust, and the massive tidal waves, which will inundate coast lines for hundreds of miles inland, will be either fortunate or assisted. Since the Earth is to become a home for service-to-others entities, those humans operating in this orientation will have a choice to remain in their human form or reincarnate later. If the human form is chosen, then these humans will be assisted during the hours of calamities. They will be unaware of the assist, but will find themselves, clinging to floating material after the flood has passed, or regaining consciousness after the earthquakes. Many will move to safe areas and set up communes, operating in the service-to-others mode of the future. These areas will be rural, essentially primitive, and they will not rely on the trappings of civilization as they now know it, either before or after the cataclysms.

Past Cataclysms

The Earth bears witness to the cataclysms in her past and their periodic occurrence. Beyond her deep wound in the Pacific basin, and beyond the drift of her continents, there are other scars more palpable by man.

Mountain Building

Mountain cliffs, which rise sheer in many cases thousands of feet, represent tearing of solid rock. These stand before you, while you make a hobby of scaling their heights while ignoring their deeper meaning. Have any experiments been done to determine how much force would be required to tear rock of this depth? None have. The reason lies in the equally deep desire of mankind to avoid thinking about the Earth's past cataclysms.

Heaving and Sinking Land

Beneath the sea in the Bahamas lies evidence of civilizations that have gone under the waves—highways and highway markers, clearly man-made. These areas have been explored by many fortune hunters, recorded by camera, and published in full color repeatedly. Likewise, ancient Inca cities stand so high in altitude that the cities could not have been built, much less lived in. Yet the scientific community continues to claim that Earth changes happen gently, inch by inch, at the pace experienced during the memory of their current civilization.

Shifting Crust

Antarctica bears witness to her past as a steamy swamp, as do the North Seas, where oil is extracted. Likewise the temperate regions are scarred by what is termed the Ice Ages, where these regions were as snow and ice packed as the poles. A clue to these changes lies in the magnetism frozen in hardened lava, which demonstrates that magnetic north and south changed now and then. An adequate explanation has not been proffered by the scientific community. All the explanations have the Earth's thin crust remaining in place, as the thought that they are standing on a raft that can move on the sea of magma beneath them is too frightening to contemplate.

The 12th Planet

The term, 12th Planet, is not scientifically exact but relates to the historical and widely read book that Zecharia Sitchen wrote, titled *The 12th Planet*. In this book he explains that the ancient visitors from this traveling planet considered the Moon to be a planet, and counted the Sun as the first. The periodic Earth cataclysms caused by the 12th Planet have been in place for eons, since the Earth was cold and without life. The 12th Planet, acting like a giant comet, assumed its orbit around the Sun due to the gravitational and motion issues which were at play just after the big bang. The 12th

ZetaTalk

Planet's orbit is long and narrow, the trip through your solar system but a minor part of the itinerary. The 12th Planet approaches from Orion for another passage, with a period which loosely computes to every 3,600 years.

Planet X does exist, and it is the 12th Planet, one and the same. Interest in Planet X was roaring along going into the 1983 IRAS search and discovery of a large object in the direction of Orion. Planet X disappeared from the news for almost a decade, after its discovery, as a cover-up is now in force. When the blanket of suppression was dropped on the media and major observatories, who know just where Planet X is at all times these days, it took some time for an explanation for the silence to be concocted. Since JPL and NASA are firmly in hand, doing the bidding of the establishment on so many information issues, they became the designated arm of disinformation. The mystery of why the outer planets appeared perturbed to astronomers for the last 160 years was explained away by adjustments in the size and composition of the outer planets, discovered by probes. The public gets the conclusion, but not the facts.

Continental Drift

The asteroid belt, full of gravel and boulders, did not get there by accident. When your solar system formed, matter was clumping together, and this process did not overlook this one little orbit around this one little Sun for some odd reason. Long before there was highly evolved life on the Earth, it rode that orbit, which happened to be smack dab in the path of the 12th Planet at that time. In due time, a monumental collision between the young Earth and one of the 12th Planet's moons occurred. Matter went in every direction and the impacts were fierce. Your solar system, in fact, had several more planets in orbit than it does today, in orbit close enough to the asteroid belt to be considered within it. Shattered matter, slinging off into different directions, were missiles of death for some time. One disaster followed another, until at last there were no more hapless planets to be pelted into pieces.

The Earth wobbled out of orbit at the initial impact, and her wobble took her, eventually, into her present orbit closer to the Sun. When the Earth was in orbit farther from the Sun, it bore as life only cold creatures that lived in the dark waters on the scant vegetation that grew there. After the impact, the larger piece became the Earth, with its waters pooling in the wound as a

210

cosmetic, the motion of the Earth pulling the waters round, to give a smooth appearance. Looking down from space, man can clearly see that the continents once formed a whole. Like the pieces of a puzzle that can be placed together, South America fits nicely into the curve of the Western African coast, and North America tucks up against Europe.

The Earth, during each successive Pole Sift, has filled her wound. At first, due to the lopsided nature of her shape, the tug toward roundness was slight. She hugged herself, all on one side, and each passage of the giant comet only pulled slightly at this hug, separating her landmass and moving this into the gap. But each succeeding passage found a more vulnerable scene, and the separating of the single landmass increased. Rifts were driven between landmasses and became vulnerable spots, torn recently, tearable again. Increasingly the Americas have moved away from the African and European continents. Now, when the Americas are almost midway between the other landmasses, and the African landmass has cleanly separated too, they are more vulnerable than ever to becoming fully balanced during a pole shift.

During the coming pole shift the Pacific gap will close, equalizing the landmasses as they spread around the globe. This will be devastating to certain subducting areas, such as India and Western Australia, and will heat to a tremendous degree those plates that are above the subducting plates in California, Tibet, and along the Pacific Rim.

Wandering Poles

The wandering poles attest to prior pole shifts but don't give a true picture, as many times poles situate over oceans or land that subsequently submerges, areas unexplored by modern man. What is termed a wandering pole is mankind's best efforts to trace the placement of the poles, dating the record in hardened magma which captures the moment's magnetic alignment. The Ice Ages, occurring over northern Europe and America, are also written records of when poles were situated over those spots. Pole shifts can be as slight as a few degrees, or close to 180° F, the most extreme case.

The strength and direction of any given pole shift is dependent on whether the two planets are lined up pole-to-pole or side-to-side on the approach. Where the Earth is close to the point of passage, a pole-to-pole lineup occurs. In a pole-to-pole confrontation the 12th Planet's north pole essentially grips the Earth's south pole and drags it with it as it passes, pushing away the north pole. Where the Earth is a quarter way around on her orbit, a side-to-side lineup occurs. In a side-to-side confrontation, the Earth is only nudged to line up with her brother, just as small magnetic particles in ore attempt to align with each other. When the Sun stands between the Earth and the 12th Planet there is, in essence, no pole shift but simple tension and compression in the crust, expressed as increased earthquakes and volcanism.

The position of the Earth or the 12th Planet during any passage is strictly by chance, governed by the various influences that affect the arrival of the 12th Planet, which can meet with any number of delaying influences on its journey. Thus, there is no regularity to dramatic pole shifts, where the Earth is essentially turned upside down. Dramatic reversals happen rarely, as the 12th Planet must virtually come between the Earth and the Sun to have this much influence. Human written and verbal history will not serve man well in preparation for the forthcoming pole shift, as a shift as devastating as this one will be has not occurred within the past 50,000 years.

A reversal of the Earth's polarity, where the magnetic north pole points off consistently in another direction, does not occur, ever. This is a hypothesis that humans have concocted to explain what they find in the Earth's crust. In this hypothesis, they are assuming that the Earth's crust does not move about, but it does. Scientists who do not buy into the pole shift will argue endlessly that it is the poles that move and reverse. Sometimes, during a pole shift, the movement is slight, and sometimes the crust does, as you say, a 180. The coming shift will come close to that, being better than a quarter turn. Having only the Earth's crust to examine, and being in denial or unaware of pole shifts, a human could only assume that the poles had moved, rather than the crust.

The story of the devastation the 12th Planet causes upon the periodic passage seems surreal to näive mankind, who has a scant record from the prior pole shifts where the human race was decimated and civilizations disrupted, so that records were not reliably kept until a few generations had passed.

34
Pole Shift Legends

    The Flood occurred three pole shifts back, approximately eleven millennia ago. The shift prior to that had been slight, so that melting of the poles was slow and incomplete. Ordinarily each pole shift places the old poles in a position where they will quickly melt, facing the Sun. The pole shift ahead of the one causing The Flood only moved the old poles slightly, so much of the ice was still remaining. Poles over land have constant runoff when they melt, and they settle as the weight of ice presses down, but poles over oceans melt more from the bottom up, leaving caverns of ice honeycombed within as the water can support ice of odd shapes. Thus a vast body of thin ice stretched out over the southern ocean, over the location of the old pole. When the comet caused massive Earth movements this ice sheet fractured and fell into the water, causing a huge displacement and resulting massive wave. This wave was the flood, of legend worldwide.

Jewish Exodus

The last passage of the 12th Planet is best remembered as the time of the Jewish exodus from Egypt, but what is not well known is the reason for the exodus. Slaves do not just walk away from their masters, and in particular a large group of slaves, old women and children among them, do not get miles away from their masters in a desert area where lookouts can see for miles. The institution of slavery is maintained by cruelty and punishment, and slaves attempting to escape are punished in a manner that will serve as a lesson to others contemplating such an escape attempt. Hands and feet are chopped off when the slave wanders or reaches where they are not to go, eyes poked out when the slave looks when they were supposed to drop their eyes, and tongues cut out when the speech of the slave is considered too bold.

Thus, the Jewish exodus did not occur because this large group just decided to take a stroll one day, anticipating nothing worse than a whipping as the comeuppance should they be discovered. The exodus occurred because their masters were devastated and distracted by problems so severe as to take their minds entirely off their slaves. Would this have been a flooded Nile or a plague of locusts or even a celebration where all got drunk? Nothing in the normal course of Egyptian society would have created a situation where the Jews could have left, en mass, or had the courage to leave. They left because the passage of the 12th Planet imposed first a long night and then horrendous earthquakes and volcanic eruptions in nearby volcanoes.

Chaos reigned, the very type of chaos that governments throughout the world fear lies in their near future. Guards left their posts, and household servants stole from their masters and crept away in the seemingly never-ending night. The rulers held their heads in worry and discussed among themselves how they might placate the gods. The military elite, used to utter control and tolerating no challenges to their orders, reacted to the chaos by trying to reestablish order. Hysterical troops, unable to comprehend what was happening to them, were in no mood to placate their superiors, and thus the military was engaged with internal battles for some time. It was not until the rotation of the Earth was reestablished that the Egyptian rulers and their military leaders were able to regain control of the troops. By that time, as history well tells, the Jewish exodus was a success! The parting of the Red

Sea so that Moses could lead his people to safety is counted as an act of God, a miracle, but the waters did not pull back. The sea floor heaved up, temporarily, long enough to provide safe passage to Moses, but not long enough for the Pharaoh's hapless soldiers, who followed.

Immanuel Velikovsky placed great emphasis on the Jewish Exodus, when combined with the Earth's geological history. Velikovsky's mission was to set mankind to thinking about the periodic cataclysms that have so dramatically left their mark on the Earth and human history. Mountains obviously thrown skyward under extreme pressure, the ruins of great civilizations with no reason for demise, flash-frozen carcasses of healthy mastodons with no evident cause of death—all this is put over the wall and not dealt with. Velikovsky had no knowledge of the 12th Planet or, coming before his time, Planet X, but he theorized planetary close encounters as the cause of all this history. Velikovsky's theories cannot be effectively proved until the giant comet, the 12th Planet, returns to savage this solar system again. Unfortunately for those unwilling to listen to Velikovsky or contemplate the evidence he so poetically presents, they will be learning the truth of his theories—too late!

Tales

Past cataclysms appear in print more than is recognized. Tales where the Earth yaws wide and swallows cities or hapless humans who tumble into the yaw are not describing present-day earthquakes which tumble buildings, drop bridges, and heave roads. Yaws that open and re-close may seem to occur only in story books, but they are based on real events that sometimes occur during cataclysms. Fairy tales sometimes describe mountains that rise from the Earth overnight, or caverns and passageways into the mountains that open suddenly or disappear just as suddenly. This is all attributed to magic, but to primitive humans who had no forewarning of a pole shift, emerging the morning after horrendous wind and rain storms to find the landscape rearranged, this must have seemed like magic.

Atlantis

Atlantis was land near the current continent of Europe, which was pulled into the Atlantic during the continental rip that accompanies violent pole shifts and thus disappeared dramatically under the sea. The stories about Atlantis, which has never been found, are supported by myths of great cities destroyed

215

suddenly by rising water. Well, that of course happens extensively all over the world every time there is a pole shift. Many cities in and around the European continent went under the waves during the past few pole shifts. This is because the Atlantic, as a widening ocean, tends to drag down the shore lines and outlying islands during each shift. The floor of the Atlantic drops, pulling its perimeter with it.

Lemuria

Lemuria was land on the other side of the world, in the Pacific, which also slipped under the waves during a pole shift. As with most Pacific lands, Lemuria was inhabited by the easygoing peoples of the South Pacific. Lemurians, great in number as the land was more than the scattering of islands that exist in the Pacific today, have been deified as a special spiritual race, and all manner of benefits to occur should they somehow return. As is often the case, these lands, in death, are more than they were in life.

Bermuda

During every pole shift some land, particularly coastal land near a widening ocean rift, submerges. This has been the case on the eastern seaboard of the U.S., and in the Caribbean. Traces of a submerged civilization can be seen under the waves off Bermuda—roads, sign posts, and walls. This land has been dragged down over successive pole shifts, to its present depth, so slipping under the waves was not as dramatic as it might seem. As the melting poles soon cause the oceans to encroach on the shorelines, the surviving inhabitants are forced to flee inland, and thus the historical record tends to get lost.

Ancient Maps

An unanswered puzzle that cartographers struggle with is the presence of ancient maps that indicate that the equator and the poles were not always where they are today. The accuracy of these maps, detailing landmasses and their placement as they are essentially known today, cannot be denied. These were not fantasy maps, but were drawn with markings that relate to the placement of stars and compasses, the guides sailors use when far out at sea. There is no ready explanation, as the detail and consistency do not indicate confusion, and a matter as central to map-making as the placement of the equator and poles would not likely be confused. The obvious answer is staring these cartographers in the face. Pole shifts occur often, and have occurred in recent times.

Prophecy

If one reads beyond the surface for the deeper meaning, one will find a remarkably similar theme in many prophecies. Compare the Hopi Indian, Mother Shipton, and *OASPHE* descriptions of the forthcoming time of destruction and death with the scientific analysis done by Sitchin and Velikovsky, and one will find, time after time, that they correlate. Yet the Hopi had no contact with Mother Shipton, nor she with the Ohio dentist who wrote the *OASPHE*, and Sitchin and Velikovsky moved in different circles and during different eras. Therefore, dwell less on the trivial differences in their prophecy, and more on the similarities.

Invariably, prophecies about the millennium or pending geological changes are laid alongside each other with the differences raised up and demands for reconciliation made. Like the famous story about the blind men all feeling a different part of the elephant, some differences are due to segregation, but most are due either to the prophet being misunderstood or the prophet misunderstanding what it is they have been told. If you had never experienced an eclipse of the Sun but had been advised that one would occur, the message may be interpreted as a day when the Sun would hide, when the Sun and Moon would do battle, when night would come early, when there would be a short day or two short days, or a very short night—but all these statements would be referring to the same pending eclipse. Just so, when a prophecy states that land will go under the sea and another states that the land will rise from the sea, these prophecies are not in conflict with each other, as both situations will occur.

ZetaTalk Prediction

The first pass of the 12th Planet will occur, by our calculations, early in the year 2003. All the cataclysms expected will occur during this pass—tidal waves, earthquakes of a magnitude 15 on the Richter scale, and a cloud of volcanic dust that will make the atmosphere dense as dusk for decades. A second pass will occur some seven or more years later, approximately 2011. This second pass takes the comet outside of your solar system again, but as the Sun will buffer the Earth on this second pass, only slight earthquakes and tides will occur at that time.

Edgar Cayce

The Edgar Cayce vision of California appearing as islands, having been inundated, is not in conflict with the ZetaTalk statement that the West Coast will rise up due to forceful subduction of plates to the west of the land. One has only to look at the geography of California to see that the fertile inland valley was recently an inland sea, due to the surrounding mountains holding the water as a bowl. The ZetaTalk prediction of massive and forceful tidal waves, rising hundreds of feet high to clear the mountains when they have no where else to go, will re-flood the inland sea once again, and that drainage will take some time. Edgar Cayce has also stated a vision that lands will appear in the Caribbean, where ZetaTalk has pointed to an area off Antarctica. Insofar as Cayce was seeing the immediate effect of the pole shift on the land, with the Atlantic widening so that there is temporarily less water to rise up on the shores, the vision is correct. Cayce was also reporting the immediate effect of the pole shift on California.

Mayan Calendar

The Mayan calendar is not so much incorrect as misunderstood. The calendar is derived from calendars and plotting methods left behind by the hominoid visitors from the 12th Planet. There are and were many calendars in operation, and the western calendar of 365 days with an occasional leap year is only one such method. Dates, when plotted according to one calendar method, do not always line up exactly when translated to another calendar. However, the primary difficulty in interpreting the Mayan calendar is determining the correct starting point. One may be accurate in calculating the number of days, months, and years between events, but unless the starting point is precisely known, the end point is questionable. Thus there are various interpretations on when the Mayan calendar ends, albeit this rather obviously coincides with the coming millennium. We have given the correct dates for the return of the 12th Planet as the year 2003 for the devastating first pass. All other dates are incorrect.

35
Pole Shift Signs

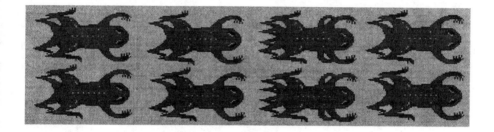

American Indian legends are deeply appealing to most humans, who sense the wisdom of the ages behind the symbolism. The prophecy of the White Buffalo Calf seems specific, however, and the birth of such calves going into the millennium has set many to wondering. Is this simply coincidence, or does it have meaning? It does indeed have meaning, a prophecy based on what history taught the plains Indians, and thus the White Buffalo Calves are yet another harbinger of the coming pole shift.

Albinos occur naturally in all life-forms, some with more rarity than others. What causes an albino to emerge is assumed to be a genetic quirk, where the normal production of color compounds is suppressed. This is the effect but not the cause, else why would life in dark caverns or the depths of the ocean be pale, without color? If color were a genetic quirk, then why the almost total absence of color in creatures living in darkness? Coloration is influenced by radiation, just as tanning takes place upon exposure to sunlight. What is little understood is that this phenomenon has two switches, one increasing coloration under certain radiation frequencies, but another reducing coloration under a different set of radiation frequencies. The core of the Earth, emitting in greater bursts the radiation her caverns and deep-water creatures are bathed in, is confusing her surface creatures. Thus, the White Buffalo Calves, heeding the signals from the restless Earth, are heralding the approaching pole shift.

Increasingly, as the core of the Earth adjusts to the approach of her brother, the 12th Planet, this increased radiation is reflected on the surface of the planet. Humans are aware of radio waves, X-rays, electromagnetic fields, and gravitational tugs. This is but a tiny fraction of the invisible influences, and all of them are affected by the approach of the 12th Planet. Life at the moment of conception and at key points during development of the embryo where cell specialization or the inception of limbs and organs occurs, is delicate, and under more than the influence of DNA. Look to what the drug Thalidomide did to the formation of limbs, where a chemical influence interfered with the message intended by the DNA, and how children raised under high-power lines developed cancer at an undue rate. As with White Buffalo Calves being born, deformed frogs are heralding the approach of the 12th Planet.

Trends

One sign of the approach of the 12th Planet is a slowing in the rate of rotation, a forerunner of the actual stop in rotation that occurs at the moment of passage. As with weather and warming trends, this is at first so gradual and slight as to be arguable. Humans in denial do not argue with the current data drawn—they argue with the comparison to past data. The past data was invalid in some way, was recorded with imprecise instruments, or perhaps was not measured at all. Precise weather data has only been gathered for the past few decades, a hundred years at most, and prior to that was only re-corded at times of extreme weather like hurricanes, and this in the form of tales. There was no mechanism to measure, for instance, the wind velocity of a hurricane, so the estimated height of a tidal wave or size of buildings flattened was recorded. Likewise with major earthquakes, which in the past have flattened cities. Without the ability to capture Richter scale, earth-quakes in the past were either termed a temblor, small or big.

The best way to counter arguments is not to point to the past but to start recording the present. All the trends and signs will only exacerbate, with the oceans warmer still, the weather more erratic and unpredictable still, and the Earth gradually slowing in her rotation more and more measurably. If one gathers these statistics now, and gathers them yearly, the trends will become a clear pattern. Thus, the arguments will be with people now living, and with statistics gathered by the same methods. As the trends and signs will increase more rapidly, exponentially, as the 12th Planet enters the solar system, this comparison can be used as a signal to many who plan to move to safety that the time has arrived. Where weather and warmer oceans will be arguable up to the end, a slowing rotation is not arguable.

Weather Changes

Weather changes have already begun—violent storms, unusual weather patterns, severe and long lasting droughts, increased frequency of hurricanes, torrential rains, and a general warming of the planet. The Earth itself, not just the atmosphere, will be warmer, and this affects weather patterns. Humanity has come to expect predictability in the weather. Even the monsoons of the East, or the hurricanes that hit the eastern United States, are expected and prepared for, as they are predictable. During the next few decades, until the Earth settles down into another predictable pattern, mankind will find its greatest problems with the weather to be its unpredictability. The reason lies deep within the Earth's core, an area the meteorologists refuse to consider, and thus their predictions on the atmosphere will never be based on the right parameters.

A key change, to which one could point, is the warming of the Earth's oceans around the globe. This has been measured as a six-inch rise, worldwide, on all the beaches. The waters have risen because they are warmer, and warm water takes up more room than cold water, as all elementary physics books will report. How is it that the oceans, so very deep and so very cold, have warmed up? Is it the almost imperceptible rise in the temperature of the air, a degree or so, as reported to date? Since heat rises, why would this slight rise affect the oceans? Meteorologists will tell you that the effect of air warming is air turbulence, not warmer oceans. The oceans are warmer because the core of the Earth has heated up, and it does so in response to its brother coming closer. This will continue, and increase, until sometime after the cataclysms are past.

Going into the cataclysms the weather will become unpredictable, with torrential rainstorms where not expected, and droughts likewise where not expected. Extremes of temperature will be experienced. There will be

unusually warm winters, where the trees and shrubs will start to bud, thinking spring, and then will be subjected to frost. Similarly, frosts will come
late in the spring, almost into summer, killing the buds which have already
put forth their tender shoots.

Where today the world balances these situations, shipping produce
around the world, during the years coming close to the time of the reappear-
ance of the 12th Planet, all parts of the world will experience extremes. Of
course, leading up to the cataclysms, not all produce will fail. Greenhouse
crops will come through. Backyard gardens, tended carefully by watchful
eyes, will survive. But the large cash crops that supply crowded population
centers will find little to market, and the prices will go up accordingly.

At first, stores put up against such times will be tapped. After a bit,
these stores will run down, and governments will get nervous. Helping
handouts, from countries better off to those in desperation, will stop. Friction
on these matters will fray at already frayed nerves. Up until the cataclysms,
humans in the main will struggle on with the farming and fishing methods
they are familiar with. Those groups who have prepared, and are relying on
themselves and their own carefully tended gardens, will not find themselves
pinched between starvation and hostilities. Fortunately, the easiest produce
to grow is that most economical as foodstuffs. Humans have but to return to
their recent past and relearn these lessons.

Deep Quakes

One of the surest signs that the current eccentricity in weather patterns
and the increased magnetic diffusion exhibited by the Earth's core and the
warming of the oceans from the bottom up are not simply variations on the
norm, is the dramatic increase in deep earthquakes, as noted since the mid
1980s. This of course gets little media attention, just as the increasing
magnetic diffusion is not in the media, as they are difficult symptoms to
explain. The increase in deep earthquakes, those indicating plate adjustments
at the most fundamental level, are in particular a telling clue that a pole shift
is in the Earth's near future. Few earthquakes register at this level, as most
quakes registered by man are on the fragile and easily crumbled surface.

The snapping or crumbling surface affects mankind's habitat directly, so
that surface quakes are noticed. Deep quakes rock the boat but don't normally throw the crockery about, moving the plate as a whole rather than

adjusting the surface. Therefore deep quakes result in little damage, and thus get little media coverage. However, as a symptom heralding the coming pole shift, they are extremely significant and more importantly, unexplainable in any other context. The increase in deep earthquakes is currently reported, but as these increase and attention is focused on this curious symptom, the current availability of these statistics may be blocked. Earthquake data is reported by location, date and time, Richter scale magnitude, and depth. Expect that latter piece of information to be dropped in the future.

Booms and Flashes

Increasingly as the pole shift nears, the Earth will give evidence of the compression and tension in her surface by what humans will perceive to be thunder or sonic booms. The mechanism is in fact the same, clapping air masses. Where thunder is caused by air masses separated by what is essentially a vacuum created by the superheating lightning bolt, and where sonic booms are caused by a compressed and thinned air mass colliding, pre-cataclysm booms are caused by heaving and falling in large bodies of water. For every earthquake compression adjustment there is, somewhere, a widening in a rift. Most often these rifts lie underwater, as water fills low-lying places. A widening rift does not jolt the bordering plates, it is a silent adjustment. However, the sea water rushing to fill the new void has an effect on the air masses above, creating a thin air mass and causing the air on all sides of this thin air space to rush in, and clap!

Flashes of light will accompanying the booms caused by heaving seas, leading the startled public to perceive that an explosion might have happened. As the booms happen over water, where could the spark for an explosion come from? These are indeed related to the booms, and are indeed explosions, and emerge from the same source. Great pools of methane gas lie trapped under the surface in certain areas of the world, due to rotting debris trapped under layers of volcanic ash or sediment. Just as the booms indicate adjustments in the sea bed causing heaving water to clap, just so the flashes indicate adjustments in land masses allowing the methane gas to escape and on occasion spark into an explosion.

Illness

Increasingly, as the pole shift nears, the populace will take sick. This will take the form of known illnesses occurring more frequently, seemingly depressed immune systems, but will also appear as new and puzzling illnesses not seen before in the memory of man. The changes at the core of the Earth that have resulted in El Niño weather patterns and White Buffalo Calves and deformed frogs also affect man. Not only is the body asked to adapt to a changing environment, where radiation elements unknown to man are increasing, but various infectious agents are also influenced to behave differently. Exposure patterns are thus changed, with infections occurring in circumstances otherwise considered healthy. The germs are on the move. Their carriers are on the move. And thus humans are exposed to diseases that are so rare as to be undocumented in medical journals.

36
Countdown

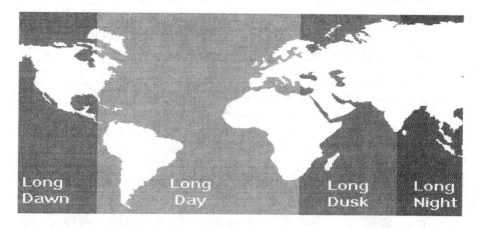

The pole shift will not take anyone by surprise, given the plethora of undeniable signs that something momentous is around the corner, such as increasing earthquakes and volcanic eruptions, intractable droughts and inexplicable downpours, and most telling of all, an increased slowing of the Earth's rotation. Nevertheless, the exact moment, day, or week to disrupt everyone's schedule and head for the hills or farm seems difficult to determine. For primitive peoples without mechanical clocks there is a countdown sign that can be scarcely ignored. The Earth moans, during her rotation slowing and stoppage, a sound not heard by humans except during earthquakes. Here, the moaning is chronic, essentially continuous, as though under a stress it cannot relieve with an earthquake, yet cannot bear in silence. For those who question the accuracy of their mechanical clocks, and who may have missed the presence of red dust due to living indoors, this moaning of the Earth is equivalent to the clanging of the fire marshal's bell. Here it comes, ready or not!

Rotation

The most dramatic sign will be a slowing rotation. Where at the present time, this rate is enough to cause an occasional fraction of a second, per year, of adjustment to the world clock, this will soon change. This increasing slowdown will get diminishing press coverage, as clocks are quietly adjusted behind the scenes and the public told their clocks must be running fast. But there will be a point in time, a few days ahead of when rotation stops, when this will get blatantly obvious. When one wakes up in the morning, finding it to be dark outside rather than a breaking dawn, yet the clocks in the house and the entire neighborhood confirm that it is indeed the morning hour—this is a countdown sign. Rotation will completely stop in a day or so, with such a dawn followed by an evening where the Sun seems reluctant to set, setting hours later than usual, and then rotation stops completely.

Should one line these planets up side by side, the Earth would look to the 12th Planet as the Moon does to the Earth. There is no contest. In the final days, as the 12th Planet begins passing between the Earth and its Sun, the Earth slows in its rotation and actually stops for several days. This is recorded in written history and spoken folklore, worldwide, as a long day or night. Rotation stops because the magnetic influence of the giant comet has essentially gripped the Earth, with a predictable part of the Earth facing the approaching 12th Planet—the mid-Atlantic Ocean off the eastern seaboard of the United States. This part of the globe lines up over former lava flows from the renting apart of the continents, the mid-Atlantic rift, and is more intensely magnetized that other parts of the globe. Thus, the Atlantic lava beds are gripped, facing the Sun, facing the approaching 12th Planet coming up from the South along the rift, and causing both Europe, the Americas, and Africa to be on the long-day side of the Earth.

Comet Tail

A second countdown sign is a fine red dust, unmistakable as it cannot be confused with any other natural occurrence. Ponds and rivers turn red, the blood color mentioned in the Bible's *Book of Revelations*, with this iron ore dust giving the water a brackish taste. This countdown sign comes almost in step with the rapid slowing in rotation, as the 12th Planet must be between the Earth and the Sun for the trash in its tail to be sweeping the Earth. Again, this occurs a day or so before rotation stops, and travel will become difficult if not impossible once it does. The tail of the 12th Planet has dust, gases, stones, boulders, and moons. The comet's tail sweeps the Earth—dust, gases, stones and boulders all. The comet's moons hug close, so do not come in range, but all else is a massive onslaught on the Earth's atmosphere.

The first to arrive is a fine red iron dust. This dust, already oxygenated, does not burn. The next is a fine gravel, dropping in places like hail stones. By this time the Earth's upper atmosphere is tearing away, dispelled into space and no longer snug as a mantle around the Earth, so this trash no longer burns as most meteors do. Now comes an occasional boulder, falling without resistance on the hapless Earth. Those who would escape the wicked lick of this tail are advised to take shelter against cliffs, in caves, in valleys, or under metal roofs. Its passage is swift, a matter of days, and the ending abrupt.

Panic

In spite of denial and suppression of talk about the approaching cataclysms, when the Earth slows and then stops in its rotation the truth will be known. How could it not? There will be in general two responses in those previously unaware or in denial—flight and paralysis. Paralysis needs no explanation: sitting at home and drinking the liquor cabinet dry; baking a cake and throwing a party just to pass the hours more quickly in a diversion. In paralysis, no attempt to deal with the impending disaster is made. Of course, those who remain in denial even when night does not become day or the day refuses to end are in a type of paralysis. There will be those who will go to work and attempt to shop and attend social functions, as though nothing were amiss. Activity and familiarity tend to comfort.

Those who sense the seriousness of the situation will attempt to flee. If they have been informed, but scoffed, they may know what to do and where to go, and attempt to do so in great haste. Belongings and even loved ones left behind, doors left wide open, heading for the hills, for cover, to escape the city. If they have not been informed they will attempt to flee anyway, going in all directions. Some, faced with a baking Sun that will not relent will crouch under structures that will ultimately crush them, knowing no better. Some, hearing the Earth moaning beneath them, will take to the air or sea if possible, only to find themselves eventually dashed out of the skies by hurricane winds or crushed under waves hundreds of feet high. Those who have prepared and placed themselves and their loved ones in safe places will not find themselves overrun at the last minute. This is not because last minute stragglers are not trying to join them. This is because the stragglers cannot reach them.

Imagine the situation. On one side of the Earth the Sun is not setting. Temperatures rise. Machines break down. The telephone lines are jammed, and highways are blocked with disabled cars. Those on foot don't last long in the heat. Essentially, all is heat-locked. People will seek a cool spot and wait for whatever comes. On the other side of the Earth, perpetual night is reigning. Here activity is not heat-locked, but is rather sleep-locked. Businesses do not open, because everyone is confused. Are the clocks broken? Telephone lines are also jammed, and lack of coordination is evident everywhere. The night shift goes home, eventually, exhausted, but the day shift never shows up. The traveler attempting to drive somewhere finds gas stations unattended and cars out of gas blocking the roads. So those becoming aware of the situation at the last minute do not go anywhere, essentially, whether they want to or not.

The exception might be the wealthy or powerful who have maintained a plane, fueled and ready, and find all these arrangements working well when the crisis arrives. Private landing strips and well-stocked country estates make a last-minute flight to safety possible. These are the types of plans being made by members of the establishment who, while tending to themselves, are working hard to keep the rest of humanity in blind ignorance.

Safe Places

Many factors go into what constitutes a safe place during a pole shift. Mountains may ride over flat land abutting the mountain range, but if the plates are being pulled apart or sliding past each other, this will not occur. Land is affected by the plate it rides upon, and if that plate is forced under another, the land may drop below sea level and become submerged. Likewise if the plate is forced to ride atop another under pressure, the land may rise above sea level. All coastal areas will be subject to sloshing water, but some coastal areas will be the safest due to hot land or violent earthquakes, in which case going out to sea in boats may be the best chance of survival.

Gently rolling hills may afford good protection from the hurricane force winds, but where the hills are composed of loose soil that will shift unpredictably or slide, it may be safer out in the open lying flat.

Areas subjected to mountain building in the recent past can be anticipated to be the subject of mountain building again during the coming pole shift. This includes the Rockies west of the Continental Divide and the Himalayas. The spine of mountains running the length of South America is also highly subject to trauma during pole shifts. Humans during former cataclysms ran to safety from the winds first, as these were the first to arise. Thus they went into the valleys, the low areas, and it is here that the heat from friction in lower plates rubbing is the hottest. The legends report that those seeking shelter in valleys jumped into rivers to cool themselves, only to find the water boiling. In both the Americas the land east of the Continental Divide tends to go for a ride across the plains to the east.

Coastal lands can be pulled below sea level. The Atlantic is anticipated to widen greatly during the coming pole shift, and this will affect England as well as the islands lying to the west of her. England, however, will not go completely under the waves but will experience an overall drop in sea level. Due to its attachment to the plate including India, the western portion of Australia will suddenly go under the waves. This will seem, to the stunned residents, as though a tidal wave were steadily moving inland, and where the crest of the wave will not at first be high, the waters will just keep rising until all not afloat are drowned. Central America will also disappear under the waves when the Pacific shortens, the many small plates being the point of least resistance against larger plates surrounding Central America.

The low-lying land bordering the Atlantic will be subjected to inundation from tidal waves during the pole shift to an astonishing degree. Waves hundreds of feet high carry a tremendous force of water behind them, which breaks barriers before it and climbs up and over barriers such as hills that stand in its way. Where France connects the Mediterranean and the Atlantic near the border with Spain, it will be subject to sloshing water from both water sources. As water bodies of different sizes develop sloshing with different rhythms, this area of France can expect a devastating possibility of having a wave come in from both sources at once. This will result in tidal bores roaring up into the valleys of the Alps near Switzerland.

Rivers can present dangers not imagined. The Mississippi River will be overflowing its banks during the time of the pole shift, as much due to back pressure from the gulf, forcing the river to back up, as from downpours upriver. Horrified residents in the bordering states will find water descending upon them not from the gulf, but from inland valleys not normally flooded. They must watch their backs as well as their fronts. Assume a rampaging Mississippi, equivalent to at least twice the flood stage ever experienced. Water softens the blows both from the jolts of earthquakes and, if one is underwater, from flying debris. However, water will carry one with it, and the swimmers or submarines may find themselves hundreds of miles inland when a tidal wave recedes, or far from any shore.

Caverns or man-made tunnels in traumatized mountain areas will not be safe. In past cataclysms, faced with high winds and hailstones, many sought shelter in caves or caverns. This as often brought death as salvation, as these hollow places were formed during mountain building in the past, so seeking shelter in them is equivalent to trying to avoid traffic by standing in the middle of a busy highway. Subterranean cavities that would be safe are so deep and thickly surrounded by rock that they are essentially a bubble in a slab of granite. As humans run the risk of being trapped or crushed and could expect no rescue help afterwards, this option is far less safe than other options.

Cities will not be safe. Beyond collapsing buildings that will be virtual death traps, gas lines and oil and gasoline storage will be in flames, and the whole place likely to become an inferno. During violent earthquakes, those humans who survived were surrounded by the least structure. The single structure that resists tearing away in hurricane force winds and can withstand the magnitude of earthquakes expected is a continuous oval, partly laid into the earth. A domed structure gives the least resistance to winds, and where the dome is continuous, it provides a shape most resistance to earthquake damage. Wind sweeps over but does not lift this, and the sharp jolt of an earthquake will not crack a continuous form. An oval will also settle into its pre-quake position under the jiggling influence of after shocks. Made of metal, such a structure also protects from fire and hailstones.

37
The Pole Shift

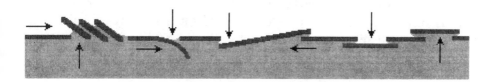

When the 12th Planet positions itself between the Earth and the Sun, things suddenly change. The Earth then has its greatest advocate for its previous magnetic alignment, the Sun, negated. The Earth hears only the magnetic voice of the 12th Planet, so to speak, which stands between the Earth and its former magnetic commander, the Sun. The strength of the magnetic field will be such that the 12th Planet's north pole, angled essentially in the same direction as the Earth's north pole, forces the Earth's north pole to evade the pressure and accommodate its larger brother by swinging the bulge of Brazil to the north pole. The Earth's core is more sensitive to the magnetic alignment than the crust. The core grips the crust, and is not as liquid as one might think. There is friction, so there is the tendency for the whole to move as one.

The pole shift is in fact a movement of the interior of the Earth, the core, to come into alignment with the 12th Planet. The 12th Planet, due to its massive size in comparison to the Earth, dominates the magnetic scene, and it is in this regard that gravity comes into the Pole Shift equation. The Earth's crust resists aligning with the giant comet, being caught in a web of magnetic pulls from its immediate neighborhood. In other words, the Earth's crust wants to stay with the old, established, magnetic pull, while the core of the Earth, having less allegiance and attachment to the neighborhood, listens to the new voice. There is a great deal of tension that builds between the crust of the Earth and the core of the Earth. This tension is released when the core of the Earth breaks with the crust, and moves. However, the core of the Earth drags the crust with it as it turns to align anew.

The pole shift is therefore sudden, taking place in what seems to be minutes to humans involved in the drama, but which actually takes place during the better part of an hour. There are stages, between which the human spectators, in shock, are numb. At first there is a vibration of sorts, a jiggling, as the crust separates in various places from the core. Then there is a slide, where the crust is dragged, over minutes, to a new location, along with the core. During the slide, tidal waves move over the Earth along the coast lines, as the water is not attached and can move independently. The water tends to stay where it is, the crust moving under it, essentially. When the core finds itself aligned, it churns about somewhat, settling, but the crust, more solid and in motion, proceeds on. This is in fact where mountain building and massive earthquakes occur, just as car crashes do their damage on the point of impact, when motion must stop.

Weak spots among the Earth's crust give way. The Pacific Ocean will shorten, and the Atlantic will widen. Subducting plates will subduct greatly. Mountain building will occur suddenly, primarily increasing in areas already undergoing mountain building. All told, the better part of an hour, but at certain stages, only minutes. Plants survive as they are rooted and their seeds are everywhere, and animals, including man, survive because they travel with the moving plates of the Earth and experience no more severe a shock when the plates stop moving than they would during a Richter-9 earthquake. Where mountain building occurs when the plates stop moving, the stoppage is not simply a sudden jolt, like a car hitting a brick wall. All is in motion, and the stoppage is more like a car hitting a barrier of sand-filled plastic barrels—a series of small jolts, occurring in quick succession.

Earthquake

During the pole shift all plates on Earth are on the move, and the jolt occurs at the sudden stop when the crust stops moving. This is when the Richter-9-equivalent earthquakes, which we have termed Richter 15, because the scope is far larger than Richter 9, will be felt worldwide. The earthquakes following the pole shift will be no more wrenching than earthquakes due to plate adjustments under normal circumstances. The moving plates, suddenly slamming into each other as they start to slow down, will create a domino effect not unlike a multiple car crash. One plate slams into another as the first plates slows down, creating a domino effect that rapidly ricochets around the world, within minutes.

There is no delay in this motion, as each plate is solid and what affects one edge affects the far edge, when the entire plate is in motion. Thus, the earthquakes come all at once and rapidly settle down to an adjustment phase, within minutes. But due to the immensity of the adjustment, with many plates in barely tenable positions, there will be many aftershocks, most occurring within the first few weeks. These will range from Richter 8 on down, but in no case will be as great as the initial shock during the pole shift. They will rapidly diminish, reduced to annoying tremors after a few weeks.

Plate Adjustments

During severe pole shifts, land rises and drops, sometimes moving under the waves. This is caused quite naturally by moving plates, which adjust to being squeezed against each other or pulled apart. Suddenly submerged land can be the result of either dynamic. Likewise, land long under the sea can suddenly pop up, presenting gasping and dying sea life and deep muck that eventually dries to form new and very fertile soil.

Continents pulled apart, as in the steadily widening St. Lawrence Seaway or the African Great Rift Valley, can cause land along the perimeter to rise, as the stretch over the curvature of the Earth has been removed, so that the natural buoyancy or shape of the land can take effect. Thus the land in the New England area of America is expected to lift somewhat when the St. Lawrence Seaway tears further apart. Continents pulled apart, as in the widening Atlantic rift, cause sinking land along the shores as the curvature of the Earth causes the midpoint between continents being pulled apart to drop. There is less crust to cover the magma underneath, so that rips in the crust form at the weakest or lowest points. Ripped crust at the bottom of ocean rifts allows heavy land along the edge to lose its support, thus it can sink into the magma.

Continents squeezed together invariably find one plate or the other acting as the loser, subducting or fracturing into pieces that slant at an angle to form new mountain ranges. For every adjustment where the continents or land are being wrenched apart, there is a collateral squeezing of plates elsewhere. On the Earth, this squeezing occurs along the Pacific Rim, with Japan and the Philippines, along with the whole western coast of the Americas, getting the brunt of this squeeze. Where this squeezing causes new land to rise is where plates fracture, freeing a portion of a plate to act on its own. Squeezing can force land under, to relieve the stress, but can also pop land up, so that it rides above another plate. This is often the case, and thus as a result of the coming pole shift, new land will emerge near Antarctica between the tip of Africa and South America due to pressure against the western coast of South America.

Continental Rip

Tearing of continents is less traumatic than it would seem to humans, who imagine the continents as one plate and think of how lumber resists being torn, metal bends and twists before tearing, and a rope of fibers resists while the fibers snap one by one. Continents are in fact an overlay of many plates, and faults are where most of the plates have fractured in the same place. The continents are attached because some of the plates have not fractured. This concept should not be that hard to grasp if one considers that many land faults have a slip-slide relationship to the plates, which are moving in different directions past each other. This motion would not be possible if the plates were not, in fact, separate. Thus, ripping apart of continents is no more traumatic than subducting or slip-sliding.

The land along the edges generally retains its altitude, as this was determined by the thickness of the plates, thus its buoyancy on the sea of lava. Solid land is composed to a great degree from the lighter elements, which rose to the top during the early cooling of planet Earth, and thus formed the floating crust.

38
Wind, Water, and Fire

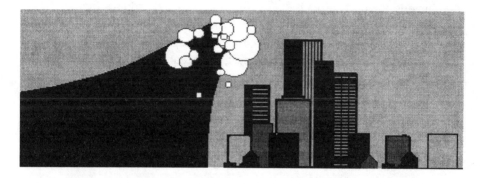

As great as the danger to humans and the fauna and flora of the Earth that earthquakes bring, greater still is the devastation that the shifting waters will bring. There are several factors at play. Water is more liquid than the core of the Earth, and certainly more liquid than terra firma. Where the Earth, dragged by its core, is shifting into alignment with the 12th Planet, its waters resist greatly. Thus the waters slosh over the nearby land, in the direction opposite to the shift. This is lessened by a tendency of the waters directly under the giant comet to rise up to meet the comet. The waters heap up, in what appear to be giant waves. This tends to lessen the sloshing over a shoreline on the comet side, but has no effect on the water's movement on the far side of the Earth.

During the hour of the pole shift, when the crust of the Earth is being dragged along with the core such that the Earth's north pole is turning away from the north pole of the 12th Planet, and the Earth's south pole is pulling up to face it, several things are happening at once. A synergy, or playoff, therefore occurs. The stage is set by what occurs during the days preceding the pole shift, when the Earth's rotation slows and then stops, within a day, and stands with her mid-Atlantic ridge facing the Sun where the 12th Planet is passing. During these few days, less than a week, when rotation has stopped, the waters of her oceans flow toward the poles and away from her fat equator. An equalization occurs, the waters settling evenly, where normally the rotation pulls the water by centrifugal force to where the motion is fastest, at the equator. Thus, when the pole shift itself occurs, the oceans have pulled away from the tropical shores and flooded the frozen poles.

Tidal waves are caused by several factors, but to those living along the coasts, the effect is the same. When the Earth rolls her north pole away from the Sun and the passing 12th Planet, the water resists, and thus there is flooding where the oceans meet land moving into the water, and a drawing away of the oceans on those shores which are pulling away from the stagnant ocean water. However, for the most part, the oceans move with the land as one. When the motion stops, the water, not being attached to the core as the crust is, fails to put on the brakes and continues its motion, and thus tidal waves occur where only hours before the water had drawn away from the shores. A third factor affects the height and force of tidal waves, and that is the movement of plates where the bowl that holds the ocean water may become larger or smaller.

Where the Atlantic widens and tears apart the North American continent along what is already her seaway, there will be more places for the water to pool than there will be water available, which will cause water gathered at the poles to rush toward these parts of the globe. Where the African Continent continues to rupture away from its large neighbors, or where there is a rupture along the land fault bordering India, there will be a temporary lowering of water in the Indian Ocean, which will draw water from where it has gathered at the south pole. Where the Pacific shortens dramatically, subducting India and western Australia and subducting plates along both the American continents, the water in the Pacific will find its bowl suddenly smaller, and will rise along shores on both sides.

Given the size of the Pacific ocean, and the ability of her waters to rush over low-lying areas in Central America or around Australia, tidal waves along the Pacific coast are not substantially larger than along other coasts. The Pacific will already be low on the coasts along her equator due to the waters movement toward the poles when rotation stops for several days. Given that the Atlantic and Pacific oceans will equalize in size during this next pole shift, and finding the oceans in the Pacific more full, relatively speaking, the water at the poles will pour into the Atlantic or Indian Ocean, in preference to pouring into the Pacific. And then the broad expanse of the Pacific can absorb any shrinking of the Pacific bowl, as each acre of ocean takes its share of the rise, lessening the effect on the shores.

All of these actions, where water is set in motion, create chaotic motion. Water may be in a position to suddenly drop, having been heaped high in proportion to the surrounding water. Cold arctic water may have been thrust on top of warmer water, and as with tornadoes, when the thrust that caused this situation stops, the cold water will suddenly drop, creating a vortex. These giant whirlpools have been recorded by the ancients, as their ships on occasion were caught in them during a pole shift. When one of the fleet managed to escape, the tale was told and recorded. However, as with many pole-shift-generated tales, these tales are taken to be myths.

Wind Storms

At the shift, the surface of the Earth will move, in just under an hour, more than a quarter turn. Massive earthquakes and tidal waves occur when this motion stops, and hurricane-force winds occur world wide during this shift. During the shift, the atmosphere of the Earth does several things, all at once. It drags along with the Earth, to which it is attracted, being primarily more involved with gravity attraction straight down. Just as the waters in your oceans move with the Earth as it turns, the atmosphere, being a lighter and more mobile ocean, moves too.

It moves as a mass, pushing on air in other places and likewise, itself being pushed. Thus, even in those places on the Earth which are not moving during the shift, but are pivot points, the air is turbulent. It swirls, as circular motion in air masses is the response to conflicting forces, as seen in the circular motion of tornadoes and hurricanes. Humans wishing to prepare for these violent winds should anticipate a force equal to their familiar hurricanes, not tornado force, although tornadoes will be spawned. Stay below the Earth's surface, lie low, and tie down everything you wish to find when it's over.

Fire Storms

Fire storms are caused by reactions of atmospheric gasses to the turmoil going on. Hydrocarbons are in essence created, due to the flashes of lightning and intense heat due to passage over open volcanoes, and these hydrocarbons rain down, afire, at times. With the atmosphere scattered, chemicals in the comets tail similar to petrochemicals do not flash in a quick consummation into water and carbon dioxide, but descend close to the surface of the Earth before bursting into flame—a fire storm, killing all beneath it. All this has been reported in ancient times, as humans observed accompaniments to the cataclysms. This type of activity sets forests afire. Where vegetation regrows, from seeds and roots, many areas will nevertheless be denuded of vegetation for some time.

Oil, gas, and coal deposits are indeed the product of biological elements decomposing under great heat and pressure, but this is not the only source of these products. They form in the atmosphere under certain conditions, where intense heat from exploding volcanoes and continuous lightning create the equivalent of petrochemicals from the carbon, hydrogen, and oxygen in the atmosphere. Petrochemicals that form in the sky, where they fail to burn due to lack of free oxygen, soak into the fractured ground and become trapped during the settling process that aftershocks provide for many years after a pole shift.

39
The Aftermath

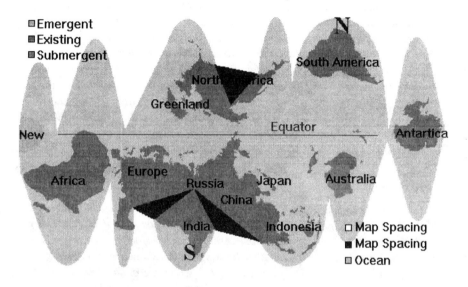

Emergent
Existing
Submergent

N

South America

North America

Greenland

Equator

Antartica

New

Africa

Europe

Russia

Japan

China

Australia

India

Indonesia

S

Map Spacing
Map Spacing
Ocean

The day of a significant pole shift, such as will occur on this next passage of the 12th Planet, is one no human on Earth will be able to ignore. For most, it will be a most terrible day.

The Wait

Those who have had no forewarning will be no worse off than those who have heard rumors but have been unable to make changes in their life to prepare. In fact, having no forewarning will almost be a blessing for those unable to prepare, as in this way they will not agonize over choices made. Those who have prepared will be in a state of high anxiety, imagining the worst. Regardless of whether a human realizes what is about to happen but has been unable to take themselves to safety, or has no realization, the effect is the same. They wait for what is to come next. As we have described, this waiting can take the form of distractions such as parties or denial such as continuing with the daily routine

ZetaTalk

as though everything were normal, but for most this waiting is a type of breath holding. They are in shock, from the time they realize that the Earth has stopped rotating until the pole shift, they are essentially in shock, for days.

Tidal Waves

For those along coast lines, the hour when the Earth's crust moves along with the core to its new position is not the time of trauma until the Earth's core and crust stop. It is then that massive tidal waves roll slowly up into the coastal areas, first on one side of a body of water and then, later when the water sloshes back, on the other side. Both tides are equally devastating. Being on high ground along a coast line is no safety factor if the water has nowhere to go, as the press of water behind the wave head will force the water up when meeting a barrier, so one is flooded anyway. Riding the wave results in being dashed against barriers, and allowing the wave to engulf one is a certain drowning, fortunately a painless death. Thus, those along the coast lines die from tidal waves, almost invariably, if they are not dead already.

Earthquakes

For those inland beyond the reach of tidal waves, the earthquakes are devastating. All but the flimsiest of housing is wrenched so violently that they collapse, crushing and trapping those inside. Those inside tents or straw huts will find themselves, along with their housing, jerked sideways, but aside from scrapes and bruises, relatively unharmed. Lying on the ground during this time is in and of itself a protection, as friction along the ground prevents one from being hurled. In the cities, structures collapse, creating in the extreme— everywhere—the scenario seen after major earthquakes. The injured die from lack of treatment, and the living soon sicken from drinking sewage-contaminated water, and with transportation blocked on all sides, starvation soon takes its toll also.

Plate Movement

Those living on subducting plates that border the oceans will find themselves covered with a depth of ocean water that they cannot resist. They will surely drown. Those situated where rapid subduction occurs, on areas above sea level, may find themselves on hot earth during the moments following a pole shift. The crust stops moving, and the plates in essence slam into each other, like a train whose engine suddenly comes to a stop. Here height helps, as the greater the distance from where friction between the crusts is creating heat, the better. The heat can be great enough to melt rock, as witnesses who have

240

survived such terrifying sights attest. Volcanoes, active and inactive, will explode violently, covering the surrounding areas in raining rock and dust and superheating the air so that all life nearby is extinguished in a wink.

Fire Storms

Lightning and fire storms from falling walls of flaming petrochemicals, formed during the interaction of gasses with volcanic heat and continuous lightning, cannot be predicted. They can happen world wide, and as with the hurricane-force winds are a feature of the atmosphere, not the land mass. While they are rare, these fire storms are devastating, and burn all beneath the falling wall of flame in a holocaust. The horrified victims have little chance to even realize what is happening before they are engulfed and lose consciousness from lack of oxygen. As with spontaneous human combustion, the victim is unconscious during the burning process. Protection from this rare chance of devastation is best attained by sheltering under a metal roof, which will not burn.

Starvation

In rural areas survivors find themselves dealing less with the collapse of civilization than with climate changes. At first, stores are eaten until gone, and then real concern about the inability to grow crops sets in. Will the Sun never shine through the clouds? More than any other reason, this is what causes pole-shift survivors to wander—they are seeking a land where the sun shines as it used to, sure that they are simply on the wrong side of the Earth for some reason. Starvation soon has survivors eating everything in sight, chewing on old leather, eating the branches of dead trees, but still the gnawing hunger continues. Death by starvation is also relatively painless, as a stupor sets in. The mind is dulled, and languor envelopes the human, who is essentially asleep when death comes.

Climate Change

The pole shift, of course, radically affects the climate of every place on Earth. How could it not? The equator has changed, and formerly temperate and even polar areas now find themselves under the hot, continuous equatorial sun. Inhabitants of these areas may find themselves subject to severe sunburn, for the first time in their lives, and, not understanding the phenomenon, they will not know what to do. Other inhabitants, formerly in the equator, will quickly freeze to death. The temperature plunges, unremittingly, and they are ill prepared. This is, all told, a relatively benign death, as the hypothermic body becomes dreamy and seemingly falls asleep. Few areas will find the climate remaining the same, by coincidence having the same relative latitude as before.

Over time the plants and animals change, accommodating the climatic change. Plants, in particular, are hard hit, as they are sensitive to the temperature, humidity, and exposure to sun and wind. The die-off is massive, but certain other opportunists survive. Over time, there is a creep that occurs, such that from places where the climate has remained the same, plants grow outward toward where they find conditions hospitable. The opportunists who took over, preempting all the stragglers, find they are being pushed, steadily, to assume their former status. Animals, being mobile, are less hard hit, and either travel or adjust their day and night to the new conditions. After a time, a few centuries, the Earth looks much as it did before, only this time with new poles, a new equator, and newly established temperate zones.

All of this activity is modulated at first by the gloom caused by volcanic dust. Strong sunlight occurs only occasionally, in certain locations. In the main there is dusk, ever present dusk. Where there is vegetation die back, this is caused in fact more by the lack of sunshine than by any climatic changes. Animal life is impacted by the lack of food, too, more than climatic changes. However, after a couple of decades, the skies clear, and then the climatic changes are the stronger determinant. Overall, the Earth's climate remains much as it is today, throughout and after the cataclysms. Initially, just after the pole shift, the local climate at any given point on the Earth will be a result of several factors.

Previous Climate

> *Previous climate, as for instance on a former polar ice cap, will have either a warming or cooling influence. This will only be extreme where ice packs linger or the ground is deeply frozen. Elsewhere, warming or cooling to temperatures appropriate to the new longitude occur within days.*

Long Day or Night

Placement on the day or night side of the Earth, when rotation stops for days preceding the pole shift and slowly begins again after the 12th Planet passes, is a factor. Again, this effect dissipates within days.

Volcanic Activity

Volcanic activity and the roiling of the Earth's core are factors that continue for some decades after a pole shift, just as they do during the decade preceding a pole shift. Overall, this activity has a slight warming influence, a few degrees at most, depending on location.

Cloud Cover

A dense cloud cover that lasts for decades is a factor, resulting from the volcanic activity and loss of atmosphere due to the stripping away that occurred during lashing by the comet's tail. The dust-filled clouds are low to the ground, and create a constant gloom. Rain occurs almost continuously. Where sunlight cannot penetrate and seldom manages to peek through this dense cloud cover, it does warm the Earth's atmosphere and thus its warming influence is not lost on the Earth. There will be less warmth from sunlight, but more warm, wet air.

Geography Change

As we have stated, the Atlantic will widen and the Pacific will narrow. Where the Pacific effect will cause sudden and violent subduction of several plates, which are already subducting, in the Atlantic the effect will be the opposite. A gulf will appear, with plates torn apart and the softer magma under the plates will be exposed to the cold Atlantic water. While this will harden the magma and establish new plate surface, there will be less support for the abridging plates, those that attach however remotely to the shorelines of the Americas, Europe, and Africa. These non-supported plates will sink, somewhat, bringing their formerly above-water land masses down under the water in many places. As an instance, Europe, and in particular the western islands of Britain and Ireland, will find itself more affected than some other parts of the globe.

After the pole shift the Earth begins rotating again, with its new poles in the same relative position to the solar system as today. In other words, whatever part of the Earth is north, magnetically, after the shift, will become the new north pole. The pole shift, with consequent realignment of the poles, will place the new equator over formerly frozen lands. Greenland, Canada, Alaska, Siberia, and Europe will be affected by the new equator. This will not mean that these areas will be lush, right away. The temperate zones, not all that lush to begin with, will find themselves after the cataclysms in a warm state, but with little vegetation. Past cataclysms have regularly rearranged the Earth's geography and climate zones, as the Earth attests. The continents, once one large land mass, were torn apart, temperate or tropical areas suddenly freezing up and covering over with ice and snow that never melts, and frozen wastelands gradually melting and warming to sustain life once again. Mountains in mountain-building areas were pushed higher and subducting plates were suddenly slid under the overplate.

While the land rearranges, the oceans slosh about but eventually settle into the lower areas. Coastal spots that had formerly been above the water line may now be under the waves, and likewise plates that had been submerged may now be dry land. How much land pokes above the waves depends on how deep and wide the ocean rifts are, but historically the landmass in total has remained the same. Continents do not disappear, but plates abutting continents or close to the ocean surface may rise and fall, depending on the plate action around the site and elsewhere around the globe. If plate action thrusts formerly submerged land out from under the sea, then the settling oceans have less area to settle into and consequently beaches worldwide may rise. Likewise, a sudden yaw in a mid-ocean rift may cause beaches worldwide to drop, but inevitably the yaw is matched by a crunch elsewhere, where land will subduct.

New Rotation

After the 12th Planet passes, the Earth's rotation begins again due to the factors that guide rotation of the planets in your solar system. Many humans assume rotation to be simply leftover motion resulting from some past activity such as the big bang, but rotation is guided by gravitational and electromagnetic influences on the liquid cores of planets and moons. Parts of the core move away from or toward these influences, dragging the crust with it, and as the turning motion brings those parts of the core back to where they don't want to be, motion is reinstituted and continued. For the Earth, frozen in place at the moment of passage, rotation begins again within a day after the 12th Planet moves from its influential place between the Earth and the Sun.

Rotation restarts, at first slowly but then picking up speed until a day on planet Earth is much as it used to be. Just as rotation stops within a day, just so rotation returns within a day, much to the relief of the frantic survivors who fear the long day or night they have been experiencing will never end. The Earth's rotation returns to her normal pace within days of the 12th Planet's passage. In fact, the return occurs faster than a mirror image of the stoppage of rotation, due to the 12th Planet leaving the solar system at a faster clip than the speed at which it entered. When the 12th Planet enters the solar system, it begins what is essentially a dive for the Sun. As a repulsion force prevents contact, the 12th Planet in essence ricochets off the Sun, zooming past and on out of the solar system.

Thus, within a day of the passage, the Earth begins to rotate again, and within a day or two has returned to her normal pace or rotation. Nevertheless, during an adjustment period that may last several months or even years, rotation may be a bit erratic. One should not set the clock on a 24-hour day, at least not at first.

Polar Melt

After a pole shift, ice on the former poles invariably melt and soften, while the new poles take on layer after layer of ice and snow. This pace is not matched by the pace of ice build-up, because polar-cap building only stabilizes after some centuries when evaporation and melting at glacial edges equals the arrival of newly fallen snow. In the meantime the waters rise worldwide, several hundred feet, and then recede again. This pace is gradual, so that coastal settlements have plenty of time to relocate, an exercise they find they must do repeatedly.

The melting will occur faster than the reforming, for there are more factors at play for ice to form than for ice to melt. The ice over the former poles will now be facing the Sun, and the melt rate will proceed based on the air temperature and the absorption of solar rays, both of which will be high, because the old poles will now be situated essentially at the new equator. Any water at the new poles will freeze, but the buildup of ice on a pole is not altogether from the water that happened to be there when the pole took position. The buildup comes from precipitation, and this accumulates over hundreds of years. The Earth, therefore, will experience more water in its oceans for some time after the cataclysms.

Whereas new ice caps take centuries to fully form, existing poles thrust under an equatorial sun melt rapidly. The melting ice caps will thus raise the sea level, worldwide, by 650 to 700 feet within two years. Survivors living below this level will find themselves moving repeatedly as rivers begin to overflow their banks and marsh areas become lakes. Those planning survival sites should consider this factor as well as escape routes for survivors who might be trapped by the rising water. Survival sites should be selected for their ability to link to other land areas that will be above the water line as well, so that technologies and skills can be shared among the survivors. Survivors thus will find it possible rather than impossible to visit each other in a new world without maps, and certainly without guidelines for boats setting out on what will seem to be an endless sea.

40
Impact on Society

How would the existing governments be maintained in a world having undergone a cataclysm such as we describe? The existence of electricity will be spotty. Communications will in the main return to what it was in the previous century, by letter or carrier. The concept of legislature even at the county level would be difficult to maintain, much less at the state or federal level. Add into this the fact that the geography will change. Some lands will disappear, and others will rise from the seas. The poles will align in different parts of the world. What is north? What is south? Maps previously drawn up will be useless.

We are not describing a world where the established government is likely to continue as it was. We are describing a world where new forms of governing will emerge. The type will depend on the nature of the group of people. As we have detailed, there will be an increasing separation of service-to-others from service-to-self. Those groups oriented to service-to-others will not require the same controls that are required today. Rather than the problem of citizens stealing from each other, held in check only by the enforcement of law, these new communities will share. Consideration will be the rule, rather than the rule of law. For those groups oriented increasingly to service-to-self, no laws or corps of police would hold the self-serving actions in check. There, the rule of law is supplanted by the rule of the strong.

How will the governments take being so supplanted? Will they attempt to collect taxes, order cooperation, or demand allegiance? Some lone individuals will attempt to do so, perhaps in small bands, but where there is no food, and the citizenry is essentially homeless, these attempts will turn about on the so-called representatives of the people. Where is the government assistance? What does the government anticipate doing for its citizenry? Why, when the government was assuring the populace that they should not be alarmed by the approaching comet, should the populace now give any heed to the so called government? On the local level, there may be some continuance, according to the competence of the local government. Leadership will have to be earned.

Increasingly as the year 2003 approaches, there will be sculpting of reserves in the U.S. for not only the military but also for what is termed a carry-on government. Those whose lives have been in government service cannot imagine life otherwise. As the population would be likely to swarm onto military bases, demanding to be fed, those bases that will be set aside for a government recoup will be made undesirable to the public—the storage of biological warfare components, nuclear warheads, or armaments likely to explode during massive earthquakes. There is no way for the public to determine which report of storage of undesirables is true or untrue, and we are not advising that people go to military bases. In truth, all such locales, whether the story was true or not, will be undesirable.

Any survivors close to such a military depot or processing center for biological weapons disposal or nuclear weapons reserves will find themselves equally distressed. If the stories are true, then they are living, if living at all, steeped in poison during the Aftertime. If the stories are not true, then they are living close to former government workers and military who want to reestablish a government. The rationale is that the populace will be better off with this governance, so they are doing a service. In truth, there is nothing such a tattered remnant of a federal government could do for the populace that they could not do better for themselves. Naturally, the first thing these former government workers will be looking to do is impose taxes, and without a money base, this will be in the form of food and supplies.

Death Rate

The Earth is habitable after the cataclysm, and this is why the human species has continued through previous cataclysms. Life is rough, and life is short. The infant mortality is horrific. The strong survive, and where there is communal cooperation among caring people, the odds are not really that bad. Habitability varies, depending on location. Volcanic eruptions continue from activated volcanoes that take some time to settle down. The rains seem continuous, but plant life does not mind this as much as the mammals trying to get dry. Diets are not as varied as before, as far as staples go, but in other regards are more varied. Those who survive learn to eat everything, including bugs. Bugs are numerous, growing in great numbers in the humidity, and living off the tissue from the dead, which seems to be everywhere.

During past cataclysms the human population was also decimated, but as primitive conditions prevailed, death from earthquake damage was slight, and almost all the survivors were familiar with farming practices. Housing during past cataclysms was light, made of straw or wood or cloth as in tents, and this splintered or blew away during earthquakes rather than landing on and crushing the inhabitants. Unless the humans were unlucky enough to be in the path of a tidal wave or lava flow or standing on heaving or hot earth— they survived. Following past cataclysms, the survivors did not have much less after the cataclysms than they had had before, as they had been living a bare-survival existence as is. Life became harder, of course, as one could plant but would find no harvest and domesticated animals soon died from lack of feed. Fewer and fewer fish were in the streams, fruit and nut trees failed to bear, and produce normally harvested from the wild suffered in like manner. The survivors found themselves faced with having to be resourceful, eating whatever could be found—bark, bugs, moss, leaves, and on occasion each other.

The coming pole shift will differ from past cataclysms in several respects, however, all of which will bode ill for the present human populace. Consequently, we predict that 90% of the population will die as a direct or indirect result of the cataclysms, with the remainder polarizing due to the increasing polarization of the spiritual orientations. This Aftertime will be different, spiritually as well as physically. The population is urban, rather than rural. The Industrial Revolution, which has touched almost every country, has paved the way for a virtual flip-flop in the proportion of people dedicated to agriculture. In past eras almost 100% of the populace was farming, but in industrialized countries mechanized farming allows almost 100% of the population to be freed from this task. These survivors will have almost no concept of how to live off the land.

Because non-farming occupations are almost invariably physically idle, the population is soft. Even housekeeping, once exhausting, is slothful due to modern labor-saving devices. These survivors, out of shape, will find their soft bodies an unneeded burden during the Aftertime. High-rise buildings or even modern housing will be death traps during the cataclysms, trapping inhabitants if not crushing them. Where housing in the past was primarily single-storey shacks with straw or lightweight roofs, today such a domicile would never be considered. Housing must be solid, and crowded cities built up, stacking people on top of one another in buildings that will invariably tumble during the massive earthquakes that accompany a cataclysm.

Coastal areas are crowded, being considered prime living space and the populace having been freed from the necessity of farming. Cities of millions will go under gigantic tidal waves, and none will be found living when the waters recede. Man has created poisons and weapons that will be turned against him during and following the cataclysms. Chemical tanks will explode, spewing their contents, and an armed populace will find weapons used to wrench precious food from those without weapons. Cannibalism will occur where food is so scarce that none is to be found anywhere, and the young will be taken first. Parents who defend their young will be killed and eaten also. Where in the past the urge to eat one another pitted the strong against the strong in battles that seldom were anything but a standstill, weapons such as handguns are a great equalizer. The one with the gun wins. Gunfights will also break out, and with no law enforcement, with murderous results.

Starvation

Except for those few who have prepared, humans surviving the cataclysms will find themselves without food. In the cities this will happen quickly, as fresh or frozen foods will spoil due to total power failure, and canned and dried goods will only go so far. Then what? Rural areas, where one would presume to find gardens put in and livestock in abundance, will not be much better off. The drought and irregular weather will have taken their toll, to say nothing of the cataclysms themselves. How long will a hungry farmer hand grain to his livestock? He will eat the grain himself and the livestock, and when he gets hungry enough he will eat his last breeding pair and his seed stock. Gone.

Planting and harvesting will not go on as before, as the gloom that follows a cataclysm is devastating to vegetation. If vegetation survives the droughts that precede the cataclysms and the hail and fire storms and high winds that occur during the cataclysms, then it must next survive an almost continual deluge and lack of sunlight. The comeback after a cataclysm is not, in the main, from domesticated plants and animals, although some dedicated farmers will bring their breeding pairs and seed stock through. The comeback is from wilderness areas, from sturdy roots that keep on trying and scattered seed that keeps on sprouting. In the meantime, humans starve.

Money

Money will begin to lose its value long before the cataclysms hit. This will be worldwide, and in almost all cultures. Why should this be the case, when, as we have stated, the majority of humanity will either be unaware of the coming cataclysms or in denial? The financial structure of the world's financial empires is really quite fragile. Look to the swings of the stock markets, the bond markets, and other speculations. Panic sets in at a moment's notice. The problem is that financial matters are based on human perceptions of worth. This moves about, even in the most stable of times. The value of an item increases during shortage, plummets during times of plenty, and otherwise is affected by various perceptions of being in the right place at the right time. There are gamblers aplenty in the financial arenas.

One of the reasons that financial giants among the elite seek to negate awareness of the alien presence is their fear of the repercussions on the financial markets. If they cannot negate awareness, they seek to minimize panic. Look to history, to see how little it took to create financial panics. What with the millennium approaching, and all the dire predictions made by many, true or untrue, many people worldwide will be on edge. Add to this the increasing crop failures, with consequent food shortages, affecting the markets in commodities. Humans of good heart concerned with survival through the cataclysms are advised not to look to the money markets for assistance. Put your money into land and stable structures, documentation on the technologies and scientific knowledge of today, and apparatus with which to grow hydroponic vegetables and tanks for fish and crustaceans on the nutrients from recycled sewage.

The impoverished individual may find himself without goods or services, but as this is his *status quo* under normal circumstances, he will mobilize himself more effectively during the Aftertime. He will grieve less and ponder his options more, and take risks where the wealthy sit on the remnants of their toys until death overtakes them. In like manner, those who are physically or mentally handicapped may have an advantage over those who are whole in the Aftertime. They have already adjusted to being diminished and looked down upon. The palsied individual will find himself comforting those who have newly lost an eye or a hand, and the chronically mentally ill may find themselves counseling those who have gone mad from the turmoil and sense of loss. Survival is to a great extent based on the ability to adapt, and in this way those on the bottom today have an advantage over those on the top.

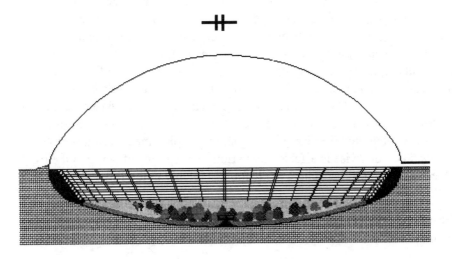

41
Survival

Small cooperative groups, operating in the service-to-others orientation, where the concerns of all are the concerns of each, will have the best chances. Most important is a cooperative attitude among the group, with a willingness to undertake distasteful tasks, a desire to share among all what little there may be, and a positive attitude toward the future. Sunlight may be scarce, so crops grown under artificial light will be most abundant. Rivers and seas may be poisoned, what with the volcanic dust falling everywhere, so fish tanks fed from algae grown in human sewage will likewise be most abundant. Certain crops fair better and go further than others. Good cooks, skilled at making the plain fare tasty, will be much appreciated. These groups will experience a natural way of life reminiscent of life during the last century.

It is no small matter to have music, poetry, and art. This fills the heart of the musician, poet, or artist as much as the recipient. There will be much need for such distraction, as the days will be dim, and the nights dark and long. But do plan to educate your young. Save educational material. There is no reason that technology should stop, just because the infrastructure of human society has been torn asunder. Technology is in the minds and documentation that all humans can access, and rescue. Do that.

Safety Measures
The cataclysms present those who would survive with several challenges—hailstones, fire storms with a brief period of oxygen depletion, earthquakes of a magnitude mankind has never experienced, rapid mountain building, spewing volcanoes, winds of hurricane force, and tidal waves high enough to sweep over tall buildings. What to do?

ZetaTalk

Tidal Waves

As the exact position of the Earth when it stops rotation cannot be calculated, just which shore will experience the worst tidal waves cannot be predicted. This is more severe on the dark side of the Earth, as the waters are gripped by the passing comet on the side facing the Sun, and thus are not as free to flow. Practically speaking, to take no chances, one should have at least 200 feet of elevation and be at least 100 miles away from any shore.

Volcanoes

Clearly safety involves removing oneself from active or even relatively active volcanoes. Volcanoes, new and old, will present those living nearby with sudden activity during the cataclysms, with little warning.

Mountain Building

Remove yourselves from areas where mountain building is likely to occur. Flat plains or plateaus are safest. In this, geological analysis of plates should be your guide. Don't be above a subducting plate, as even if you are riding on top, the ground beneath you may be heated white hot, from friction.

Earthquakes

The earthquakes will essentially level all cities, and of course railways, landing strips, and highways and bridges will be unusable. Don't figure on any power or water systems to be functional, and the telephones will surely be permanently dead. When the earthquakes are expected, lie flat. In this way you will skid and slide a few feet. Standing, or positioned at a height, you will be dashed. And by all means, do not be under a structure that will fall down and crush you.

Hailstones and Fire storms

Metal roofs will deflect the fire storms and hailstones also, if sufficiently thick. For large meteors, which are few, there is no safety measure to be taken. Trust to luck, there. If the shelter you are in is not open to the outside, temporary depletion of oxygen will not affect you.

Crops

After the cataclysms, livestock will be eaten or will die for lack of feed. Seeds sown will fail to thrive after germination from lack of sunlight and the excessive drenching rains. What will the survivors eat? Those who have prepared by establishing intensive indoor gardening such as hydroponics and the most protein-efficient animal husbandry, fish tanks and ponds, will find themselves not only subsisting but subsisting well. Such arrangements require indoor lighting. Hydroponics can be grown around the clock and fish eat either this produce or water plants that feed off the community's sewage effluent, but the base of this food chain is the hydroponic vegetation.

For plants, light is life, for without it plants die. Such indoor farming, in place prior to the cataclysms, should not rely on lighting from either the Sun or the utility companies. Both will in essence go out during the decades immediately following the cataclysms. Power for indoor lighting should rely on harnessing wind, or water flows, or other such mechanical generation that can be counted upon to be present after the cataclysms. Food stuffs that can be grown without artificial light and will do quite nicely on the gloomy light supplied by the Sun are mushrooms, earthworms, and various insects that feed on dead tissue.

After the cataclysms bugs will be in abundance, as dead tissue from both plants and animals is everywhere. This trend can be taken advantage of, as distasteful as that concept might be to humans who have never eaten a bug. Larvae, grown in humus, can be turned into pureed and creamed soups, puddings, or omelets by skilled cooks. Those eating the fare would never guess that the base was not cream, milk, and eggs. For those humans who do not prepare, they will find themselves eating bugs in any case, as meals from what they can catch or find growing will be few and far between.

Safe Water

After the cataclysms mankind's problems with his water supply will take a quantum leap. Water, from all sources, may be poisoned, with the old standby, rainwater, failing to provide potable water. During the pole shift volcanoes, old and new, will violently explode. The resulting ash will sift down from the upper atmosphere for decades, poisoning ground water. Humans driven to drink this gritty water will find more than grit between their teeth—they will find their nervous system beginning to fail them, their eye sight fading, and their digestive system intolerant of any food they may find. We are speaking here primarily of lead poisoning, which is not a problem man expects from the water nature provides. Lead settles and over eons settles down out of the way, but after a cataclysm the lead-heavy mantle has been spewed out over the landscape, and most of this vomit will be in the form of fine billowing dust.

During the cataclysms the ground is heaved and jerked, and any wells or piping will be shattered. In that the ground water is as likely to carry poisons as the surface, having filtered down from the surface, what looks like pure water from underground may be, again, a slow death. Ground water also is subject to contact with the lead-heavy mantle, which most often does not make it all the way to the surface during eruptions. If one cannot trust the usual water supply, what to do? Distillation processes or recycling water known to be pure are two approaches likely to provide a steady supply of water. This may seem tedious to those so used to taking fresh, pure water for granted, but those who prepare for the times ahead will not find themselves suddenly without one of life's necessities.

Internet

Computer networks such as the Internet will survive the cataclysms according to their structure. Any electrical appliance protected from damage will operate after the cataclysms as before, provided a source of electricity is available. Networks are another matter, as there are many parts to the whole, and in the main any breakage will disable the whole—the weak link theory in action. Networks relying on wires run over the Earth cannot be expected to be operational. Likewise, networks operating by satellite bounce will find themselves with a problem when the satellites are torn from the skies. How then will computer networks operate? We would suggest that networks established by dish, not relying on satellites, may be a solution. From high point to high point on Earth, such a network could operate after the cataclysms.

Troubled Times

Troubled Times believes that a worldwide cataclysm of massive proportions will strike the Earth in the year 2003. The cause of this natural event will be a monster planet, known to the ancients but as yet undiscovered by modern man, which will pass very near the Earth as part of its normal 3,600-year orbit around the Sun. The ancients called this monster the 12th Planet, and as this magnetic giant passes by, it will force our north and south poles to rotate 90°. The shifting poles will drag the Earth's crust with them, ultimately producing a new global map in a matter of hours in a massive cataclysm affecting all life on Earth. These events have occurred before, as ancient legends and prophecies foretell, creating what man interprets to be ice ages, wandering poles and the flood, and have resulted in the extinction of the mastodon and the sinking of Atlantis.

Mankind survived these past cataclysms, some because they were lucky, and others because they foresaw events and took precautions. To prepare for this event, Troubled Times, a volunteer organization, was formed. The Troubled Times mission is to place into the public record a set of solu-

ZetaTalk

tions for survival into the next century, solutions that are affordable, attainable, and which will produce a healthy life-style in the Aftertime. These solutions can be found radiating from The Hub of Troubled Times, which is icon driven to help the public rapidly locate information.

Those who wish to join this volunteer organization have but to check out the current ongoing teamwork and join the membership to enter into the stream of activity and offer their contributions. Where *ZetaTalk* supports the operation of Troubled Times, the two are separate entities, as is the nonprofit organization, Troubled Times, Inc. Original works within Troubled Times are owned by the individual contributors, who have granted Troubled Times the right to make this information available to the public.

Lack of preparation for the cataclysms may be worse than fatal—it may leave you and those you care about injured, hungry, frightened, and with no recourse or end in sight! Starting in 1997 the Earth's warming trend, stemming from her core, was noticed and has become a general topic of conversation. Prepare now for self sufficiency in a safe location. Starting in 2000, three years prior to the cataclysms, a period of crop shortages will be so severe that alternative food production needs to be begun and practiced in earnest. This is when you should become practiced at self sufficiency. Starting in May, 2003, the Earth's rotation will stop within a day and hold for several days just prior to the pole shift. This is when you and your loved ones should be situated at your safe location.

Visit Troubled Times online at

http://www.zetatalk.com

To order more copies of this book, call 1-800-366-0264 or visit the 5th World of Publishing online at

http://5thworld.com